INTRODUCTION TO
THE UCSD p-SYSTEM™

INTRODUCTION TO THE UCSD p-SYSTEM™

Charles W. Grant
Jon Butah

Berkeley • Paris • Düsseldorf

CREDITS
Cover Art by Daniel Le Noury
Layout and technical illustrations by Judy Wohlfrom

This book describes UCSD Pascal™ and the UCSD p-System™, which are distributed and licensed for distribution by SofTech Microsystems, Inc., 9494 Black Mountain Road, San Diego, California 92126.

UCSD Pascal™, UCSD p-System™, and p-System™ are trademarks of The Regents of the University of California and are used under a license from SofTech Microsystems, Inc.

Altos is a trademark of Altos Computer Systems.
Apple II is a trademark of Apple Computer, Inc.
Commodore is a trademark of Commodore International.
IBM is a registered trademark of International Business Machines Corporation.
LSI-11 and PDP-11 are trademarks of Digital Equipment Corporation.
NorthStar Horizon is a trademark of NorthStar Computers, Inc.
Pascal MicroEngine is a trademark of Western Digital Corporation.

Library of Congress Card Number: 81-50655
ISBN 0-89588-061-X
Printed in the United States of America
10 9 8 7 6 5 4 3 2

TABLE OF CONTENTS

Acknowledgements — **ix**

Introduction — **xi**

1 BASIC CONCEPTS — 1

Typical Computer System Components — 1
What Is An Operating System — 5
The p-System — 8
Summary — 18

2 AN EXCURSION INTO THE SYSTEM — 21

Step 1: Booting The System — 22
Step 2: Setting The Date — 22
Step 3: Creating A Pascal Program — 24
Step 4: Listing The Directory Of A Volume — 30
Step 5: Compiling The Program — 31
Step 6: Fixing The Error — 33
Step 7: Recompiling — 34
Step 8: Running The Program — 35
Step 9: Saving The Work File — 35
Summary — 37

3   *THE FILER*   **39**

Part One: The Filer Commands   40
   Entering and Leaving the Filer   40
   Introduction to Work File Commands   47
Part Two: Filer Reference Summary   85

4   *THE EDITOR*   **109**

Part One: The p-System Editors   109
   YALOE   109
   Screen Oriented Editor   109
   L2   110
Part Two: Writing Pascal Programs   110
   Entering the Editor: The EDIT Command   112
Part Three: Writing Natural Language Text   155
   Natural Language Commands   155
Part Four: Reference Summary   176

5   *CREATING SHORT PASCAL PROGRAMS*   **201**

Part One: COMPILE, RUN, And EXECUTE   201
Part Two: The UCSD Pascal Compiler   211
   Compiler Directives   211
Summary   220

6   *PREPARING LARGE PASCAL PROGRAMS*   **223**

Part One: Managing Large Source Programs   224
   Combining Multiple Source Files   224
Source Management Summary   238
Part Two: Compiling Large Source Programs   238
   The Swapping Options   241
   Symbol Table Management   243
   Reducing Symbol Table Size   246
Compiling Summary   248
Part Three: Running Large Programs   248
   How Main Memory Is Used   248
   Main Memory Allocation   256
Summary   262

APPENDICES

Appendix A:
Disk Volume Sizes   **265**

Appendix B:
System Configuration   **267**

Appendix C:
Pascal Compiler Error Messages   **277**

Appendix D:
Run-time Error Messages   **283**

Appendix E:
The Librarian   **285**

Index   **297**

ACKNOWLEDGEMENTS

I am grateful to the following people for their contributions to the development of this book: Rudolph S. Langer, for suggesting that I become involved in this project; Salley B. Oberlin, for providing valuable editorial improvements to the text; and Richard A. King, for offering assistance with text and program verification.

——*Charles W. Grant*
Livermore, California

I wish to thank a number of people who have supported me as I wrote my part of this book. Jack Davis, Carol Davis, and Dave Roehr at the Computer Age store in Capitola, CA., lent out important pieces of hardware and software at critical moments. Ed Lang and Brent Olander at Applied Microcomputer Technology, Inc., in Scotts Valley, CA., put their excellent word processing facilities at my full disposal. Rodnay Zaks at Sybex offered essential editorial guidance. Sybex editor, Salley Oberlin, smoothed the preparation of the final draft with her courtesy and efficiency. Finally, my wife, Jenny, carried more than her share of family responsibilities at times when the writing kept me intensively engaged.

——*Jon Butah*
Freedom, California

The authors welcome corrections and constructive suggestions from the readers of this book.

INTRODUCTION

This book comprehensively explains the UCSD p-System™—the operating system that supports the Pascal programming language on many microcomputer systems. It offers a hands-on tour through all the features of the file system and the screen editor; it also guides the reader through an exploration of certain features of the UCSD Pascal™ compiler and explains the ways to write, compile and run large and small Pascal programs.

The best way to read this book is seated at your computer. If you try each example as you read about it, you will quickly become a proficient p-System™ user. In particular, you will learn how to:

— create and maintain files

— edit programs and documents

— compile and run small and large Pascal programs.

On the other hand, if you are away from your computer, you will still be able to follow the examples, thanks to the generous use of screen illustrations.

Because it is a complete description of the p-System, this book is also useful as a reference document. You will find it of value whether you are a beginner, a hobbyist, or a professional.

CONTENTS

Chapter 1 (*Basic Concepts*) discusses the basic features of any operating system and, in particular, those of the p-System. It also explains the terms for the p-System used throughout the book.

Chapter 2 (*An Excursion Into The System*) takes you on a step-by-step excursion into the system and through the nine steps necessary to create and run a typical Pascal program.

Chapter 3 (*The Filer*) explains the p-System file system. It shows you how to use the Filer commands to create, delete, copy, print, and rename files.

Chapter 4 (*The Editor*) teaches you how to use the p-System Screen Oriented Editor. With this editor, you can prepare both programs and documents.

Chapter 5 (*Creating Short Pascal Programs*) demonstrates how to compile and run small Pascal programs. Much of the information in this chapter is also applicable to other languages supported by the p-System (e.g., FORTRAN).

Chapter 6 (*Preparing Large Pascal Programs*) explains the various ways you can fit a large program into the available memory of the micro-computers that support the p-System.

Several Appendices follow Chapter 6. **Appendix A** offers important information on disk volume sizes. **Appendix B** gives a detailed explanation of a system configuration procedure. **Appendix C** lists the Pascal compiler error messages. **Appendix D** lists the run-time errors. **Appendix E** describes how to use the Librarian.

WHICH COMPUTER SYSTEMS DOES THIS BOOK APPLY TO?

The p-System is available for many microcomputers, minicomputers and microprocessors, including:

Altos™
Apple II™
Commodore CBM
Data General Nova
DEC PDP-11™
DEC LSI-11™
Heath/Zenith Data System, H-11, H-8, H-89
Hewlett Packard System 45
IBM Personal Computer
Intel 8080, 8086
Lockheed Sue
MOS Technology 6502
Motorola 6800, 6809, 68000
Nanodata QM-1
NCR Alp II
NorthStar Horizon™
OSI
Philips P2000
Radio Shack TRS-80
Terak
Texas Instruments 9900, BS200
Western Digital Pascal MicroEngine™
Xerox 820
VAX
Zilog Z-80, Z8000

and other custom microcoded processors.

The examples in this book are from Version II.0 of the p-System. If you have a different version, the displays on your computer may differ slightly from those appearing here. But the information presented in this book is valid for all versions of the p-System, up to and including Version IV.

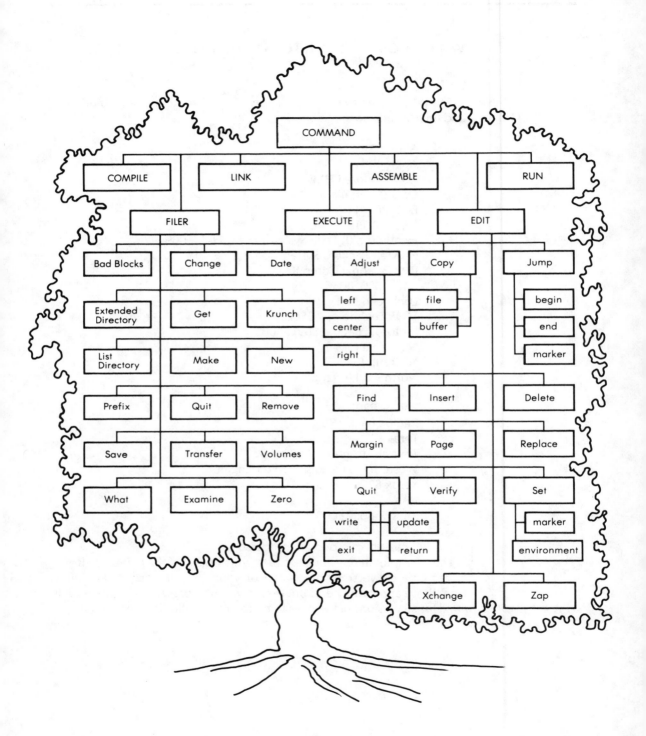

BASIC CONCEPTS 1

THIS CHAPTER INTRODUCES you to the basic concepts necessary to understand the p-System. There are three main sections. The first describes the structure of a typical computer system that runs the p-System. It defines the components of the system and describes their functions. The second section describes operating systems in general and the functions they can perform. The third section provides some important background information about the p-System, which you will need to know as you learn specific commands.

TYPICAL COMPUTER SYSTEM COMPONENTS

The structure of a typical computer system that runs the p-System is shown in Figure 1.1. The system has five main parts: the central processing unit (CPU), the main memory, the secondary memory, the console (video screen and keyboard) and the printer. We will now describe the functions of each part of the computer.

Figure 1.1: Components of a Typical Computer System

Central Processing Unit

The central processing unit (CPU) is the "brain" of the computer; it does all of the "thinking" in the system. The CPU works in the following way:

1. The CPU reads an instruction from the main memory.
2. It decodes the instruction to determine what actions to take.
3. It performs the actions specified by the instruction.
4. It repeats the process for the next instruction.

Typical instructions are: read a value from a main memory location into a register; write a value from a register to a main memory location and add two values, then store the result in a main memory location. These instructions are called *machine language instructions,* since they are instructions in the "language" understood by the machine.

A sequence of instructions is called a *program.* Executing a sequence of instructions as described above is called running a program. The CPU can only execute machine language programs.

Main Memory

Memory is a device that stores information for later recall by coding it into a form that can be kept on some physical medium. The *main memory* in your computer codes the information into electrical charges, which are stored in tiny electronic circuits. Each electronic circuit can store one of two charge values, which represent one of two values of information (for example: one or zero, yes or no, on or off, black or white, or any other two values you may wish to encode).

Information can be measured. The smallest unit of information is the *bit*. A bit can be used to distinguish between two possible values. Eight bits are called a *byte*. A byte is a larger unit of information, which can be used to distinguish between 256 possible values. Computer systems that run the p-System typically store information in main memory in units of 8-bit bytes. The term *word* in the p-System means a two byte quantity of information (i.e., 16 bits).

In order for your computer to run the p-System it must have a sufficient amount of main memory to hold the programs and data that comprise the system. The amount of main memory required to hold the system is from 48K bytes to 64K bytes. K is short for *kilo.* In computer jargon, kilo means *1024,* rather than its usual meaning of 1000.

Any program that the computer is going to run must first be loaded into main memory. This is because the CPU gets instructions to execute only from main memory. This in turn means that all of a program must fit in the available main memory, or that the program must be brought into main memory a piece at a time and each piece must be run separately.

The memory commonly used as main memory for computers is called *random access memory (RAM).* It is called random access because the CPU can read or write locations in any random order as quickly as it can read or write locations in sequential order. RAM is usually volatile. This means that when the power is turned off, all the information stored in the RAM is lost. (It evaporates, so to speak.) Therefore, RAM is only useful for temporary storage. This is sufficient for main memory, since its purpose is to provide fast temporary storage for programs and data, while the programs are being run.

Secondary Memory

On the other hand, *secondary memory* is used to permanently store programs and data for eventual reloading into main memory. Secondary memory does not need to be as fast as main memory, but it needs to be non-volatile. When the power is turned off, it must retain the information stored in it.

Secondary memory keeps information in the same manner as main memory: by encoding the information into a form that can be recorded on some sort of physical medium. The typical secondary memory medium for computer systems that run the p-System is the floppy disk. Other types of disks are in use on such systems, but the floppy disk is the most common because of its low cost.

Floppy Disks

A *floppy disk* is a flexible circle of mylar plastic, coated with a thin magnetic covering, permanently packaged in a lined plastic envelope. Information is stored on the floppy disk (and other types of disks) in a series of microscopic magnetic regions on the coating of the disk. A floppy disk is shown in Figure 1.2.

Figure 1.2: Floppy Disk

A floppy disk can store from 50 to 1000 K bytes of information depending on its size (8 inch or 5¼ inch), the format of the information stored on it, and whether or not information can be stored on both sides. Appendix A lists the amount of information that can be stored on the various types of disks used on p-Systems.

Disk Drives

A *disk drive* is a device that writes information from the computer onto a disk, and reads information stored on a disk back into the computer. A *floppy disk drive* is a device that reads from, and writes to, floppy disks.

Console

The *console* is the part of the computer system that makes communication between you and the computer possible. The console consists of two parts: one for input and the other for output. The *keyboard* is the input part of the console. You type information into the computer with the keyboard. The *cathode ray tube (CRT)* screen (similar to a television set) is the output part of the console. It displays the computer's responses to your actions.

Some computer systems use consoles that print information on paper, rather than display it on a CRT screen. The p-System was designed to be used on systems that have a CRT screen. It can, however, be used on a system with a printing console, but it will not be as convenient as using a CRT screen. For example, the p-System includes a powerful program called the *screen oriented editor*. This program lets you manipulate textual[1] data with the computer, while watching the results of your actions on the CRT screen. You will not be able to use this program without a CRT screen. In the demonstrations in this book, we assume that you have a system with a CRT screen and that you are using the screen oriented editor.

Printer

The *printer* is just as you would expect, a device that writes information from the computer onto paper in human-readable form. A printer is an optional part of a computer system. You do not need a printer to use the p-System, but it is nice to have one.

Now that we have looked at the basic system components, let's go on to discuss operating systems.

---

[1]In this context, "textual" means composed of lines of characters. Textual data is usually intended for a human reader.

WHAT IS AN OPERATING SYSTEM

An *operating system* is a collection of programs that act as tools for the users of the computer system. The purpose of the operating system is to make life easier for programs and programmers. The operating system provides services that are needed over and over again. Some of the services typically performed by an operating system include:

- accepting commands from the keyboard, decoding them, and performing the indicated actions (the shell)

- loading programs into main memory and causing the CPU to start executing them (the loader)

- maintaining the information stored on secondary memory in an organized, easy-to-use manner (the file system)

- providing standard services for operations commonly performed in programs, such as output to devices (the library)

- allowing the user to manipulate textual material stored on the computer (the editor)

- translating programs in various languages into a form that can be run on the machine (compilers and assemblers).

The services supplied by the operating system do not need to be redefined in every new program. They are kept in one place in the operating system for all programs to use. This makes life for a program and the programmer much simpler. A program does not have to keep track of certain details, such as knowing precisely where the data is stored on disk, or even which disk or what kind of disk it is. Instead, it can concentrate on the problem that it was designed to solve and let the operating system worry about the details that are not relevant to the problem.

The operating system conceals from the program the peculiarities of the devices in the system. Because of this, the same program can be run with different devices without having to be modified. Since all the device-dependent information is in the operating system, programs can be device-independent.

Without an operating system, a user would have to load a program into main memory by hand (with a front panel, or by some other method) every time a program is run. The user would also have to remember exactly where each piece of data is stored on every disk, and include in each program the instructions required to read and write data to and from the disks.

Let's now examine some of the main features of an operating system.

The Shell

After turning on the computer, the first thing that you do when you sit down at the console is to start typing commands. If the system is to respond to these commands there must be a program that reads them from the keyboard, decodes them and then calls on the other parts of the operating system to carry out the operations specified in the commands. The program that interprets the commands you type is called the *shell*.

The Loader

The *loader* reads a program from secondary storage into main memory and causes the CPU to start executing the program. This service is also used internally by the operating system to read different parts of itself into main memory.

The File System

The *file system* stores information on, and retrieves information from, secondary storage. An important function of the file system is to group information into units, called files, and to associate each file with a *file name*. The file can then be referred to in programs by its file name alone, without having to specify its location on disk.

The file system maintains information about file names and locations in an area on the disk called the *directory*. Usually each disk has a directory that contains information about the files stored on it.

The Library

The *library* contains a collection of subprograms that can be combined with other users' programs. There are two types of libraries: resident and non-resident. A *resident* library is a group of subprograms that are kept in main memory. Programs may just "assume" that this library is there and available for use. A *non-resident* library is a group of subprograms kept in a file. The process of combining a program with subprograms from a library is called *linking*. The operating system utility that performs this service is called a *linker*.

The Editor

The *editor* enables you to enter and change textual material. You will typically employ an editor to prepare programs and documents. (In fact, the manuscript for this book was prepared using the p-System screen oriented editor.) The editor is the most frequently used feature of most operating systems. For this reason, users often judge the convenience of using an operating system by the ease of using its editor.

The process of translating programs requires further discussion.

Program Translation

The CPU can only execute machine language programs. Programs in languages other than the machine language for a particular machine must first be translated into the machine's machine language before they can be run.

If a program is in a high-level language, such as Pascal, BASIC or FORTRAN, this translation process is called *compiling*. The program that provides this service is called a *compiler*. It is easier to program with high-level languages because they allow you to concentrate on the problem at hand, rather than on the peculiarities of the machine. High-level languages tend to produce programs that are larger and slower than the same programs written in low-level languages. On the other hand, programs in high-level languages can be written much more quickly, and are more apt to be correct than their low-level counterparts.

Assembly language is a low-level language, very close to machine language. If your program is in assembly language, then the process of translating it to machine language is called *assembling*. The program that provides this service is called an *assembler*. In fact, assembly language is merely a more convenient way of writing machine language programs. Since you are practically writing in machine language, you have control over everything and can choose the shortest and fastest sequences of instructions for your problem. However, programs in low-level languages are harder to write, debug (remove errors), and understand than programs in high-level languages.

There is one other way for a computer to execute a program in a language other than its machine language: *interpretation*. Interpretation is an indirect method of running a program. With this method the CPU executes a program called an *interpreter*, which is written in machine language. The function of the interpreter is to read your program, which is in some other language, and to perform the actions specified in the program. The CPU does not directly execute your program, instead, the CPU and the interpreter program, together, simulate another CPU that has the language of your program as its "machine" language.

Programs that are run using interpretation are generally slower in execution than those run after compiling or assembling. This is because the interpreter must translate and execute each command at run time. On the other hand, for compiled or assembled programs, the translation is done ahead of time by the compiler or assembler. Thus, at run time only execution takes place.

(*Note:* The programming language BASIC is usually implemented by an interpreter, rather than a compiler. This is the case for most of the common microcomputers. For example, the Radio Shack TRS-80, the Apple computer, and the Commodore PET all implement BASIC with an interpreter. The programming languages Pascal and FORTRAN are usually implemented by compilers, not interpreters. However, in the p-System, BASIC, FORTRAN and Pascal are all implemented by compilers.)

THE p-SYSTEM

Let's now examine the basic characteristics and features of the p-System. We give detailed explanations of specific parts of the system in later chapters.

The UCSD p-System was initially developed at the University of California at San Diego (UCSD). The primary purpose of the system was to support the Pascal programming language on microcomputers. For this reason the p-System has many features that assist in the creation and execution of Pascal programs. In fact, the system itself is written in the UCSD Pascal programming language.

In the late 1970's, the p-System became commercially available through SofTech Microsystems in San Diego. It is currently in use on a wide variety of microcomputers.

The p-System is based on the concept of *operating modes.* An operating mode is a state or condition that the system may be in at a given time. Examples of modes are the RUN and EDIT modes. Each mode has a different set of commands that are valid only while the system is in that mode.

The p-System is *menu* driven. This means that you select the command that you want from a list presented on the screen, just as you might select an entree from a menu in a restaurant. You make the selection by pressing a single letter key on your console's keyboard. The letter that you use is usually the first letter of the command that you want.

The menu that the computer displays is one form of a *prompt.* A prompt is simply something that the computer displays to help you decide which command or what data to enter into the computer next. We will refer to the menus as prompts from now on.

Each mode has its associated prompt, which is a menu of the valid commands for that mode. The COMMAND mode is the top-most level of the p-System command structure. This mode corresponds to the shell function of an operating system, described earlier. We will now examine the prompt of the COMMAND mode:

Command: E(dit, R(un, F(ile, C(omp, L(ink, X(ecute, A(ssem, D(ebug, ? [II.0]☐

(*Note:* the cursor symbol (☐) appearing on the screen indicates the position of the next character to be inserted or deleted.)

The prompt of the COMMAND mode is typical of p-System prompts. The current mode is identified on the left. It is now the COMMAND mode. After the mode identification, some of the available commands are listed in abbreviated form. For example, 'E(dit' means use the E key to select the EDIT command and 'X(ecute' means use the X key to select the EXECUTE command. Near the end of the line, in square brackets, is the version number of the program that implements this mode. In this example, II.0 is the version number. At the very right end of the line is the cursor, which indicates that the system is waiting for you to type a character as input.

There may be more valid commands than can be listed on one screen line. When this occurs, only the most common commands appear in the prompt. The other commands are still available for use even though they are not shown. In some modes the question mark (?) command will display an auxiliary prompt, which lists the additional commands that were not included in the main prompt. This is the case for the COMMAND mode. All of the commands shown in both prompts are available for use, regardless of which prompt is currently being displayed. Here is the auxiliary prompt for the COMMAND mode:

Command: U(ser restart, I(nit, H(alt [II.0]☐

Depending on the version of your system and the width of your console's screen, the prompt that appears may differ from the one shown above. In this book, the prompts that are shown are those from Version II.0 of the p-System, configured for an 80 character-wide CRT screen. One command prompt that you might see if you have a screen less than 80 characters wide, looks like this:

Command: E, R, F, C, L, X, A, D, ? ☐

The commands listed in the prompts for the various modes are of three basic forms. Commands like INIT, the system reinitialization command, return the system to the same mode when they are finished (the COMMAND mode in this case). Some commands, however, switch to different modes. For example, the EDIT command switches the system into the EDIT mode. Each mode also has an escape command that terminates the current mode, and returns you to the mode that you were in before you invoked the current mode. The QUIT command is the usual command for this function. The COMMAND mode is the highest-level mode and does not have any previous mode to return to. However, the HALT command is practically equivalent to an escape command, since it terminates the current mode and returns you to the point where you started. On some systems this command returns you to the manufacturer's operating system.

The modes of the p-System have been arranged in a tree[2] structure. A diagram showing this structure appears in Figure 1.3. The mode selection commands drop you down a level in the tree. The escape commands move you up a level in the tree. Let us look at an example of how to move around in this mode tree.

We always start at the COMMAND mode, which is at the root of the tree. From the COMMAND mode we have the option of selecting the commands displayed in the COMMAND prompt. For this example, we select the FILER command by pressing the F key. This moves us down one level in the tree to the FILER mode.

The FILER is a program used to manipulate the files in the p-System's file system. We will introduce the file system shortly, and we will explain the FILER in detail in Chapter 3. Let's look at the prompt for the FILER mode:

Filer: G(et, S(ave, W(hat, N(ew, L(dir, R(em, C(hng, T(rans, D(ate, Q(uit [C.4]☐

The prompt line is not long enough to hold all of the options. Use the '?' option to display the remaining commands. Select the '?' option by pressing the question mark key. The prompt then changes to show those options that didn't appear on the original prompt:

Filer: B(ad-blks, E(xt-dir, K(rnch, M(ake, P(refix, V(ols, X(amine, Z(ero [C.4]☐

Press '?' again to return to the original prompt. All of the FILER commands are valid when either prompt is displayed. Switching the prompts simply serves as a convenient reminder of the commands available.

From the FILER mode you can select the VOLUMES command by pressing the V key. The VOLUMES command is a command that returns to the current mode. The VOLUMES command displays the current volumes that are on-line. (We will explain the concept of a volume shortly.) After selecting the VOLUMES command, you will find yourself back in the FILER mode. The system will be waiting for another valid FILER command.

The QUIT command in the FILER mode is the escape command for this mode. Select the QUIT command by pressing the Q key. This returns you (back up the tree) to the COMMAND mode, where you started.

---

[2]It is interesting to note that in computer science, trees are always drawn with the root at the top, the branches in the middle, and the leaves at the bottom.

Now that we understand the basics of the p-System command structure, let's examine the basics of the p-System's file system.

The p-System's File System

The p-System's file system manages information stored on secondary memory and handles input and output of information to devices. The information in the file system is grouped in units called *files*. A file is a sequence

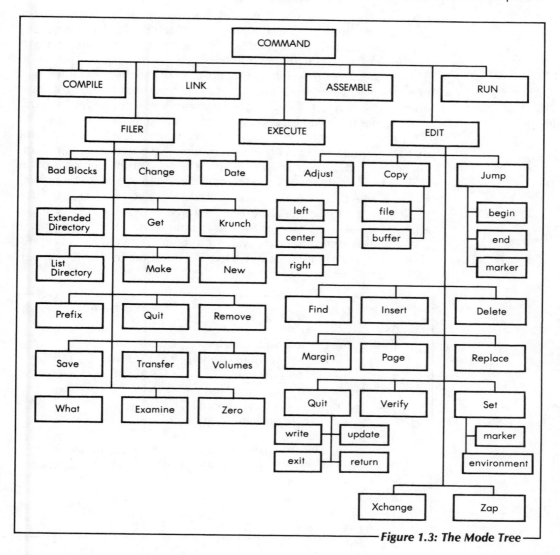

Figure 1.3: The Mode Tree

of information. The information can be of many forms: machine language instructions, textual data and other types of data. The type of information in the file determines the type of the file. Machine language instructions are kept in code files. Textual data are kept in *text* files. Most other types of data are kept in *data* files.

Devices, Unit Numbers, Volumes and Volume Names

The file system manages all the devices in the system. A device is a piece of machinery interfaced to the computer. Each device has a fixed unit number associated with it. A disk drive, a console, or a printer are all examples of devices with unit numbers.

The p-System's file system consists of a set of *volumes*. A volume is an object that allows information (in the form of files) to be stored on it, input from it, or output to it. The difference between volumes and *devices* is that the volumes have names, and the devices have only unit numbers.

All devices, except disk drives, are also volumes. The printer is a volume that accepts output. The console is a volume that accepts input (from the keyboard) and displays output (on the screen). (For the purposes of the p-System, the data input from the console is considered to be coming from a file.) A disk drive is not considered to be a volume because information is not stored in the disk drive; it is stored on the disk. For this reason each of the disks is considered to be a separate volume with its own name.

A volume name is associated with each volume. All volumes, except for disk volumes, have fixed names. Here is a list of the fixed unit numbers and volume names.

Unit #	Device	Volume Name
0 —	not used	
1 —	the console with echoing	CONSOLE:
2 —	the console without echoing	SYSTERM:
3 —	the graphics device	GRAPHIC: (for a TERAK computer)
4 —	a disk drive (usually floppy)	
5 —	a disk drive (usually floppy)	
6 —	the printer	PRINTER:
7 —	an auxiliary device for input	REMIN: (usually hooked
8 —	an auxiliary device for output	REMOUT: up to a modem)
9 —	a disk drive	
10 —	a disk drive	
11 —	a disk drive	
12 —	a disk drive	

A disk volume has a volume name, but it is not fixed. You can change it by using the change command in the FILER.

Let's suppose that you have a disk volume named X. If you request the operating system to read something from X, then the operating system will examine the disks currently in the disk drives in order to find one named X. Because of this search, it is possible to refer to a disk volume by name, independent of the disk drive it happens to be in. It is important to note the distinction here. Disk drives are devices with unit numbers. Disks are volumes with volume names.

All of these devices are not always implemented in all versions of the p-System. For example, in Apple Pascal (the Apple Computer version of the p-System), up to six of the disk drives are implemented as floppy disk drives, if you have them. The printer and the remote device are implemented if you have the proper interface cards installed. The console is implemented either as the Apple's screen and keyboard, or as a remote terminal if you have a serial interface installed. The graphics device is not implemented for the Apple.

The volumes capable of storing blocks of information for later recall are called *block structured* volumes. In the p-System, only the disk volumes are block structured.

As previously mentioned, the most important function of the file system is to allow information to be accessed by name, rather than by specific locations on the disk. Let's now examine the file naming structure in the p-System.

File Names

File names consist of two parts: the *volume specification* and the *file specification* within the volume. You may leave out either or both of these parts under some circumstances. The two parts of the file name are separated by a colon (:).

The Volume Specification   The volume specification can occur in several forms. The usual form is a *volume name*. A volume name can be up to seven characters in length. A sharp sign (#) and unit number can also be used as a volume specification. A volume specification using the unit number of a disk drive refers to whatever disk volume is currently in that unit.

The Root Volume   The asterisk symbol (*) is used to represent a special volume called the *root volume*. The root volume is the volume that the system was booted from. (*Booting* or *bootstrap loading* is the process of bringing the operating system into main memory and causing the CPU to start running it.) The root volume is expected to contain some files that the operating system needs for certain functions.

The Prefix Volume If you do not specify any volume in a file name, the operating system will prefix your file specification with a special volume specification called the *prefix volume.* This saves you from having to type volume specifications if a file is on the volume currently designated by the prefix. The prefix volume name is set at boot time to be the same as the root volume name. The prefix volume name can be set to any volume name by using the PREFIX command in the FILER mode.

File Specifications A file specification is the name of a file on some volume. The file specification can be up to 15 characters in length. File specifications usually contain a descriptive suffix as their last 5 characters. The suffix describes the type of the file. For example, A.TEXT is a text file; B.CODE is a code file; and C.DATA is a data file. It is not absolutely necessary to follow this convention, but it is a good idea. In order for a file to be designated as the work file, its specification must end in either .CODE or .TEXT (the work file will be explained shortly). Most of the operating system files have the prefix SYSTEM. in their names; SYSTEM.COMPILER, SYSTEM.EDITOR and SYSTEM.FILER are examples.

Recall that a file name consists of a volume specification and a file specification separated by a colon. Here are a few examples of file names.

File Name	*Meaning*
DISKA:FILE1.CODE	the file FILE1.CODE on the volume DISKA
#4:GAME.CODE	the file GAME.CODE on whatever volume is in the disk drive with unit #4
*SYSTEM.WRK.TEXT	the file SYSTEM.WRK.TEXT on the root volume
LETTER.TEXT	the file LETTER.TEXT on the prefix volume
FOO:	the entire volume named FOO
:	all the files on the prefix volume
#6:	unit #6, the printer the same as PRINTER:
PRINTER:ABD.TEXT	the same as PRINTER:

These examples illustrate some important points about file names:

- When using an asterisk to specify the root volume, the colon is optional, e.g., *SYSTEM.WRK.TEXT

- If no volume is specified, the prefix volume is assumed, e.g., LETTER.TEXT

- If no file specification is given, the entire volume is assumed, e.g., FOO:

- The file specification is optional for non-block structured devices and is ignored if given, e.g., PRINTER:ABC.TEXT

Each block structured volume contains a directory of the files on that volume. Each directory can contain a maximum of 77 entries. Therefore, the maximum number of files on a volume in the p-System is 77.

When you specify a file name, the operating system performs the following steps to read the data from the file. First, it looks in the disk drives to find the volume with the correct volume name. Then, when it has the correct volume, it reads the directory of the volume and looks for the file name that matches the one in the file specification. If a matching name exists, then the operating system reads the information in the directory that specifies where the data for the file is stored on the volume. The operating system then reads the data from the file from those locations. (Aren't you glad the operating system does all this work, and that you don't have to worry about it?)

Wild Cards

The wild card characters used in file specifications—the equal sign (=) and the question mark (?)—permit you to manipulate a group of files with a single command. You can use a wild card with the EXTENDED DIRECTORY, LIST DIRECTORY, REMOVE, CHANGE, and TRANSFER commands in the FILER mode. You can use a wild card to replace one or more characters of a file name that you type in response to a prompt. A wild card will match any sequence of characters in a file specification. It is like a hand full of jokers in a game of poker.

For example, if you type

B = A

you are specifying all of the files (on the prefix volume) with names that begin with the letter B and end with the letter A. (*Note:* For clarity, throughout this book, all user responses appear in **UPPERCASE BOLDFACE** type.) It is never possible, in the p-System, to use two wild cards in one specification. In other words, you may never type something like =A= to refer to a group of files.

The question mark (?) wild card works exactly like the equal sign (=), except that the computer will ask you to verify every file before executing the command. The question mark wild card is the preferred wild card for the REMOVE, CHANGE, or TRANSFER commands, since it can prevent you from removing, changing, or transferring a file inadvertently. Let's look at an example of how a wild card works with the EXTENDED DIRECTORY command.

Example of WILD CARD   Let's assume that the prefix volume has the following files:

> TEST.TEXT
> TEST.CODE
> PROPOSAL.TEXT
> MEMO.TEXT
> SUM.TEXT
> SUM.CODE
> SAMPLE.TEXT

In this example, we want to display information about the .CODE type files only, using the EXTENDED DIRECTORY command of the FILER.

If you use a wild card in the file specification, for example

> **= .CODE**

then only the files with the suffix .CODE will be selected. In other words, the computer will only display information about TEST.CODE and SUM.CODE. The other files will be ignored.

Only one wild card is permitted in a file specification. It can appear in one of four positions. Figure 1.4 shows examples of the four ways a wild card can appear in a file specification and lists the group of files that it will select from the directory displayed above. Study it and then experiment with your own system.

The Work File

In order to explain the function of the work file, let's imagine a "typical" session with the computer.

— You sit down at the computer.

— You enter a program using the editor.

— You try to compile the program, but it has errors.

— You use the editor to fix the errors.

— You try to compile the program again, but you find new errors.

— You use the editor to fix the new errors.

— You try to compile the program again, and you find no errors.

— You try to run the program, and it does not work.

— You edit the program to try to make it work.

— You try to compile the program, and you find that you have introduced yet more errors.

— You edit the program once more to try to fix those errors.

— You try to compile again, and once again you have no errors.

— You try to run the program, and it works!

— You write your working program out to a disk for safe keeping.

You type:	*Files selected:.*	*Meaning:*
= .TEXT	TEST.TEXT PROPOSAL.TEXT MEMO.TEXT SUM.TEXT SAMPLE.TEXT	all files ending with .TEXT
S =	SUM.TEXT SUM.CODE SAMPLE.TEXT	all files starting with S
S = TEXT	SUM.TEXT SAMPLE.TEXT	all files starting with S and ending with TEXT
=	TEST.TEXT TEST.CODE PROPOSAL.TEXT MEMO.TEXT SUM.TEXT SUM.CODE SAMPLE.TEXT	all files

Figure 1.4: Wild Card Examples

During this process you used the one or two files that you were working on, over and over again. If you had to specify which file you were using at each step of this process, you would be doing a lot of repetitive typing, and you might even introduce errors by specifying a wrong file.

The work file provides a shortcut for such situations. The work file is a file that the commands EDIT, COMPILE, RUN, ASSEMBLE and LINK will use as a default file. If you designate the file you are working on as the work file, then the process becomes much simpler.

The P-Machine

The p-System is based on (and written in) the UCSD Pascal programming language. The UCSD Pascal compiler (as well as the UCSD BASIC and FORTRAN compilers) translates programs into a machine language called P-code. This P-code is interpreted in the p-System by an interpreter.

The P-code interpreter simulates a machine that uses P-code as its machine language. This simulated machine, a combination of the intepreter and the CPU, is called a pseudo-machine or P-machine. Thus, the language of the P-machine is known as pseudo-code or P-code.

The P-machine is the heart of the p-System. All of your Pascal, BASIC and FORTRAN programs are compiled into P-code by a compiler, and an interpreter executes the P-code. In fact, the only p-System code files that are not P-code are the code files produced by the assembler. These files are actually in the machine language for the CPU in your computer.

SUMMARY

This chapter has presented the basic concepts necessary for understanding computer systems and operating systems. It has offered important definitions, descriptions of typical computer system components, and necessary background information for understanding the p-System. We will use this information in Chapter 2, as we go on an excursion into the p-System.

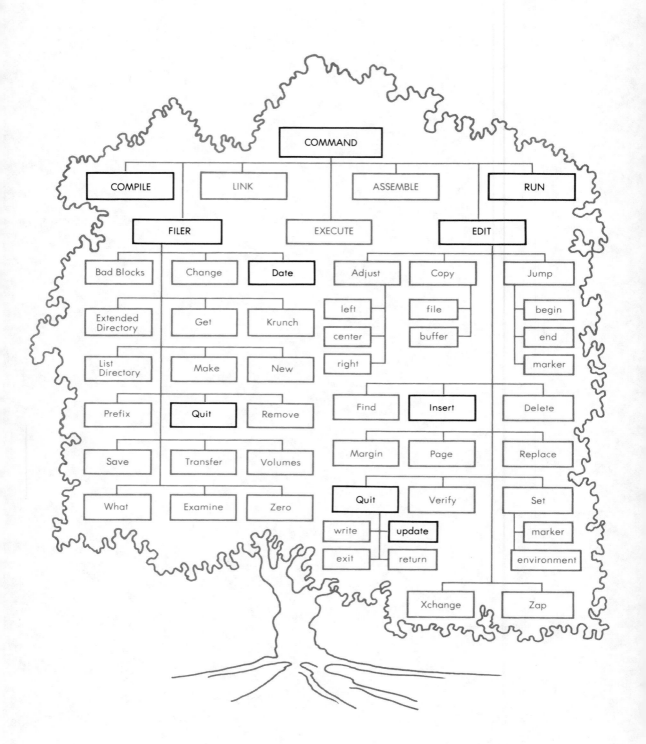

AN EXCURSION INTO THE SYSTEM 2

As YOU READ THIS CHAPTER, you should be sitting at a computer. By carefully following all the operations suggested, you will learn to use the p-System to write and run a sample Pascal program. There are nine major steps. You will:

1. Boot the p-System into your computer.

2. Set the current date.

3. Create a sample Pascal program, including an intentional syntax error.

4. List the directory of the disk.

5. Attempt to compile the sample program. The mistake will produce an error message.

6. Fix the error.

7. Recompile the program.

8. Run the program.

9. Save the program under a new file name.

In performing these steps, you'll get an overview of some of the major commands and features of the p-System.

In this chapter, as well as throughout this book, it is assumed that you have the p-System up and running on your computer system. It is also assumed that the p-System is properly configured to the characteristics of your system, especially to your CRT, so that you can use the screen oriented editor. All of the examples in this book use this editor, so you will need to use it to follow along.

With luck, your system came from the store already configured. If this is the case, GREAT! Read on. If not, then you must stop and configure your system before you can proceed. If you know someone who is experienced with the p-System, ask them to help you—a system configuration can be rather tricky. But if no one is available to help you out, Appendix B will. It contains an explanation of the configuration procedure. You will also need your p-System manual and the manuals for your computer system.

All the examples in this book assume that you have an 80 character-wide CRT screen, since this is the size the p-System was designed to work best with. If your screen is a different size, the displays on your screen will be very similar, but not identical to, those in this book. Also, it is assumed that your console has keys for all the standard p-System functions. If it does not, you can configure your system to use the keys you do have. However, if you do this, keep in mind that the keys you use will not exactly correspond with the keys in the examples in this book. Consult your system's reference manual for any differences.

STEP 1: BOOTING THE SYSTEM

You boot the p-System into your computer when you insert the p-System disks into the disk drives and turn the computer on. It is not possible here to describe the details of this operation for every microcomputer capable of using the p-System. For guidance, use the documentation supplied by the manufacturer of your computer. When booting is finished, a welcome message appears at the center of your screen. This three-line message gives the name of the root volume and, on the bottom line, it displays the current date. Let's go on to Step 2 and learn how to set the date.

STEP 2: SETTING THE DATE

The first time you boot the p-System the current date will undoubtedly be wrong. You will want to change this date. This is a routine operation you should undertake whenever starting a new day or night's work. The current date is recorded every time you create or update a file. If this information is accurate, it can help you to keep track of your work.

When booting is completed, the top of the screen displays the prompt for the COMMAND mode:

Command: E(dit, R(un, F(ile, C(omp, L(ink, X(ecute, A(ssem, D(ebug, ? [II.0]☐

Right now we are only interested in the FILER command. It invokes the FILER mode that contains the DATE command. The DATE command will allow us to set the current date.

Select the FILER command by pressing the F key. The screen goes blank.

After a moment, a new line appears at the top, replacing the prompt for the COMMAND mode. It is the prompt for the FILER mode:

Filer: G(et, S(ave, N(ew, L(dir, R(em, C(hng, T(rans, D(ate, Q(uit [C.4]☐

The FILER commands will be described in Chapter 3. Here, we are intent on the DATE command represented on the prompt by the letter D in 'D(ate'.

Now select the DATE command from the FILER prompt by pressing the D key. The FILER prompt vanishes and is replaced by three new lines:

Date set: <1 . . 31>-<Jan . . Dec>-<00 . . 99>
Today is 12-Nov-80
New date?☐

The date on the second line is the current system date when you select the DATE command. In the sample, it is November 12, 1980. Your screen, of course, may show a different date.

The first line tells you the *format* (i.e., the permissible characters) for the date. The third line asks you to enter a new date. Here is a translation of the first line: the date consists of the day, the month, and the year, separated by hyphens. The day must be a number between 1 and 31. The month must be abbreviated to three letters. The year must be a two-digit number.

Now type in the actual current date. For example, if the date is December 25, 1981, you would type 25-DEC-81 immediately after the question 'New date ?':

Date set: <1 . . 31>-<Jan . . Dec>-<00 . . 99>
Today is 12-Nov-80
New date ? **25-DEC-81**☐

If you make a typing mistake, use the backspace key. Each time you press it, the cursor will move back one space on the screen and erase a character. You can then retype the correct character.

Now, look at the date you have typed. Make sure it fits the required format. Then press the RETURN key. You have just executed a p-System command. The date you typed is now the current system date. A fourth message line appears confirming this, and the prompt for the FILER mode reappears:

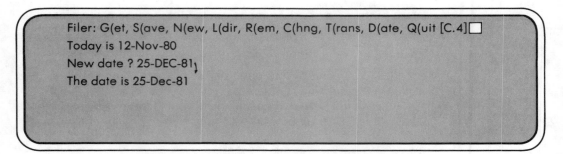

Filer: G(et, S(ave, N(ew, L(dir, R(em, C(hng, T(rans, D(ate, Q(uit [C.4]☐
Today is 12-Nov-80
New date ? 25-DEC-81⌋
The date is 25-Dec-81

The computer is ready to execute another FILER command.

If the date on the last line is the old current date, you have made a mistake in the format of the date you typed. Press the D key, selecting the DATE command, and try again. The DATE command is explained in more detail in Chapter 3.

Now, we must leave the filer. The letter Q on the prompt for the FILER mode represents the QUIT command, which is precisely the command we need. Press the Q key to invoke the QUIT command. The screen goes blank and the prompt for the COMMAND mode reappears:

Command: E(dit, R(un, F(ile, C(omp, L(ink, X(ecute, A(ssem, D(ebug,? [II.0]☐

Now that we have reset the current date, we can move ahead to bigger and better things. Let's use the editor to write a sample Pascal program.

STEP 3: CREATING A PASCAL PROGRAM

Select the EDIT command by pressing the E key. Since this is the first time you have used the system, there should be no SYSTEM.WRK.TEXT file on the root volume. The COMMAND prompt will disappear and the screen will look like this:

>Edit:
No workfile is present. File? (<ret> for no file <esc-ret> to exit)
:☐

If your root volume has a file SYSTEM.WRK.TEXT, or if another file has been designated as the work file, the screen will be filled with text. You will need to quit the EDIT mode with the EXIT option (described in Chapter 4) and use the NEW command of the FILER mode to clear the work file (described in Chapter 3).

Let's examine the screen more closely. The top line tells you that you have selected the EDIT mode. The arrow-head character (>) is the direction marker (explained in Chapter 4). The second line tells you that there is no work file present. The question 'File?' asks if there is some file on disk you wish to edit. (There isn't.) In parentheses, the message '<esc-ret> to exit' informs you that by pressing the ESCAPE key and then the RETURN key, you can leave the EDIT mode and return to the COMMAND mode. (You don't want to.) The message '<ret> for no file' tells you that by pressing RETURN you can create a new file. That's exactly what you want to do.

Press the RETURN key. A new line appears at the top of the screen. It is the prompt for the EDIT mode:

>Edit: A(djst C(py D(lete F(ind I(nsrt J(mp R(place Q(uit X(chng Z(ap [E.6g]
□

The screen below the prompt for the EDIT mode is blank and the text buffer in the main memory of the computer has no text in it. In a moment, we are going to put something on the screen and in the text buffer.

The text buffer is a section of main memory that contains the text you are editing. Part of the text buffer is displayed on the screen during the editing process.

Notice the prompt for the EDIT mode. It is a menu of available commands. ADJUST, COPY, DELETE, etc., are all commands in the editor that manipulate written text in various ways. Chapter 4 will explain the EDITOR commands in detail. Here, we will use the INSERT command to write a short Pascal program. INSERT lets you put text into the computer's text buffer.

Select the INSERT command by pressing the I key. This invokes the INSERT mode. The prompt for the INSERT mode appears at the top of the screen:

>Insert: text [<bs> a char, <del> a line] [<etx> accepts <esc> escapes]
□

The INSERT mode will be explained in Chapter 4. For the moment, we will use the options of the INSERT mode as we need them.

Notice that the cursor has not moved from the screen position it occupied when the prompt for the EDIT mode was displayed. Now, however, you are in the INSERT mode. Any letter key you press will appear on the screen and go into the text buffer.

We will use the Pascal program GREETING as a sample program. This program appears in the first chapter of *Introduction To Pascal* by Rodnay Zaks (Ref. 310 in the Sybex Library at the end of this book). Begin by typing in the first few letters on the first line. Then type in three incorrect characters:

> \>Insert: Text [<bs> a char, <del> a line] [<etx> accepts <esc> escapes]
> **PROGXXX**☐

Now press the backspace key three times to erase the incorrect letters. Backspace is the recommended key for the function of deleting a character. You may have to use a different key on your system. Check your documentation.

> \>Insert: Text [<bs> a char, <del> a line] [<etx> accepts <esc> escapes]
> PROG☐

Finish typing the first line correctly. Then press RETURN:

> \>Insert: Text [<bs> a char, <del> a line] [<etx> accepts <esc> escapes]
> PRO**GRAM GREETING**; ↵
> ☐

(*Note:* the symbol (↵) represents pressing the RETURN key at the end of the line.)

Now, type the second line and press RETURN:

>Insert: Text [<bs> a char, <del> a line] [<etx> accepts <esc> escapes]
PROGRAM GREETING;
BEGIN ⌡
◼

Press the space bar three times to indent the next line. Then type the line. (*Note:* be sure to omit the second quote mark. This intentional mistake will help us learn about important p-System features.)

>Insert: Text [<bs> a char, <del> a line] [<etx> accepts <esc> escapes]
PROGRAM GREETING;
BEGIN
    WRITELN ('HELLO)◻

Now press RETURN and notice what happens to the cursor. It lines up under the first non-blank character ('W') of the line it came from. This is the Auto-Indent feature, which causes the indentation of the new line and the previous line to be the same. This is very handy when a sequence of Pascal statements have the same indentation.

>Insert: Text [<bs> a char, <del> a line] [<etx> accepts <esc> escapes]
PROGRAM GREETING;
BEGIN
    WRITELN ('HELLO) ⌡
    ◼

However, for this program the final line should align with the second line, so we must press the backspace key twice. This moves the cursor to the left screen margin. Now type in the third and final line, and press RETURN:

```
>Insert: Text [<bs> a char, <del> a line] [<etx> accepts <esc> escapes]
PROGRAM GREETING;
BEGIN
     WRITELN ('HELLO)
END.
```

The text of GREETING is complete. Check it over. Make sure the second quote mark in the third line is missing. Then press the ETX key. ETX is the recommended key for the editor accept function. ETX is generated on most terminals by holding down the control key and pressing the C key. This is sometimes called CRTL-C. Your system may be configured to use a different key for this function. Again, check your documentation.

The prompt for the EDIT mode reappears. This terminates the INSERT mode and accepts the text we have written into the computer's text buffer.

```
>Edit: A(djst C(py D(lete F(ind I(nsrt J(mp R(place Q(uit X(chng Z(ap [E.6g]
PROGRAM GREETING;
BEGIN
     WRITELN ('HELLO)
END.
```

We will now store the text of GREETING on the root volume as the file SYSTEM.WRK.TEXT (the work file). Then we will check the root volume's directory.

First, select the editor QUIT command by pressing the Q key. The screen offers this new display:

>Quit:
       U(pdate the workfile and leave
       E(xit without updating
       R(eturn to the editor without updating
       W(rite to a filename and return
  ☐

Note that we have four options to choose from:

1. UPDATE puts the text in the text buffer on the root volume as the file SYSTEM.WRK.TEXT (the work file).
2. EXIT discards the text in the text buffer and exits to the COMMAND mode.
3. RETURN keeps the text in the text buffer and returns you to the EDIT mode.
4. WRITE puts the text in the text buffer on a disk under a file name you specify.

Chapter 4 describes these options in detail. For this example we want to use the first option: UPDATE. Select the UPDATE option by pressing the U key. As the system writes the text in the text buffer onto the root volume, the following message appears:

Writing . . ☐

When the process is complete, the COMMAND prompt reappears and a message indicates the size of the file in bytes:

Command: E(dit, R(un, F(ile, C(omp, L(ink, X(ecute, A(ssem, D(ebug,? [II.0]☐
Writing . .
Your file is 56 bytes long.

Our sample Pascal program GREETING is now stored on the root volume under the file name SYSTEM.WRK.TEXT. Let's verify this by using the EXTENDED DIRECTORY command in the FILER mode. This command displays the directory of a volume.

STEP 4: LISTING THE DIRECTORY OF A VOLUME

Enter the filer by pressing the F key. The prompt for the FILER mode appears. Although the letter E—representing the EXTENDED DIRECTORY command—does not appear on the prompt for the FILER mode, you can select the command anyway.

Press the E key. The prompt for the FILER mode is replaced by this question:

Dir listing of what vol ? ☐

The system is asking for the name of the volume whose directory you wish to see. We wish to see the directory of the root volume, which should now contain the file SYSTEM.WRK.TEXT (i.e., the GREETING program). Type an asterisk. This indicates the root volume, as you might remember from the section on the file system in the last chapter.

Dir listing of what vol ? *☐

Now press RETURN. The screen clears, and after a moment, it displays the name of the root volume and a list of all the files in its directory. The prompt for the FILER mode reappears at the top of the screen:

Filer: G(et, S(ave, W(hat, N(ew, L(dir, R(em, C(hng, T(rans, D(ate, Q(uit [C.2]☐
BOOT:

SYSTEM.PASCAL	33	10-Feb-79	10	512	Datafile
SYSTEM.MISCINFO	1	10-Feb-79	43	192	Datafile
SYSTEM.COMPILER	68	8-Feb-79	44	512	Codefile
SYSTEM.EDITOR	45	22-May-79	112	512	Codefile
SYSTEM.FILER	28	22-Jul-79	157	512	Codefile
SYSTEM.LIBRARY	14	7-Mar-80	185	512	Datafile
SYSTEM.SYNTAX	14	2-May-79	199	512	Textfile
SYSTEM.WRK.TEXT	4	25-Dec-81	213	512	Textfile
< UNUSED>	277		217		

8/8 files< listed/in-dir>, 217 blocks used, 277 unused, 277 in largest

We will study the details of this display in Chapter 3. It is full of useful information. Here, we will only confirm that the file SYSTEM.WRK.TEXT containing the GREETING program is indeed present. It is 4 blocks long—the minimum length for a .TEXT file—and was created (or updated) on the date set as the current date in Step 2 above.

Now we will use the FILER mode's QUIT command to return to the COMMAND mode. Unlike the editor QUIT, the filer QUIT presents no options.

Press the Q key. The command executes immediately. The prompt for the COMMAND mode reappears on screen. We are ready to compile the GREETING program.

STEP 5: COMPILING THE PROGRAM

We will now use the COMPILE command to translate the source code of GREETING into the machine code comprehensible to the computer. But, the compilation won't work because of the syntax error—the missing quote mark—in the program.

In response to the COMPILE command, the system automatically searches the root volume for the file SYSTEM.WRK.TEXT (the work file) and compiles its contents. The results of a successful compilation are stored on the root volume as the file SYSTEM.WRK.CODE (the other half of the work file). The details of the COMPILE command and the UCSD Pascal compiler will be explained in Chapter 5.

Now select the COMPILE command from the prompt of the COMMAND mode by pressing the C key. A message appears on screen:

Compiling... ☐

After a moment, compilation begins. As source code (or the original mnemonic or high-level statement version of a program) is translated into machine code, messages appear on the screen indicating the stages of the process. When the compiler encounters the error, it stops and displays the offending line of code with an error message and three options.

Compiling...

Pascal compiler [II.0.A.1]
<   0> . .
GREETING [2124 words]
<   2> . .
BEGIN
     WRITELN ('HELLO)<<<<
Line 2, error 202: <sp> (continue), <esc> (terminate) E(dit ☐

The four < pointers call your attention to the line with the missing quotation mark. The bottom line reports the number of the text line where the error is located and an error code number. It also indicates the three options now available to you. You can:

1. Press the space bar to continue compilation.

2. Press the ESC key to terminate compilation and return to the COMMAND mode.

3. Press the E key to start the chain of events described below.

Chapter 5 will fully describe all three of these possibilities. For this example, we want to use the third.

Press the E key. The system automatically:

- quits the COMPILE mode

- invokes the EDIT mode, which will put SYSTEM.WRK.TEXT (i.e., the GREETING program) into the text buffer and display it on the screen

- positions the cursor next to the mistake

- displays an explanation of the error at the top of the screen.

The result of all this activity is the following display on the screen:

```
String constant must not exceed source line. Type <sp>
PROGRAM GREETING;
BEGIN
     WRITELN ('HELLO)□
END.
```

The p-System has placed you in position to conveniently correct the error in your Pascal program.

The message at the top of the screen is the description of error number 202. (All the syntax error numbers and messages appear in Appendix C of this book.) Now press the spacebar. The prompt for the EDIT mode appears and the cursor remains in position:

```
>Edit: A(djst C(py D(lete F(ind I(nsrt J(mp R(place Q(uit X(chng Z(ap [E.6g]
PROGRAM GREETING;
BEGIN
      WRITELN ('HELLO)□
END.
```

We are ready to correct our intentional mistake.

STEP 6: FIXING THE ERROR

We will use the INSERT command to fix the syntax error in the GREETING program.

First, move the cursor one space leftward by pressing the backspace key once. The cursor is now sitting on the right parenthesis:

```
>Edit: A(djst C(py D(lete F(ind I(nsrt J(mp R(place Q(uit X(chng Z(ap [E.6g]
PROGRAM GREETING;
BEGIN
      WRITELN ('HELLO□]
END.
```

Now press the I key, selecting the INSERT command. The right parenthesis moves to the right screen margin:

```
>Insert: text [<bs> a char, <del> a line] [<etx> accepts <esc> escapes]
PROGRAM GREETING;
BEGIN
      WRITELN ('HELLO□                                                    )
END.
```

Type the quote mark and then press the ETX key. The right parenthesis moves back, and the INSERT mode is terminated. The prompt for the Edit mode reappears:

```
>Edit: A(djst C(py D(lete F(ind I(nsrt J(mp R(place Q(uit X(chng Z(ap [E.6g]
PROGRAM GREETING;
BEGIN
     WRITELN ('HELLO')
END.
```

The quote mark you typed is now part of the text in the text buffer.

As in Step 4 above, select the editor QUIT command by pressing the Q key. Then press the U key for the UPDATE option. The text in the text buffer is written on the root volume as a new SYSTEM.WRK.TEXT file. The old SYSTEM.WRK.TEXT is erased from the directory. The prompt for the COMMAND mode reappears at the top of the screen.

STEP 7: RECOMPILING

We will now use the COMPILE command once more to recompile the GREETING program. This time, there shouldn't be any errors. Invoke the COMPILE command by pressing the C key. Again, as we saw in Step 5, the screen displays a series of messages during the compilation process. There are no Pascal syntax errors. Compilation is successful:

```
Compiling...



Pascal compiler [II.0.A.1]
<   0> . .
GREETING [2124 words]
<   2> .
3 lines, 3 secs, 60 lines/min
Smallest available space = 2124 words
```

The significance of the bottom line will be explained in Chapter 5. The second-to-last line indicates the total number of text lines compiled and the time spent compiling. If your system does not have a clock you will not see the information about the time.

There is now a file SYSTEM.WRK.CODE on the root volume that contains the machine code for the GREETING program. Verify this for yourself, if you wish, by using the EXTENDED DIRECTORY command in the FILER mode (see Step 4 above). Let's see if GREETING works.

STEP 8: RUNNING THE PROGRAM

We are going to use the RUN command to execute the compiled code of the GREETING program. When RUN is selected, the system will search the root volume for the file SYSTEM.WRK.CODE and execute its contents. The details of the RUN command are discussed in Chapter 5.

Select the RUN command from the prompt of the COMMAND mode by pressing the R key. A message appears to let you know the program is being executed:

Running...

Then the screen displays the program output and the prompt for the COMMAND mode reappears:

```
Command: E(dit, R(un, F(ile, C(omp, L(ink, X(ecute, A(ssem, D(ebug,? [II.0]☐
Running...
HELLO
```

GREETING worked! There are no *run-time errors*.

Our excursion is nearly over. One step remains. We are going to save the GREETING program under a new file name and thus free the work file for some other use.

STEP 9: SAVING THE WORK FILE

You should save the work file whenever you have successfully compiled and run a program and want to move on to something else. You do this by renaming the root volume files SYSTEM.WRK.TEXT and SYSTEM.WRK.CODE, by using the FILER command SAVE.

First, enter the FILER mode by pressing the F Key from the COMMAND mode. Then select the SAVE command by pressing the S key. The system will ask:

Save as what file ? ☐

Now type the new file name *GREETING without any suffix and press RETURN:

Save as what file ? ***GREETING** ⏎

The prompt for the FILER mode reappears above a message that indicates that the file names SYSTEM.WRK.TEXT and SYSTEM.WRK.CODE have become GREETING.TEXT and GREETING.CODE on the root volume:

```
Filer: G(et, S(ave, N(ew, L(dir, R(em, C(hng, T(rans, D(ate, Q(uit [C.4]☐
Text file saved & Code file saved
```

Let's check this with the EXTENDED DIRECTORY command described in Step 4.

As before, select the EXTENDED DIRECTORY command by pressing the E key. Then type the asterisk (*) and press RETURN. The directory of the root volume appears. Notice the files GREETING.TEXT and GREETING.CODE:

```
Filer: G(et, S(ave, N(ew, L(dir, R(em, C(hng, T(rans, D(ate, Q(uit [C.4]☐
BOOT:
SYSTEM.PASCAL      33    10-Feb-79    10    512    Datafile
SYSTEM.MISCINFO     1    10-Feb-79    43    192    Datafile
SYSTEM.COMPILER    68     8-Feb-79    44    512    Codefile
SYSTEM.EDITOR      45    22-May-79   112    512    Codefile
SYSTEM.FILER       28    22-Jul-79   157    512    Codefile
SYSTEM.LIBRARY     14     7-Mar-80   185    512    Datafile
SYSTEM.SYNTAX      14     2-May-79   199    512    Textfile
GREETING.TEXT       4    25-Dec-81   213    512    Textfile
GREETING.CODE       2    25-Dec-81   217    512    Codefile
< UNUSED >        275                 219
9/9 files<listed/in-dir>, 219 blocks used, 275 unused, 275 in largest
```

Actually, GREETING.TEXT and GREETING.CODE are still designated as the work file. If you invoked the EDIT command, for example, the contents of GREETING.TEXT would appear on screen. To "undesignate"

GREETING.TEXT and GREETING.CODE, you must use the FILER command NEW. This command clears the work file.

Select the NEW command by pressing the N key. The command executes immediately and a message appears on the screen:

Workfile cleared

The GET command is the converse of the NEW command. Use it when you want to designate a file or pair of files on any volume as the work file.

SUMMARY

Having worked your way through all nine steps of a first encounter with the p-System, you should now be familiar with the basics that let you write, compile, correct, and run Pascal programs. In subsequent chapters, you will learn a great deal more about each of these operations. Before reading on, however, you might want to practice the material in this chapter by repeating the nine steps, using a new program. Here is another short program from *Introduction To Pascal* (Ref. 310):

```
PROGRAM SUM;
VAR A, B, TOTAL: INTEGER;
BEGIN
    WRITELN ('ENTER TWO NUMBERS TO BE ADDED... ');
    READ (A, B);
    TOTAL: = A + B;
    WRITELN ('THE SUM OF ',A,' AND ',B,' IS ',TOTAL)
END.
```

We will use the SUM program in Chapter 4 to examine the editor in detail.

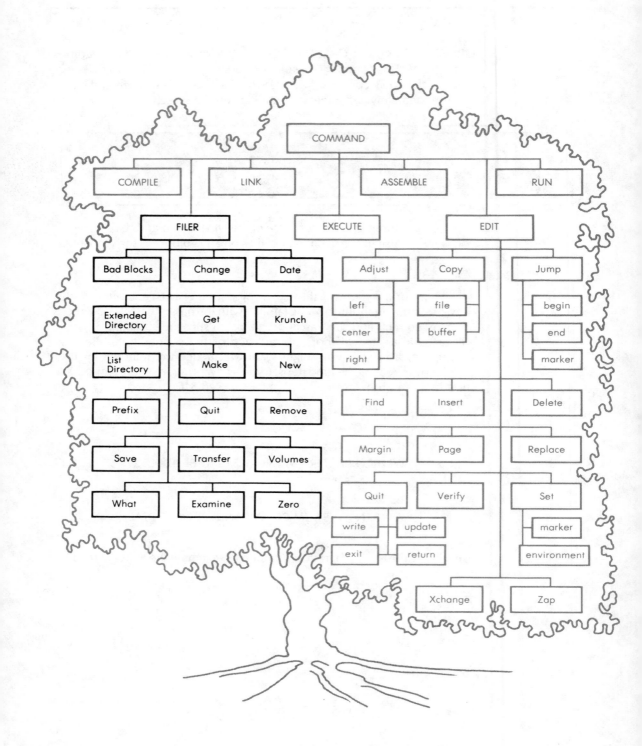

THE FILER 3

IN THE p-SYSTEM, the FILER is a program that contains commands which perform many useful operations on disk volumes, and on the files stored on disk volumes. For example, you can use FILER commands to:

- designate or clear the work file
- rename, move, or erase files
- make a backup copy of a volume
- copy a file onto another volume
- print a file
- identify and fix bad areas on a disk.

This chapter consists of two parts. Part One discusses the FILER commands. Part Two is a reference summary of the chapter. As always, you will best understand and retain the material presented if you actually practice the commands as you read about them.

PART ONE: THE FILER COMMANDS

We will organize our discussion in this section according to the scope and function of the various FILER commands. Specifically, we will examine groups of commands that will:

- display information—the VOLUMES, PREFIX, EXTENDED DIREC-TORY, and LIST DIRECTORY commands

- affect the work file—the GET, WHAT, NEW, and SAVE commands

- alter the directory—the REMOVE, CHANGE, MAKE, and ZERO commands

- operate on contents—the TRANSFER command

- operate on the disk—the KRUNCH, BAD BLOCKS, and EXAMINE commands

- do housekeeping—the DATE command

Figure 3.1 lists the FILER commands in alphabetical order and gives a brief description of each command.

We will now learn how to invoke and quit the filer.

Entering And Leaving The Filer

Recall from Chapter 1, that in order to enter the filer you must be in the COMMAND mode and have the prompt of the COMMAND mode on your screen:

Command: E(dit, R(un, F(ile, C(omp, L(ink, X(ecute, A(ssem, D(ebug, ? [II.0] ☐

Then you can select the FILER command by pressing the F key. This enters the FILER mode and displays the FILER prompt:

Filer: G(et, S(ave, W(hat, N(ew, L(dir, R(em, C(hng, T(rans, D(ate, Q(uit [C.4] ☐

Leaving the FILER and returning to the COMMAND mode is simplicity itself; just press the Q key. This selects the QUIT command which returns you to the COMMAND mode. The prompt for the COMMAND mode immediately replaces the prompt for the FILER mode.

We will now examine a group of commands that display information: VOLUMES, PREFIX, EXTENDED DIRECTORY, and LIST DIRECTORY.

The VOLUMES Command

The VOLUMES command tells you the numbers and names of the volumes currently on line as well as the names of the root and prefix

Command	Description
BAD BLOCKS	scans the blocks on a disk volume and identifies those with faulty contents or other problems.
CHANGE	renames a file or a volume.
DATE	sets the system date.
EXAMINE	attempts to repair faulty blocks on a disk volume.
EXTENDED DIRECTORY	lists the names of the files on a volume and gives other information.
GET	designates a file as the work file.
KRUNCH	moves files so unused areas of a volume are consolidated.
LIST DIRECTORY	lists the names of the files on a disk.
MAKE	establishes dummy files on a volume.
NEW	clears the current work file.
PREFIX	designates a new default prefix volume.
QUIT	quits the filer.
REMOVE	removes files from a volume.
SAVE	saves the work file under a new file name.
TRANSFER	copies a file to another volume or device.
VOLUMES	lists the names of the current volumes, the root volume, and the prefix volume.
WHAT	indicates the status of the work file.
ZERO	initializes the directory of a volume.

Figure 3.1: The Filer Commands

volumes. You can use VOLUMES to quickly check the name of a volume in a particular drive, or to recall the name of the prefix volume.

Executing VOLUMES To execute VOLUMES, select the VOLUMES command from the FILER prompt by pressing the V key. There is no VOLUMES prompt. After a moment, a list of the volume numbers and names appears on screen. At the bottom of the list, the root volume is listed as the ROOT VOL; the prefix volume is called the PREFIX. Figure 3.2 shows a sample VOLUMES display. A sharp sign (#) before a volume name indicates that the volume is a block-structured device (i.e., a disk).

Use the VOLUMES command to look at your own system. First make sure that you are in the FILER mode and that the prompt for this mode is on the screen. Then press the V key. A display like the sample display in Figure 3.2 will appear.

The PREFIX Command

The PREFIX command displays or changes the name of the current prefix volume. The root volume is automatically designated as the prefix volume when you boot the system. You must use PREFIX to establish a new prefix volume.

Executing PREFIX To execute PREFIX, select the PREFIX command while in the FILER mode by striking the P key. This produces the PREFIX prompt:

Prefix titles by? ☐

```
Vols on-line
1      CONSOLE:
2      SYSTERM
4 #    DEMO:
6      PRINTER:
11 #   SYS:
12 #   BOOK:
Root vol is - SYS:
Prefix is    - BOOK:
```

Figure 3.2: The VOLUMES Command—A Sample Display

You now have two options. You may:

1. display the name of the current prefix volume by typing a colon (:) and pressing RETURN. The name of the prefix volume will appear under the FILER prompt.

2. change the prefix volume to a different volume by typing in the new volume name followed by a colon and then pressing RETURN. Check the message that appears under the FILER prompt to confirm that your typing was accurate.

Let's look at an example of the PREFIX command.

Example of PREFIX   When the system is booted, the root volume is automatically specified as the prefix volume. We will now set the volume DEMO as the prefix volume.

Press the P key to select the PREFIX command. Answer the prompt by typing 'DEMO:'. Then press RETURN. A message appears under the FILER prompt, confirming the new prefix volume:

Prefix titles by ? **DEMO:**

Prefix is DEMO:

Two Hints   If you are using a two-drive system, you can leave the system disk (the root volume) in place and make the volume in the second drive the prefix volume. Then, in response to some prompt, you can refer to the root volume with an asterisk (*) and the other volume with a colon (:).

If you are changing disks frequently, you may want to set the unit number of the disk drive as the prefix volume. This will allow you to refer to any volume that happens to be in the drive, as the prefix volume. When you change disks, the new disk will automatically become the prefix volume.

To set the unit number of the drive as the prefix, first make sure that the drive is empty. Then execute the PREFIX command by pressing the P key, and type in the volume number of the drive. You must include the sharp sign (#) and the colon. For example, suppose drive 5 has no disk in it. If you reply to the PREFIX prompt by typing # 5 and pressing RETURN:

Prefix titles by ? **#5:**

then *any* disk you put in drive 5 will be the prefix volume.

Note that this will not work in the p-Systems that use a CP/M BIOS for the disk I/O routines. CP/M is set up to hang (wait for you to put a disk in) if you attempt to access a disk drive when there is no disk present. You can get around this problem on these systems by putting a disk into the drive that does not contain a valid p-System directory. A formatted but not yet ZEROed disk will work, as will a disk that has a CP/M directory on it.

The EXTENDED DIRECTORY Command

The EXTENDED DIRECTORY command displays the contents of a volume directory. (You used the EXTENDED DIRECTORY command in Chapter 2.) The information it gives can help you make a variety of decisions about when to use other FILER commands. For this reason, you will probably find yourself using the EXTENDED DIRECTORY command frequently.

Executing EXTENDED DIRECTORY To execute EXTENDED DIRECTORY, select the EXTENDED DIRECTORY command while in the FILER mode by pressing the E key. This produces the EXTENDED DIRECTORY prompt:

Dir listing of what vol ? ☐

You now have five options. You may:

1. display the directory of the prefix volume by typing a colon (:) and pressing RETURN.

2. display the directory of the root volume by typing an asterisk (*) and pressing RETURN.

3. display the directory of some other volume by typing the name of the volume followed by a colon, and then pressing RETURN.

4. display the directory of *any* volume that is currently in a particular drive by typing the unit number of that drive, preceded by a sharp sign (#) and followed by a colon.

5. display a subset of the files on any of the above volumes by using a wild card in a file specification.

Error Message If the volume you specify isn't on line (i.e., in a drive), the following error message will appear:

VOLNAME: No such vol on line <source>

Information Displayed What does the EXTENDED DIRECTORY display tell us? The name of the volume appears at the top left of the display. The column under the volume name lists the file names in the directory and the unused areas of the volume. The column to the right of the file names shows the number of blocks in each file or unused area. The third column shows the date the file was created or last updated. The fourth column indicates the starting block number for each file and unused area. The fifth column shows how many bytes of the last block are used. (There are 512 bytes in a block.) The last column displays the system designation of the type of material in the file. The bottom line of the EXTENDED DIRECTORY display tells us four things:

1. the number of files listed on the screen and the number of files in the directory; these numbers are not necessarily the same

2. the total amount of space used by the files listed on the screen

3. the total amount of unused space on the volume (this number may be incorrect if you are using a wild card to specify a subset of the files in the directory)

4. the number of blocks in the largest unused area on the volume. This is the maximum size of any new file (this number may also be incorrect if you are using a wild card).

A directory may contain more files than a single screen can display. In such a case, the top of the screen will display a message to 'Type <space> to continue'. If you press the spacebar, the rest of the directory will appear.

Let's consider an example of the EXTENDED DIRECTORY command.

Example of EXTENDED DIRECTORY   In this example, we will look at the directory of the prefix volume DEMO.

Select the EXTENDED DIRECTORY command by pressing the E key. Answer the prompt by typing a colon and pressing RETURN:

Dir listing of what vol ? :

The screen fills with the directory of DEMO under the file prompt:

```
Filer: G(et, S(ave, W(hat, N(ew, L(dir, R(em, C(hng, T(rans, D(ate, Q(uit [C.4] □
DEMO:
<UNUSED>          8                    6
TEST.TEXT         4      12-Nov-80     14   512    Textfile
TEST.CODE         2      12-Nov-80     18   512    Codefile
<UNUSED>          10                   20
PROPOSAL.TEXT     4      26-Nov-80     30   512    Textfile
<UNUSED>          25                   34
SUM.TEXT          4      26-Nov-80     59   512    Textfile
SUM.CODE          2      26-Nov-80     63   512    Codefile
<UNUSED>          2                    65
SAMPLE.TEXT       4      21-Mar-81     67   512    Textfile
<UNUSED>          209                  71
6/6 files<listed/in-dir>, 20 blocks used, 254 unused, 209 in largest
```

The bottom line of this display shows that 6 out of the 6 files on the volume are listed. A total of 254 blocks are unused, and 209 blocks make up the largest unused area. It also shows that the first file in the directory is TEST.TEXT. It takes up 4 blocks and was last updated on November 12, 1980. It starts at block number 14 on the volume.

Using The Information There are many ways the information on the EXTENDED DIRECTORY display can prove useful. For example, before moving a file from one volume to another with the TRANSFER command, you can make sure there is sufficient unused space on the destination volume. Also, before invoking EDIT to create a new SYSTEM.WRK.TEXT file, you can verify that the root volume has at least four contiguous unused blocks, the minimum number required by the p-System. And, before using the KRUNCH command, you can look at the number and position of the unused areas on a volume.

Listing A Directory To The Printer Or A File You can also use the EXTENDED DIRECTORY command to print a listing of a volume's directory. To do this, simply reply to the EXTENDED DIRECTORY prompt as above, but this time add a comma and the volume name or number of the printer, followed by a colon. Then press RETURN.

For example, suppose you want to print the directory of the volume named GAMES. Press the E key, selecting the EXTENDED DIRECTORY command. Now answer the prompt

Dir listing of what vol ? ☐

by typing

Dir listing of what vol ? **GAMES:,PRINTER:** ↲

or

Dir listing of what vol ? **GAMES:,#6:** ↲

The directory of GAMES will be printed out on the printer. This option fails, of course, if your printer is not connected, turned on, and loaded with paper.

In a similar fashion, you may store a listing of a directory as a file on any volume. To do this, you simply specify a file name after the comma. For example, suppose you want to store the directory of the volume GAMES, as a file named GAMESDIR.TEXT on the volume named MASTER. Press the E key for the EXTENDED DIRECTORY command. Then answer the prompt

Dir listing of what vol ? ☐

by typing

Dir listing of what vol ? **GAMES:,MASTER:GAMESDIR.TEXT** ↲

The volume MASTER now has a new file named GAMESDIR.TEXT that contains the directory of the volume GAMES.

If you have lots of floppy disks on hand, you might wish to put the directory of each on a single reference volume.

The LIST DIRECTORY Command

The LIST DIRECTORY command is identical with the EXTENDED DIRECTORY command in every respect, except that it displays less information. In particular, LIST DIRECTORY does *not* give you information about the unused blocks, the starting block numbers, or the type of each file.

Executing LIST DIRECTORY   To execute LIST DIRECTORY, select LIST DIRECTORY from the FILER mode by pressing the L key. The LIST DIRECTORY prompt and the ways you may respond to it correspond exactly to the EXTENDED DIRECTORY prompt and its options.

As an example, here is the directory of the volume DEMO as it appears on screen when LIST DIRECTORY is used:

```
Filer: G(et, S(ave, W(hat, N(ew, L(dir, R(em, C(hng, T(rans, D(ate, Q(uit [C.4] ☐
DEMO:
TEST.TEXT            4      12-Nov-80
TEST.CODE            2      12-Nov-80
PROPOSAL.TEXT        4      26-Nov-80
SUM.TEXT             4      26-Nov-80
SUM.CODE             2      26-Nov-80
SAMPLE.TEXT          4      21-Mar-81
6/6 files<listed/in-dir>, 20 blocks used, 254 unused, 209 in largest
```

Notice that the unused areas on the volume are not shown, nor are the starting block numbers of the various files.

Introduction To Work File Commands

Before discussing the frequently used filer commands, WHAT, NEW, GET and SAVE, we will review an important feature of the p-System: the work file.

As we have seen, the work file is a file that the system uses automatically when you select EDIT, COMPILE, ASSEMBLE, or RUN from the

COMMAND mode. The work file may be a pair of files on the root volume, named SYSTEM.WRK.TEXT and SYSTEM.WRK.CODE, or it may be only one of these. It may also be some other file or pair of files that you have designated as the work file, using the GET command.

In general, the p-System uses the work file when:

— you select EDIT from the COMMAND mode. The system loads a copy of the work file into the text buffer and displays it on the screen;

— you select COMPILE. The system attempts to compile the contents of SYSTEM.WRK.TEXT. If the compilation is successful, then the new file SYSTEM.WRK.CODE will appear on the root volume. If SYSTEM.WRK.TEXT is subsequently updated from the editor, SYSTEM.WRK.CODE will be removed;

— you select RUN. The system puts the machine code from the file SYSTEM.WRK.CODE, if it exists, into main memory and executes it. If it does not exist, then the system will first attempt to compile the contents of the file SYSTEM.WRK.TEXT, thus producing the file SYSTEM.WRK.CODE. The system will also invoke the LINKER, if the SYSTEM.WRK.CODE file needs to be linked before execution.

We will now examine the commands that designate a file as the work file (GET), display the name of the current work file (WHAT), clear the work file (NEW), and rename SYSTEM.WRK.TEXT and SYSTEM.WRK.CODE (SAVE).

The GET Command

The GET command designates a file as the work file. The file name itself is not affected; it is simply "tagged" as the work file. You will use GET when you want to work extensively on a file. If a file is designated as the work file, the contents of the file will appear on the screen every time you invoke EDIT.

Executing GET To execute GET, select the GET command from the FILER mode by pressing the G key. This produces the GET prompt:

Get what file ? ☐

Then type the file name without any suffix. You don't need to type the suffix part of the file name (i.e., .TEXT or .CODE) because the system will designate both file types as the work file. Then press RETURN. You may omit the volume specification and colon if the file is on the prefix volume. After you press RETURN, the following message appears:

Text & Code file loaded

> This message tells you that GET has been executed. The FILER prompt reappears at the top of the screen. If there is only a text version of the file that you have named on the volume, then the message:

Text file loaded

> appears. Similarly, the message

Code file loaded

> appears, if the volume has only a code version. Let's look at an example of the GET command.

> **Example of GET** We want to designate the files SUM.TEXT and SUM.CODE on the prefix volume DEMO, as the work file.
> Press the G key to select the GET command. Answer the prompt by typing:

Get what file ? **SUM**₎

> You don't need to type 'DEMO' since it is the prefix volume.
> A message then appears confirming the designation:

Text & Code file loaded

> The pair of files SUM.TEXT and SUM.CODE are now the work file. You can verify this by using the WHAT command (described shortly).

> **An Important Variation** Now consider this important variation. Suppose the root volume contains a file named SYSTEM.WRK.TEXT or SYSTEM.WRK.CODE. We want to use GET to designate some other file as the work file.
> Press G to invoke GET, and the following question appears:

Throw away current workfile ? ☐

> In other words, the system is asking if you want to destroy SYSTEM.WRK.TEXT and SYSTEM.WRK.CODE. You may answer 'YES' by pressing the Y key and SYSTEM.WRK.TEXT and SYSTEM.WRK.CODE will disappear. The system will then ask:

Get what file ? ☐

> You should respond with the name of the file you want to designate. Then press RETURN.
> You may answer 'NO' to the 'throw away current workfile?' question by pressing any other key. This will abort the GET command and return you

to the FILER mode. SYSTEM.WRK.TEXT and SYSTEM.WRK.CODE will remain unchanged. You can now use the SAVE command to rename them appropriately, and then invoke GET once more.

Another Example The directory of the root volume BOOT shows the files SYSTEM.WRK.TEXT, SYSTEM.WRK.CODE, GREETING.TEXT, and GREETING.CODE.

Filer: G(et, S(ave, W(hat, N(ew, L(dir, R(em, C(hng, T(rans, D(ate, Q(uit [C.4] □
BOOT:

SYSTEM.PASCAL	33	10-Feb-79	10	512	Datafile
SYSTEM.MISCINFO	1	10-Feb-79	43	192	Datafile
SYSTEM.COMPILER	68	8-Feb-79	44	512	Codefile
SYSTEM.EDITOR	45	22-May-79	112	512	Codefile
SYSTEM.FILER	28	22-Jul-79	157	512	Codefile
SYSTEM.LIBRARY	14	7-Mar-80	185	512	Datafile
SYSTEM.SYNTAX	14	2-May-79	199	512	Textfile
GREETING.TEXT	4	7-Sep-81	213	512	Textfile
GREETING.CODE	2	7-Sep-81	217	512	Codefile
SYSTEM.WRK.TEXT	4	25-Dec-81	219	512	Textfile
SYSTEM.WRK.CODE	2	25-Dec-81	223	512	Codefile
< UNUSED >	269		225		

11/11 files<listed/in-dir>, 225 blocks used, 269 unused, 269 in largest

We want to designate the GREETING files as the work file and discard SYSTEM.WRK.TEXT and SYSTEM.WRK.CODE in the process.
Press the G key to select GET. The system asks:

Throw away current workfile ? □

Answer 'YES' with the Y key. The system then asks for the name of the new work file:

Get what file ? □

Type the file name without a suffix, preceded by the asterisk, to indicate the root volume:

Get what file ? ***GREETING** ₎

A message appears confirming the designation of GREETING.TEXT and GREETING.CODE as the work file:

Text & Code file loaded

Now use the EXTENDED DIRECTORY command to verify that SYSTEM.WRK.TEXT and SYSTEM.WRK.CODE have been erased from the directory.

One GET After Another   If some file other than SYSTEM.WRK.TEXT and SYSTEM.WRK.CODE is already the designated work file, then you can use GET to change the designation directly to another file. In other words, the GET command moves the "tag" from one file to another. The file previously designated will not be thrown away.

The WHAT Command

The WHAT command tells you the current status of the work file. A message indicates the presence of SYSTEM.WRK.TEXT and SYSTEM.WRK.CODE on the root volume, or the name of the file designated as the work file. Use WHAT when you aren't sure what the current work file is, or even if there is one.

Executing WHAT   To execute WHAT, select the WHAT command while in the FILER mode by pressing the W key. There is no WHAT prompt. The command executes immediately. A message, determined by the actual status of the work file, appears under the FILER prompt. Examples include:

Message displayed:	Work file status:
No workfile	No SYSTEM.WRK.TEXT, SYSTEM.WRK.CODE or designated work file
not named (not saved)	Root volume contains a file named SYSTEM.WRK.TEXT or SYSTEM.WRK.CODE and no other file is designated as the work file
Workfile is VOLNAME:FILENAME	Some volume contains a designated work file, and SYSTEM.WRK.TEXT and SYSTEM.WRK.CODE do not exist on the root volume
Workfile is VOLNAME:FILENAME (not saved)	Root volume contains SYSTEM.WRK.TEXT or SYSTEM.WRK.CODE, which is the most current copy of the designated work file

Example of WHAT   In a previous example, we used GET to designate the files GREETING.TEXT and GREETING.CODE on the root volume as the work file. We will now use WHAT to verify this.

Press the W key. The following message appears:

Workfile is BOOT:GREETING

The NEW Command

The NEW command clears the work file from the system. That is, it removes the work file designation from a file or erases the files SYSTEM.WRK.TEXT and SYSTEM.WRK.CODE from the root volume. After you use the NEW command, the WHAT command will produce the message 'no workfile'. You will use NEW whenever there is a work file, and you want to employ EDIT to create a new file.

Executing NEW   To execute NEW, select the NEW command from the FILER prompt by pressing the N key. One of two things will happen, depending on the status of the work file:

1. If some file is designated as the work file and it is saved, the designation is removed and the following message appears under the FILER prompt:

Workfile cleared

The message also appears if there is no work file in the system.

2. If either SYSTEM.WRK.TEXT or SYSTEM.WRK.CODE exist on the root volume, the system asks:

Throw away current workfile ? ☐

In other words, it is asking if you want to discard SYSTEM.WRK.TEXT and SYSTEM.WRK.CODE? You may answer 'YES' by pressing the Y key. The system will then erase the file names SYSTEM.WRK.TEXT and SYSTEM.WRK.CODE from the root volume directory and mark the blocks they occupied, as unused.

You may answer 'NO' by pressing any other key. This will cancel the NEW command and the FILER prompt will reappear. SYSTEM.WRK.TEXT and SYSTEM.WRK.CODE will be untouched. If you wish, you can use the SAVE command (described later in this chapter) to rename them, and then perform NEW again. Let's consider an example.

Example of NEW   We previously designated the GREETING files on the root volume BOOT as the work file. We have checked this designation with the WHAT command. Now we want to clear the work file.

Press the N key to select NEW. A message appears below the FILER prompt:

Workfile cleared

Now try the WHAT command once more by pressing the W key. The following message indicates that GREETING.TEXT and GREETING.CODE are no longer the work file.

No workfile

The SAVE Command

The SAVE command renames the files SYSTEM.WRK.TEXT and SYSTEM.WRK.CODE. The contents of the files are unaffected. You may then create an entirely new work file.

Use SAVE when you want to store the contents of SYSTEM.WRK.TEXT and SYSTEM.WRK.CODE under a file name of your own choosing. You did this in Chapter 2 when you saved the Pascal program GREETING as the files GREETING.TEXT and GREETING.CODE.

Executing SAVE   To execute SAVE, select the SAVE command from the FILER prompt by pressing the S key. The SAVE prompt appears:

Save as what file ? ☐

Type in the file name you wish without a .TEXT or .CODE suffix, and press RETURN. When the root volume has both SYSTEM.WRK.TEXT and SYSTEM.WRK.CODE, the following message appears under the FILER prompt:

Text & Code file saved

SYSTEM.WRK.TEXT and SYSTEM.WRK.CODE are now renamed according to the name you typed. The system supplies the .TEXT and .CODE suffixes automatically.

When only SYSTEM.WRK.TEXT is on the root volume, the following message appears:

Text file saved

If the volume already has a file with a name identical to the one you typed, the system will erase the older (previous) file from the directory.

Error Messages   If you execute SAVE when the work file is a designated file, the following message appears:

Workfile is saved

If you select SAVE when there is no designated file, and there is no SYSTEM.WRK.TEXT and SYSTEM.WRK.CODE on the root volume, the system will tell you:

No workfile to save

Let's consider an example.

Example of SAVE　Suppose the root volume BOOT contains the files SYSTEM.WRK.TEXT and SYSTEM.WRK.CODE, and we want to save these files as RACE.TEXT and RACE.CODE.

Press the S key to select SAVE. Answer the prompt by typing an asterisk and the unsuffixed file name, and then pressing RETURN.

Save as what file ? ***RACE**

A message appears beneath the FILER prompt, and the file SYSTEM.WRK.TEXT is now renamed RACE.TEXT, and SYSTEM.WRK.CODE is renamed RACE.CODE:

Filer: G(et, S(ave, W(hat, N(ew, L(dir, R(em, C(hng, T(rans, D(ate, Q(uit C.[C.4] ☐
Text & Code file saved

Now use the EXTENDED DIRECTORY command to check the directory of the root volume. Note the file name changes in the directory:

Filer: G(et, S(ave, W(hat, N(ew, L(dir, R(em, C(hng, T(rans, D(ate, Q(uit [C.4] ☐
BOOT:

SYSTEM.PASCAL	33	10-Feb-79	10	512	Datafile
SYSTEM.MISCINFO	1	10-Feb-79	43	192	Datafile
SYSTEM.COMPILER	68	8-Feb-79	44	512	Codefile
SYSTEM.EDITOR	45	22-May-79	112	512	Codefile
SYSTEM.FILER	28	22-Jul-79	157	512	Codefile
SYSTEM.LIBRARY	14	7-Mar-80	185	512	Datafile
SYSTEM.SYNTAX	14	2-May-79	199	512	Textfile
GREETING.TEXT	4	7-Sep-81	213	512	Textfile
GREETING.CODE	2	7-Sep-81	217	512	Codefile
RACE.TEXT	4	8-Sep-81	219	512	Textfile
RACE.CODE	2	8-Sep-81	223	512	Codefile
< UNUSED >	269		225		

11/11 files< listed/in-dir>, 225 blocks used, 269 unused, 269 in largest

SAVE Doesn't Mean NEW   SAVE doesn't entail the NEW command. In other words, the saved file is now the designated work file. To clear the work file, you must use the NEW command. In our example, the designated work file is RACE.TEXT and RACE.CODE. Verify this with the WHAT command:

Workfile is BOOT:RACE

Saving An Updated File   There is one case where the SAVE prompt will differ from the prompt we have described. Suppose you use the GET command to designate a file as the work file, and then use EDIT to revise the contents of the file. You quit EDIT using the UPDATE option. This creates a new SYSTEM.WRK.TEXT file on your root volume. In other words, your system now has the original file designated as the work file and an updated version of it under the file name SYSTEM.WRK.TEXT. Now when you invoke SAVE, the prompt asks:

Save as VOLNAME:FILENAME ? ☐

In other words, do you want to rename SYSTEM.WRK.TEXT, using the name of the file you designated as the work file?

You may answer 'YES' by pressing the Y key. The system will rename SYSTEM.WRK.TEXT accordingly. It will also erase from the directory the original file name you designated. In effect, you now have only the latest version of the file.

You may answer 'NO' by pressing any other key. The system will ask:

Save as what file ? ☐

Respond by typing an alternate file name. Now both the original file and its updated version are available under different file names.

If you reboot the p-System before the updated SYSTEM.WRK files are saved, then the name of the designated file will not be available. Let's consider an example.

Another Example of SAVE   Suppose the root volume contains the files SYSTEM.WRK.TEXT and SYSTEM.WRK.CODE, which resulted from the update and subsequent compilation of the designated work files, HANG.TEXT and HANG.CODE. We now want to save SYSTEM.WRK.TEXT and SYSTEM.WRK.CODE as new HANG files, and discard the old HANG.TEXT and HANG.CODE.

Press the S key to select SAVE. The system asks:

Save as BOOT:HANG?

Press the Y key to answer 'YES'. A message appears confirming the operation:

Text & Code file saved

Now the EXTENDED DIRECTORY command shows that the old HANG files have been erased from the directory of the root volume.

Saving To Another Volume   You can save the work file as a file on a volume other than the root volume. In response to the SAVE prompt, simply type the volume name, a colon (:), and the file name without suffix. In this case, SAVE operates like the TRANSFER command. SYSTEM.WRK.TEXT and SYSTEM.WRK.CODE remain on the root volume. Their contents are copied to the other volume under the file name specified.

We are now ready to look at a group of FILER commands that affect the directory of a volume: REMOVE, CHANGE, MAKE, and ZERO.

The REMOVE Command

The REMOVE command erases a file name from a volume directory. The information in the file is not physically removed, but the blocks it occupies are marked 'unused' and may then be overwritten.

You can use the REMOVE command to liberate volume space. You might first transfer a file to another volume and then remove it, or you might discard a file by removing it without transferring it elsewhere. In certain circumstances it is possible to recover a file you have removed, by using the MAKE command.

Executing REMOVE   To execute REMOVE, select the REMOVE command from the FILER prompt by pressing the R key. This produces the REMOVE prompt:

Remove what file ? ☐

Type in the volume name, a colon, and the full file name including suffix. You may omit the volume name and colon, of course, if the file is on the prefix volume. Then press RETURN. The following message appears:

VOLNAME:FILENAME --> removed
Update directory?

The system is asking if you want to make the removal final. If you answer 'YES' by pressing the Y key, the file name will disappear from the directory. If you answer 'NO' by pressing any other key, the REMOVE command will abort, and you will return to the FILER mode.

Error Message   If you omit the suffix or misspell the file name, the system will not be able to execute REMOVE. The following message will appear:

File not found

Let's consider an example.

Example of REMOVE   Suppose the file JUNK.TEXT is on the volume GUIDE, which is not the prefix volume:

GUIDE:

SYSTEM.PASCAL	33	10-Feb-79	10	512	Datafile
SYSTEM.MISCINFO	1	10-Feb-79	43	192	Datafile
SYSTEM.COMPILER	68	8-Feb-79	44	512	Codefile
SYSTEM.EDITOR	45	22-May-79	112	512	Codefile
SYSTEM.FILER	28	22-Jul-79	157	512	Codefile
SYSTEM.LIBRARY	14	7-Mar-80	185	512	Datafile
SYSTEM.SYNTAX	14	2-May-79	199	512	Textfile
JUNK.TEXT	4	7-Sep-81	213	512	Textfile
< UNUSED >	277		217		

8/8 files< listed/in-dir>, 217 blocks used, 277 unused, 277 in largest

We wish to remove JUNK.TEXT.
     Press the R key selecting the REMOVE command. Answer the REMOVE prompt by typing the volume name, a colon, and the complete file name including suffix:

Remove what file ? **GUIDE:JUNK.TEXT**

The system reports the removal and asks if you want to make it final:

GUIDE:JUNK.TEXT --> removed

Update directory?

> Answer 'YES' by pressing the Y key. Then use the EXTENDED DIRECTORY to look at the directory of GUIDE again. You will find that the file name JUNK.TEXT has disappeared. The blocks it occupied are marked unused:

GUIDE:

SYSTEM.PASCAL	33	10-Feb-79	10	512	Datafile
SYSTEM.MISCINFO	1	10-Feb-79	43	192	Datafile
SYSTEM.COMPILER	68	8-Feb-79	44	512	Codefile
SYSTEM.EDITOR	45	22-May-79	112	512	Codefile
SYSTEM.FILER	28	22-Jul-79	157	512	Codefile
SYSTEM.LIBRARY	14	7-Mar-80	185	512	Datafile
SYSTEM.SYNTAX	14	2-May-79	199	512	Textfile
< UNUSED >	281		213		

7/7 files<listed/in-dir>, 213 blocks used, 281 unused, 281 in largest

REMOVE With Wild Cards   You can use wild cards with the REMOVE command. The question mark (?) is the preferred wild card. With it, you can check each file before it is removed. Let's consider an example.

Wild Card Example   We want to remove the files TEST.TEXT and TEST.CODE from the prefix volume DEMO.

Press the R key to select the REMOVE command. Answer the REMOVE prompt by typing the unsuffixed file name and the ? wild card. Then press RETURN:

Remove what file ? **TEST?**

> The system asks for approval to remove the TEST.TEXT file:

Remove DEMO:TEST.TEXT ? ☐

> Press the Y key to answer affirmatively. (Press any other key to answer 'NO'.) Then the system asks:

Remove DEMO:TEST.TEXT ? **Y**

DEMO:TEST.TEXT --> removed

Remove DEMO:TEST.CODE ? ☐

Again, reply 'YES' by pressing the Y key. Finally the system asks if you want to make the removals final:

Remove DEMO:TEST.TEXT ? Y
DEMO:TEST.TEXT --> removed
Remove DEMO:TEST.CODE ? **Y**
DEMO:TEST.CODE --> removed
Update directory ? ☐

Press the Y key to respond 'YES'. The files TEST.TEXT and TEST.CODE are then erased from the DEMO directory. Verify this with the EXTENDED DIRECTORY command:

Filer: G(et, S(ave, W(hat, N(ew, L(dir, R(em, C(hng, T(rans, D(ate, Q(uit [C.4]☐					
DEMO:					
< UNUSED >	24		6		
PROPOSAL.TEXT	4	26-Nov-80	30	512	Textfile
< UNUSED >	25		34		
SUM.TEXT	4	26-Nov-80	59	512	Textfile
SUM.CODE	2	26-Nov-80	63	512	Codefile
< UNUSED >	2		65		
SAMPLE.TEXT	4	21-Mar-81	67	512	Textfile
< UNUSED >	209		71		
4/4 files<listed/in-dir>, 14 blocks used, 260 unused, 209 in largest					

Removing Unrelated File Names If there is no convenient way to specify a group of files with a wild card, you can list each file, separated by commas, after the REMOVE prompt. For example, typing:

Remove what file ? **MEMO.TEXT,GAME.CODE,OUTPUT.DATA** ↵

will cause the REMOVE command to operate on each of the three files listed.

The CHANGE Command

The CHANGE command renames a file or a volume. CHANGE substitutes a new file name for an established one in a volume directory, or a new volume name for an old one. You might use the CHANGE command, for example, to rename an old version of a Pascal program.

Executing CHANGE　To execute CHANGE, select the CHANGE command from the FILER mode by pressing the C key. The screen displays the first CHANGE prompt:

Change what file ? ☐

To rename a file, type in the full current file name including suffix. Of course, if the file is on the prefix volume, you can omit the volume name and colon. Then press RETURN. This will produce the second change prompt:

Change to what ? ☐

Now type out the new file name in full, including suffix, and press RETURN. You don't have to retype the volume name or colon. The renamed file will be on the same volume. The screen will display a message indicating that the change has been made, and the FILER prompt will reappear.

To rename a volume, in response to the first prompt ('Change what file?'), type in the old volume name, followed by a colon. Then press RETURN. In answer to the second prompt ('Change to what?'), type the new volume name, followed by a colon, and press RETURN.

You may abbreviate this procedure by typing in response to the first prompt ('Change what file?'), the old file or volume name, a comma(,), and the new file or volume name. When you press RETURN, CHANGE will execute without the appearance of the second prompt. Let's consider an example of CHANGE.

Example of CHANGE　The volume GUIDE contains the file MEMO.TEXT that we wish to rename NOTE.TEXT. GUIDE is not the prefix volume. Press the C key to select the CHANGE command. Use the abbreviated procedure. That is, answer the initial CHANGE prompt by typing the volume name and old file name, a comma, and the new file name, and then pressing RETURN.

Change what file ? **GUIDE:MEMO.TEXT,NOTE.TEXT** ⏎

A message appears under the FILER prompt indicating that the change has been made:

GUIDE:MEMO.TEXT --> NOTE.TEXT

Verify that MEMO.TEXT has been renamed NOTE.TEXT by using the EXTENDED DIRECTORY command.

Another Example of CHANGE   Let's look at another example. We have a volume named HOT that we want to rename COLD.
Press the C key to select CHANGE. Answer the CHANGE prompt by typing the old volume name and a colon, a comma, and the new volume name and a colon, and pressing RETURN.

Change what file ? **HOT:,COLD:** ⏎

A message then indicates that the change has been executed:

HOT: --> COLD:

CHANGE With Wild Cards   You can use a wild card with the CHANGE command to rename a group of files at one time. The ? wild card is preferred. With it, you can check each file before the change is made. There's one rule to remember: if a wild card appears in the old file name, a wild card—not necessarily the same one—must appear in the new file name. Let's look at an example using a wild card.

A Wild Card Example   In this example, the prefix volume DEMO contains the files SUM.TEXT and SUM.CODE. We wish to rename these files to ADD.TEXT and ADD.CODE:

Filer: G(et, S(ave, W(hat, N(ew, L(dir, R(em, C(hng, T(rans, D(ate, Q(uit [C.4] ☐

DEMO:					
< UNUSED >	24		6		
PROPOSAL.TEXT	4	26-Nov-80	30	512	Textfile
< UNUSED >	25		34		
SUM.TEXT	4	26-Nov-80	59	512	Textfile
SUM.CODE	2	26-Nov-80	63	512	Codefile
< UNUSED >	2		65		
SAMPLE.TEXT	4	21-Mar-81	67	512	Textfile
< UNUSED >	209		71		

4/4 files< listed/in-dir>, 14 blocks used, 260 unused, 209 in largest

Press the C key to invoke the CHANGE command. Answer the CHANGE prompt by typing the old file name plus wild card, a comma, and the new file name plus wild card, and pressing RETURN:

Change what file ? **SUM?,ADD?**

The system asks for verification of the first change:

Change SUM.TEXT ? ☐

Answer 'YES' by pressing the Y key. (Pressing any other key signifies 'NO'.) The screen then reports the change and asks about the next file in the group:

```
Change SUM.TEXT ? Y
DEMO:SUM.TEXT --> ADD.TEXT
Change SUM.CODE ? ☐
```

Again, answer 'YES' by pressing the Y key. A message then indicates that SUM.CODE has been renamed ADD.CODE, and the prompt for the FILER mode reappears:

```
Filer: G(et, S(ave, W(hat, N(ew, L(dir, R(em, C(hng, T(rans, D(ate, Q(uit [C.4] ☐
Change SUM.TEXT ? Y
DEMO:SUM.TEXT --> ADD.TEXT
Change SUM.CODE ? Y
DEMO:SUM.CODE --> ADD.CODE
```

You can verify the change of file names by using the EXTENDED DIRECTORY command.

You are now familiar with two useful filer commands: REMOVE and CHANGE. You will probably employ these commands frequently. We will continue our discussion by looking at two less commonly used commands that operate on the directory of a volume: MAKE and ZERO. If you wish, you may pass directly to the discussion of the *important* TRANSFER command.

The MAKE Command

The MAKE command creates a file by inserting a file name in the directory of a volume. This reserves a specified number of blocks on the volume as a file (because they are no longer marked as 'unused' in the directory).

Although you may not use MAKE frequently, you will find it indispensable for reserving an unused area on a volume for some future use or for attempting to recover the contents of a removed file.

Executing MAKE   To execute MAKE, select the MAKE command from the FILER mode by pressing the M key. This produces the MAKE prompt:

Make what file ? ☐

Now, type the new file name in full. You can, of course, omit the volume name and colon if you are making a file on the prefix volume. Then press RETURN. A message will appear under the FILER prompt indicating that the file name has been placed in the directory.

Normally, you specify the size of the file you are making by typing a number [n] in square brackets immediately after the file name. This means the file will occupy the first unused area on the volume, n or more blocks in size. If you don't specify the number of blocks in square brackets or if you use the number 0, the MAKE command will designate the largest unused area on the volume as the new file. If you use the asterisk (*) in square brackets, the new file will occupy half of the largest unused area or all of the second largest unused area, whichever is greater. Let's consider an example.

Example of MAKE   The directory of the volume BOOK now looks like this:

Filer: G(et, S(ave, W(hat, N(ew, L(dir, R(em, C(hng, T(rans, D(ate, Q(uit [C.4]☐
BOOK:

CHPT.1.TEXT	36	21-Mar-81	6	512	Textfile
NOTE.TEXT	4	23-May-81	42	512	Textfile
< UNUSED >	4		46		
CHPT.2.TEXT	48	21-Mar-81	50	512	Textfile
< UNUSED >	12		98		
INTRO.TEXT	12	21-Apr-81	110	512	Textfile
< UNUSED >	372		122		

4/4 files< listed/in-dir>, 100 blocks used, 388 unused, 372 in largest

We want to create a file named SAVED for future use in the 4 blocks immediately after NOTE.TEXT.

Press the M key to invoke MAKE. Answer the MAKE prompt by typing the volume name, a colon, the name of the file to be created, and the block size specification in square brackets. Then press RETURN:

Make what file ? **BOOK:SAVED[4]** ↙

A message appears under the FILER prompt indicating that the file SAVED has been created:

BOOK:SAVED made

Now use the EXTENDED DIRECTORY command. The directory of BOOK looks like this:

Filer: G(et, S(ave, W(hat, N(ew, L(dir, R(em, C(hng, T(rans, D(ate, Q(uit [C.4] ☐
BOOK:

CHPT.1.TEXT	36	21-Mar-81	6	512	Textfile
NOTE.TEXT	4	23-May-81	42	512	Textfile
SAVED	4	25-Dec-81	46	512	Datafile
CHPT.2.TEXT	48	21-Mar-81	50	512	Textfile
< UNUSED >	12		98		
INTRO.TEXT	12	21-Apr-81	110	512	Textfile
< UNUSED >	372		122		

5/5 files< listed/in-dir>, 104 blocks used, 384 unused, 372 in largest

When you are ready to use the space that you have saved, you can remove the dummy file SAVED and make its blocks available.

Retrieving A Removed File   In certain circumstances it is possible to use the MAKE command to retrieve the contents of a removed file. Consider the following example.

Recall that before the files TEST.TEXT and TEST.CODE were REMOVED, the prefix volume DEMO had this directory:

```
Filer: G(et, S(ave, W(hat, N(ew, L(dir, R(em, C(hng, T(rans, D(ate, Q(uit [C.4] □
DEMO:
< UNUSED >          8                    6
TEST.TEXT           4       12-Nov-80   14    512    Textfile
TEST.CODE           2       12-Nov-80   18    512    Codefile
< UNUSED >         10                   20
PROPOSAL.TEXT       4       26-Nov-80   30    512    Textfile
< UNUSED >         25                   34
SUM.TEXT            4       26-Nov-80   59    512    Textfile
SUM.CODE            2       26-Nov-80   63    512    Codefile
< UNUSED >          2                   65
SAMPLE.TEXT         4       21-Mar-81   67    512    Textfile
< UNUSED >        209                   71
6/6 files< listed/in-dir >, 20 blocks used, 254 unused, 209 in largest
```

Now the directory of DEMO looks like this:

```
Filer: G(et, S(ave, W(hat, N(ew, L(dir, R(em, C(hng, T(rans, D(ate, Q(uit [C.4] □
DEMO:
< UNUSED >         24                    6
PROPOSAL.TEXT       4       26-Nov-80   30    512    Textfile
< UNUSED >         25                   34
SUM.TEXT            4       26-Nov-80   59    512    Textfile
SUM.CODE            2       26-Nov-80   63    512    Codefile
< UNUSED >          2                   65
SAMPLE.TEXT         4       21-Mar-81   67    512    Textfile
< UNUSED >        209                   71
4/4 files< listed/in-dir >, 14 blocks used, 260 unused, 209 in largest
```

We want to retrieve the important file, TEST.TEXT. If nothing has been written on the blocks containing TEST.TEXT since it was removed, then we can use the MAKE command to restore the file. The contents of the blocks of the files are not affected by removing the file, only the entry in the directory is changed. The MAKE command operates in the same way. The contents of the blocks are not changed, but a directory entry is created so that the blocks become a file.

We know that the blocks that contain the contents of the TEST.TEXT file have not been changed since the file was removed, so we can recover the file.

To retrieve the removed file we must complete two steps. First, we must isolate the first block that we want to MAKE into a file. We can do this by using the MAKE command to create files that will contain all of the unused blocks that come before the first block that we want to retrieve. In this example, we will MAKE the first 8 blocks of the 24 block unused area into a file named DUMMY.

To do this, select the MAKE command by pressing the M key while in the FILER mode. The prompt for the MAKE command appears on the screen. Now specify the file DUMMY, and that it takes 8 blocks, and press RETURN:

Make what file? **DUMMY[8]**

The first 8 blocks are now reserved in a file named DUMMY. This can be verified with the EXTENDED DIRECTORY command:

```
Filer: G(et, S(ave, W(hat, N(ew, L(dir, R(em, C(hng, T(rans, D(ate, Q(uit [C.4] ☐
DEMO:
DUMMY              8    25-Dec-81    6    512    Datafile
< UNUSED >        16                14
PROPOSAL.TEXT      4    26-Nov-80   30    512    Textfile
< UNUSED >        25                34
SUM.TEXT           4    26-Nov-80   59    512    Textfile
SUM.CODE           2    26-Nov-80   63    512    Codefile
< UNUSED >         2                65
SAMPLE.TEXT        4    21-Mar-81   67    512    Textfile
< UNUSED >       209                71
5/5 files< listed/in-dir>, 22 blocks used, 252 unused, 209 in largest
```

Second, now that the four blocks that we wish to retrieve are isolated, we can MAKE the file TEST.TEXT in its original position. These blocks have the original contents of TEST.TEXT. Once we give them a file name, by using the MAKE command, the information they contain will once again be available.

Select the MAKE command from the FILER mode by pressing the M key. The prompt for the MAKE command appears. Now specify that the file name TEST.TEXT is to be 4 blocks long, and press RETURN:

Make what file? **TEST.TEXT[4]**

The file TEST.TEXT is now restored. The EXTENDED DIRECTORY command verifies this:

Filer: G(et, S(ave, W(hat, N(ew, L(dir, R(em, C(hng, T(rans, D(ate, Q(uit [C.4] ☐
DEMO:

DUMMY	8	25-Dec-81	6	512	Datafile
TEST.TEXT	4	25-Dec-81	14	512	Textfile
< UNUSED >	12		10		
PROPOSAL.TEXT	4	26-Nov-80	30	512	Textfile
< UNUSED >	25		34		
SUM.TEXT	4	26-Nov-80	59	512	Textfile
SUM.CODE	2	26-Nov-80	63	512	Codefile
< UNUSED >	2		65		
SAMPLE.TEXT	4	21-Mar-81	67	512	Textfile
< UNUSED >	209		71		

6/6 files<listed/in-dir>, 26 blocks used, 248 unused, 209 in largest

Now we can go back and REMOVE the file DUMMY that we made in the first step. It is no longer needed.

By the way, when you make a file with the .TEXT suffix, the p-System requires a minimum of 4 blocks of space. If you specify less than 4 in the square brackets, an error message will appear.

Shortening A File   The MAKE command lets you reduce the size of a file. For example, suppose the file OUTPUT.DATA occupies 24 blocks on a volume. You know, however, that its contents really only require 12 blocks. To recover the empty blocks, follow these steps:

- Use the MAKE command to set up dummy files in all the unused areas on the volume previous to OUTPUT.DATA.

- Remove OUTPUT.DATA. All the blocks it occupies are now part of the first unused area.

- Use the MAKE command to create a smaller OUTPUT.DATA file. Type OUTPUT.DATA[12] in response to the MAKE prompt.

- Remove the dummy files you made in the first step.

The ZERO Command

The ZERO command initializes the directory and name of a volume. Effectively, ZERO creates a blank volume. Volumes in the p-System must be ZEROed before they can be used to hold files. You might also use the ZERO command to reinitialize a volume. This will remove all files on the volume.

Executing ZERO To execute ZERO, select the ZERO command from the FILE mode by pressing the Z key. The screen then displays the ZERO prompt:

Zero dir of what vol ? □

Type in the name of the volume whose directory you wish to initialize, and a colon. If the volume has never been ZEROed before, it will not have a volume name. In this case, you must type in a sharp sign (#) followed by the unit number of the drive that the volume is in and, finally, a colon. Then press RETURN. The system will examine the directory of the volume you have specified. If the system finds that the volume has been ZEROed previously, it will warn you that if you proceed, you will destroy the information that may be on that volume. The system then asks if you wish to proceed:

Destroy VOLNAME: ? □

'VOLNAME' is the name of the volume you specified. You may answer 'YES' by pressing the Y key, or 'NO' by pressing any other key, and thus abort the ZERO command.

If you answer affirmatively, the system then asks a series of questions about the blank volume you are creating. First, it queries:

Duplicate dir ? ☐

It is asking you if you want a duplicate directory in blocks 6–9 of the volume. This duplicate is a backup copy of the directory in blocks 2–5. A utility program, COPYDUPDIR, lets you have access to it in case the original is damaged. *Not all implementations of the p-System support this feature. Check the documentation for your system before answering this prompt.* Press the Y key to indicate a 'YES' answer; press the N key for 'NO'.

Next, the system verifies the number, n, of blocks on the volume you are zeroing with the question:

Are there n blks on the disk ? (Y/N) ☐

The number of blocks depends on the sort of disk your system uses. If the number on the screen isn't correct, the old directory is probably damaged. Answer 'YES' with the Y key or 'NO' with the N key. Next, the system asks you to name the volume being zeroed, with the prompt:

New vol name ? ☐

Type in a volume name and a colon (of course, there is nothing to prevent you from using the previous volume name), then press RETURN. Finally, the system displays the name you have typed and asks you to check it, with the question:

VOLNAME: Correct ? ☐

Again, answer 'YES' by pressing the Y key, or 'NO' by pressing the N key. An affirmative answer will cause the ZERO command to execute.

You may abort the ZERO command at any time by hitting the ESC key after any of the prompts.

Zeroing An Unused Volume   In some systems, you can ZERO a fresh, never-used volume. Other systems, however, require that the volume must first be formatted before it can be ZEROed. Check your documentation. In this circumstance, the system replaces the question

Are there n blks on the disk ? (Y/N) ☐

with the query

# of blocks on the disk ? ☐

Type the number of blocks on the volume you are using and then press RETURN.

We have now examined all the Filer commands that operate on the directory of a volume: REMOVE, CHANGE, MAKE, and ZERO. We will continue by looking at the TRANSFER command, which affects the actual contents of a file.

The TRANSFER Command

This powerful and important command lets you perform a variety of useful tasks. With the TRANSFER command you can:

- copy a file or group of files onto another volume
- print a file on a line printer
- display a text file on the screen
- move a file to a new position on a volume
- make a backup copy of an entire volume.

We will first consider the TRANSFER command in general, and then look at each of these possibilities.

Executing TRANSFER To execute TRANSFER, select the TRANSFER command from the FILER mode by pressing the T key. This produces the first TRANSFER prompt:

Transfer what file ? ☐

The system is asking for the *source* of the transfer operation. After you type in the source and press RETURN, the second TRANSFER prompt appears:

To where ? ☐

The system is now requesting the *destination* of the transfer operation. This could be another file where you wish the file to be copied, or some other volume in the system. When you type in the destination and press RETURN, the TRANSFER command is executed. A message, showing the transfer, appears under the FILER prompt.

You may abbreviate this process by typing the source and destination, separated by a comma (,), in response to the first TRANSFER prompt ('Transfer what file ?'). The second prompt will not appear. Let's look at some examples.

Copying A File To Another Volume We will now copy a file to another disk volume under a new file name. The file PROPOSAL.TEXT is on the prefix volume DEMO. We want to copy it onto the largest unused area of the volume ARCHIVE, as the file OLDPROP.TEXT.

Press the T key to select the TRANSFER command. Answer the initial TRANSFER prompt by typing the source, a comma, and the destination. Then press RETURN:

Transfer what file ? **PROPOSAL.TEXT,ARCHIVE:OLDPROP.TEXT**

A message confirming the transfer appears on screen:

DEMO:PROPOSAL.TEXT --> ARCHIVE:OLDPROP.TEXT

The source file PROPOSAL.TEXT is *not* erased or changed in any way by this operation. It is intact on the DEMO volume. A copy of its contents, however, is now on the ARCHIVE volume under the file name OLDPROP.TEXT. In this case, TRANSFER might be better named COPY.

We can put the source file into a particular unused area on the destination volume, by specifying a block size, n, in square brackets. Then the file will be copied into the first unused area on the destination volume, n blocks or larger. For example, to place OLDPROP.TEXT in the first unused area of 10 or more blocks on the volume ARCHIVE, you would answer the prompt by typing:

Transfer what file ? **PROPOSAL.TEXT,ARCHIVE:OLDPROP.TEXT [10]**

Both volumes must be on line for the TRANSFER operation to work. In a one drive system, you must start with the source volume in the drive. The system will prompt you to put in the destination volume.

Copying A File Under The Same File Name   Next, we will copy a file to another volume under the same file name. The file HANGMAN.TEXT is on the root volume BOOT. We want to copy it onto the prefix volume, DEMO, and keep the same file name. The p-System provides a typing shortcut for this sort of operation: the dollar sign ($). The dollar sign means "repeat the source file name." It lets you avoid typing the same file name twice.

Press the T key to select TRANSFER. Answer the TRANSFER prompt by typing an asterisk to specify the root volume, the file name, a comma, a colon to specify the prefix volume, and a dollar sign. Then press RETURN:

Transfer what file ? ***HANGMAN.TEXT,:$**

TRANSFER executes, and the following message appears:

BOOT:HANGMAN.TEXT --> DEMO:HANGMAN.TEXT

Both disks, BOOT and DEMO, now have the file HANGMAN.TEXT.
Two words of caution:

1. Don't forget to type the dollar sign. You can destroy the directory of

the destination volume if you omit it. The system will warn you if you are about to do this and will request confirmation.

2. Check the destination volume with the EXTENDED DIRECTORY command, before using TRANSFER. Make sure there is sufficient space available for the incoming file. Again the system will detect this and an error message will be given. No harm will occur.

Wild Cards With TRANSFER Wild cards can be used with the TRANSFER command. This means you can copy a group of files from a source volume to a destination volume. As always, it is better to use the ? wild card, so that each file may be checked just before it is copied. It may not be possible to use TRANSFER with a wild card if your system has only one disk drive. Consider the following example.

The prefix volume DEMO has the files ADD.TEXT and ADD.CODE. We want to use a wild card to put both files on the volume PASCAL without changing the file names.

Press the T key to invoke TRANSFER. Answer the TRANSFER prompt by typing the name of the source file plus wild card, a comma, and the name of the destination volume, followed by a colon and the dollar sign. Then press RETURN. (The normal rule that requires a wild card in the destination, if one appears in the source, is relaxed when you use the dollar sign.)

Transfer what file ? **ADD?,PASCAL:$**ⱼ

The system asks you to verify the first transfer:

Transfer ADD.TEXT ? ☐

Answer 'YES' with the Y key. Transfer executes and the confirming message appears. The system then asks about the second transfer:

Transfer ADD.TEXT ? **Y**
DEMO:ADD.TEXT --> PASCAL:ADD.TEXT
Transfer ADD.CODE ? ☐

Again, answer 'YES' with the Y key. (Pressing any other key would be a 'NO' answer.) A final confirming message then appears under the FILER prompt:

Filer: G(et, S(ave, W(hat, N(ew, L(dir, R(em, C(hng, T(rans, D(ate, Q(uit [C.4] ☐
Transfer ADD.TEXT ? Y
DEMO:ADD.TEXT --> PASCAL:ADD.TEXT
Transfer ADD.CODE ? **Y**
DEMO:ADD.CODE --> PASCAL:ADD.CODE

The TRANSFER command may be aborted at any time by pressing the ESC key in response to any of these prompts. Note that you can use a wild card to *add* all the files from one volume to the files already on another volume. Suppose you want to copy all the files on DEMO to the volume ARCHIVE without affecting anything already on ARCHIVE.

To do this simply select TRANSFER by pressing the T key, and then answer the prompt by typing:

Transfer what file ? **?,ARCHIVE:?**

The isolated wild card now specifies all the files on the prefix volume DEMO. Since you used ? instead of =, you will be able to check each file before it is copied.

Printing A File   You can use the TRANSFER command to print a text file. First, make sure the line printer is properly attached to the system, turned on, and loaded with paper. Next, select the TRANSFER command. In response to the prompt ('Transfer what file ?'), type the source in the usual way, a comma, and the printer as the destination. You may use either the printer's volume name or number. Let's consider the following example.

An Example   In this example we will print the file NOTE.TEXT from the volume BOOK.

Press the T key invoking TRANSFER. Answer the TRANSFER prompt by typing the volume and file name, a comma, and the volume name of the printer. Then press RETURN:

Transfer what file ? **BOOK:NOTE.TEXT,PRINTER:**

You could also use the volume number of the printer:

Transfer what file ? **BOOK:NOTE.TEXT,#6:**

TRANSFER executes. The file NOTE.TEXT is printed and a confirming message appears on the screen under the FILE prompt:

Filer: G(et, S(ave, W(hat, N(ew, L(dir, R(em, C(hng, T(rans, D(ate, Q(uit [C.4] ☐
BOOK:NOTE.TEXT --> PRINTER:

When you are transferring a file to a non-block-structured volume, such as a printer, you don't have to type a file name in the destination.

Displaying A Text File   Instead of printing a file, you can use TRANSFER to send it to the screen for viewing. This option is a nice shortcut when you want to quickly check the contents of a text file without invoking the editor. Here's how.

Select TRANSFER and specify the screen as the destination. Use the volume name CONSOLE: or the unit number #1:. Let's consider the following example.

An Example   In this example we will view the contents of NOTE.TEXT on the volume BOOK.

Invoke TRANSFER by pressing the T key. Respond to the TRANSFER prompt by typing the volume and file name, a comma, and the screen's volume name. Then press RETURN:

Transfer what file ? **BOOK:NOTE.TEXT,CONSOLE:**

Or use the screen volume number:

Transfer what file ? **BOOK:NOTE.TEXT,#1:**

The file NOTE.TEXT appears on screen under the FILE prompt.

If a text file is lengthy, the system will scroll it rapidly across the screen. You can use the CTRL-S command—or your system's equivalent—to stop and restart this scrolling. Simply hold down the CTRL key and strike the S key.

Moving A File On The Same Volume   In certain circumstances, you may wish to transfer a file within the same volume. When the source and destination volume are identical, a file may be relocated to a new position on the volume or duplicated under a new file name. Let's consider some examples of situations where this option might prove useful, for example:

1. if you want to move a file into a large unused area near the beginning of the directory

2. if you want to duplicate a file on the same volume under a new file name.

Let's examine each situation in turn.

Situation 1   The volume prefix DEMO contains the file SAMPLE.TEXT. It is 4 blocks long and located near the end of the volume:

Filer: G(et, S(ave, W(hat, N(ew, L(dir, R(em, C(hng, T(rans, D(ate, Q(uit [C.4]☐
DEMO:

< UNUSED >	8		6		
TEST.TEXT	4	12-Nov-80	14	512	Textfile
TEST.CODE	2	12-Nov-80	18	512	Codefile
< UNUSED >	10		20		
PROPOSAL.TEXT	4	26-Nov-80	30	512	Textfile
< UNUSED >	25		34		
SUM.TEXT	4	26-Nov-80	59	512	Textfile
SUM.CODE	2	26-Nov-80	63	512	Codefile
< UNUSED >	2		65		
SAMPLE.TEXT	4	21-Mar-81	67	512	Textfile
< UNUSED >	209		71		

6/6 files<listed/in-dir>, 20 blocks used, 254 unused, 209 in largest

We want to move it into the volume's first unused area, which is 8 blocks long. Invoke TRANSFER by pressing the T key. Answer the prompt by typing:

Transfer what file ? **SAMPLE.TEXT,$[8]**₎

The file SAMPLE.TEXT is moved into the first 8 block unused area on DEMO. It disappears from its position at the end of the volume: ·

Filer: G(et, S(ave, W(hat, N(ew, L(dir, R(em, C(hng, T(rans, D(ate, Q(uit [C.4]☐
DEMO:

SAMPLE.TEXT	4	21-Mar-81	6	512	Textfile
< UNUSED >	4		10		
TEST.TEXT	4	12-Nov-80	14	512	Textfile
TEST.CODE	2	12-Nov-80	18	512	Codefile
< UNUSED >	10		20		
PROPOSAL.TEXT	4	26-Nov-80	30	512	Textfile
< UNUSED >	25		34		
SUM.TEXT	4	26-Nov-80	59	512	Textfile
SUM.CODE	2	26-Nov-80	63	512	Codefile
< UNUSED >	215		65		

6/6 files<listed/in-dir>, 20 blocks used, 254 unused, 215 in largest

In this case, the TRANSFER command is accurately named. The file is moved from one place to another; it is not duplicated. If you don't specify a block size in square brackets, the file will be transferred to the largest unused area on the volume.

Situation 2 The prefix volume DEMO contains the file PROPOSAL.TEXT:

Filer: G(et, S(ave, W(hat, N(ew, L(dir, R(em, C(hng, T(rans, D(ate, Q(uit [C.4]☐
DEMO:

SAMPLE.TEXT	4	21-Mar-81	6	512	Textfile
< UNUSED >	4		10		
TEST.TEXT	4	12-Nov-80	14	512	Textfile
TEST.CODE	2	12-Nov-80	18	512	Codefile
< UNUSED >	10		20		
PROPOSAL.TEXT	4	26-Nov-80	30	512	Textfile
< UNUSED >	25		34		
SUM.TEXT	4	26-Nov-80	59	512	Textfile
SUM.CODE	2	26-Nov-80	63	512	Codefile
< UNUSED >	215		65		

6/6 files<listed/in-dir>, 20 blocks used, 254 unused, 215 in largest

We want to make a copy of it in the largest unused area of DEMO under the file name OLDPROP.TEXT.

Select TRANSFER with the T key. Next, answer the prompt by typing:

Transfer what file ? **PROPOSAL.TEXT,OLDPROP.TEXT**⌋

The message:

DEMO:PROPOSAL.TEXT --> DEMO:OLDPROP.TEXT

indicates the duplication is complete. The prefix volume DEMO now has both the PROPOSAL.TEXT and OLDPROP.TEXT files:

```
Filer: G(et, S(ave, W(hat, N(ew, L(dir, R(em, C(hng, T(rans, D(ate, Q(uit [C.4]□
DEMO:
SAMPLE.TEXT           4    21-Mar-81     6    512    Textfile
< UNUSED >            4                 10
TEST.TEXT             4    12-Nov-80    14    512    Textfile
TEST.CODE            2    12-Nov-80    18    512    Codefile
< UNUSED >           10                 20
PROPOSAL.TEXT         4    26-Nov-80    30    512    Textfile
< UNUSED >           25                 34
SUM.TEXT             4    26-Nov-80    59    512    Textfile
SUM.CODE            2    26-Nov-80    63    512    Codefile
OLDPROP.TEXT         4    26-Nov-80    65    512    Textfile
< UNUSED >          211                 69
7/7 files<listed/in-dir>, 24 blocks used, 250 unused, 211 in largest
```

Backing Up A Disk   You can use the TRANSFER command to perform the vital operation of backing up (i.e., copying) an entire disk volume. Since disks are very delicate and can be easily damaged, all of your important disks—especially those containing the p-System itself—should be backed up. Then, use the copy—never the original. If something happens to the copy, you can always make another backup copy from the original. In this manner the original will never be modified.

Disk backup is performed by using the TRANSFER command, specifying the original volume as the source and the backup volume as the destination. The system then asks you to verify the number of blocks on the source volume, and to approve the destruction of anything on the destination volume. Consider this example.

We want to back-up the 280 block volume GUIDE on the volume BLANK. In response to the TRANSFER prompt, type:

Transfer what file ? **GUIDE:,BLANK:**↲

The system then asks:

Transfer 280 blocks ? □

where 280 is the number of blocks on the GUIDE volume. Answer 'YES' by pressing the Y key. (If the number is not correct, the directory of GUIDE may be damaged.) Answer 'NO' with any other key.

When you press the Y key, the system queries:

Transfer 280 blocks ? **Y**⌋
Destroy BLANK: ? ☐

It is asking if it is alright to discard the old name and directory of the destination volume. Answer 'YES' with the Y key. (You can answer 'NO' with the N key if you get cold feet.) Answering 'YES' to this final prompt causes the TRANSFER command to execute. When execution is complete, the destination volume is named GUIDE and contains an exact duplicate of the directory and files from the source volume GUIDE.

Since you now have two identical volumes on line, it is wise to pull out the original volume, label it, *and store it somewhere safe from extremes of temperature, magnetic fields, or other hazards.*

With a one drive system, you will have to swap the source and destination volumes in and out of the drive many times. Backing up a disk on a one drive system is awkward and inconvenient. The system will prompt you when it wants its volumes swapped. You start with the source volume on line.

We have now examined the TRANSFER command and the numerous ways you can use it. We will continue by looking at three FILER commands that affect the entire contents of a volume: KRUNCH, BAD BLOCKS, and EXAMINE.

The KRUNCH Command

The KRUNCH command moves the files on a volume so that unused areas are consolidated. KRUNCH reads a file and then rewrites it on the volume in a new position. You will use KRUNCH when the EXTENDED DIRECTORY command reveals that a volume has several small unused areas scattered throughout its directory.

Make sure there will be no interruptions during execution of the KRUNCH command. Avoid fiddling with the reset key, the power switch, or the disk drive door while KRUNCH is underway. It is also a good idea to use the BAD BLOCKS command before invoking KRUNCH, to make sure all the blocks on the volume are usable.

Executing KRUNCH   To execute KRUNCH, select the KRUNCH command from the FILER mode by pressing the K key. This produces the KRUNCH prompt:

Crunch what vol ? ☐

Respond then by typing the name of the volume you wish to KRUNCH, followed by a colon. Then press RETURN.

On some systems this is followed by an additional prompt:

From end of disk, block n ? (Y/N) ☐

where n is the number of blocks on the volume.

Type Y to answer 'YES' to collect the free space at the end of the volume. If you wish to collect the free space at some other location on the volume, then type N to answer 'NO'. The system will then prompt you for the location where you wish to collect the free space:

Starting at block # ? ☐

Type in the block number of the area where you wish to collect all the free space of the volume, and press RETURN. The KRUNCH command will start to execute. When execution is complete, a confirming message appears under the FILER prompt. Let's consider an example.

Example of KRUNCH   The EXTENDED DIRECTORY command displays this directory for the prefix volume DEMO:

```
Filer: G(et, S(ave, W(hat, N(ew, L(dir, R(em, C(hng, T(rans, D(ate, Q(uit [C.4] ☐
DEMO:
SAMPLE.TEXT        4    21-Mar-81     6    512    Textfile
< UNUSED >         4                 10
TEST.TEXT          4    12-Nov-80    14    512    Textfile
TEST.CODE          2    12-Nov-80    18    512    Codefile
< UNUSED >        10                 20
PROPOSAL.TEXT      4    26-Nov-80    30    512    Textfile
< UNUSED >        25                 34
SUM.TEXT           4    26-Nov-80    59    512    Textfile
SUM.CODE           2    26-Nov-80    63    512    Codefile
OLDPROP.TEXT       4    26-Nov-80    65    512    Textfile
< UNUSED >       211                 69
7/7 files<listed/in-dir>, 24 blocks used, 250 unused, 211 in largest
```

We wish to consolidate all the unused areas on DEMO into one unused area. Press the K key selecting KRUNCH. Answer the KRUNCH prompt by typing a colon to indicate the prefix volume. Then press RETURN:

Crunch what vol ? :

A message appears when execution is complete:

DEMO: crunched

Now use EXTENDED DIRECTORY once more to look at the directory of DEMO:

Filer: G(et, S(ave, W(hat, N(ew, L(dir, R(em, C(hng, T(rans, D(ate, Q(uit [C.4]☐
DEMO:

SAMPLE.TEXT	4	21-Mar-81	6	512	Textfile
TEST.TEXT	4	12-Nov-80	10	512	Textfile
TEST.CODE	2	12-Nov-80	14	512	Codefile
PROPOSAL.TEXT	4	26-Nov-80	16	512	Textfile
SUM.TEXT	4	26-Nov-80	20	512	Textfile
SUM.CODE	2	26-Nov-80	24	512	Codefile
OLDPROP.TEXT	4	26-Nov-80	26	512	Textfile
< UNUSED >	250		30		

7/7 files<listed/in-dir>, 24 blocks used, 250 unused, 250 in largest

An Alternate KRUNCH   As mentioned previously, some versions of the p-System allow you to consolidate unused areas into one area *anywhere* on the volume, not just at the end. After you respond to the first KRUNCH prompt (CRUNCH?) by typing the volume name and pressing RETURN, the system asks:

From end of disk, block n ? (Y/N) ☐

where n is the number of blocks on your volume. If you press the Y key to answer 'YES,' KRUNCH will operate in the normal way and move all the files forward. If you answer 'NO' with the N key, however, the system will then ask:

Starting at block # ? ☐

Type in the block number you have chosen and press RETURN. KRUNCH will then move those files in lower numbered blocks, forward, and those files in higher numbered blocks, backward (i.e., toward the end of the volume). Effectively, you will create a consolidated unused area in the middle of the volume at the block you have specified.

The BAD BLOCKS Command

The information stored on a magnetic disk can be degraded by a number of causes: poor connection between the system and the disk drive, a voltage surge, a damaged area on the surface of the disk, etc. The

BAD BLOCKS command identifies those blocks on a volume that contain degraded information.

It is a good idea to use the BAD BLOCKS command whenever you:

— introduce a fresh volume into your system

— plan to KRUNCH a volume

— find an unexplainable error in program output.

Executing BAD BLOCKS To execute BAD BLOCKS, select the BAD BLOCKS command from the FILER mode by pressing the B key. The screen displays this prompt:

Bad block scan of what vol ? ☐

Type in the name of the volume you want scanned, followed by a colon. Then press RETURN. The system asks:

Scan for n blocks ? (Y/N) ☐

where n is the number of blocks on the volume. If you answer 'YES' by pressing the Y key, all the blocks on the volume will be scanned. If the number of blocks indicated is incorrect, the directory may be damaged. If you answer 'NO' with the N key, the system will then ask:

Scan for how many blocks ? ☐

Type in the number indicating the number of blocks you wish scanned and press RETURN.

As BAD BLOCKS executes, a message appears on screen whenever a bad block is located. When the scan is finished, the total number of bad blocks is displayed, together with an indication of the files, if any, occupying the faulty blocks. Let's consider an example.

Example of BAD BLOCKS In this example, we will use BAD BLOCKS on the 280 block volume GAMES. Select the command by pressing the B key. Answer the prompt by typing:

Bad blocks scan of what vol ? **GAMES:** ⟩

If you answer the question

Scan for 280 blocks ? (Y/N) ☐

affirmatively (by pressing the Y key), BAD BLOCKS will execute. The following messages appear, finally, under the FILER prompt:

```
Block 25 is bad
Block 49 is bad
2 bad blocks
File(s) endangered
BLKJACK.TEXT   22   25
```

There are two bad blocks: 25 and 49. The file BLKJACK.TEXT occupies blocks 22 through 25 on the volume. It is "endangered" because one of its blocks, 25, is bad. The bad block 49 is in an unused area. It isn't part of any file.

We will now use the EXAMINE command and attempt to fix the bad blocks on GAMES.

The EXAMINE Command

The EXAMINE command tries to repair bad blocks on a volume. If EXAMINE can't fix a block, you then have the option of marking it 'BAD' in the directory so that it is retired to the sidelines.

EXAMINE operates by reading a block, writing it at the same position on the volume, and then reading it again. If the first and second readings are identical, the screen indicates that the block 'May be ok'. The message is conditional because the actual information on the block may still be garbled. If the first and second reading are *not* identical, the system asks if you want to mark the block as 'BAD' in the directory.

Executing EXAMINE   To execute EXAMINE, select the EXAMINE command from the FILE prompt by pressing the X key. The system queries:

Examine blocks on what vol ? ☐

Type a volume name, a colon, and then press RETURN. The system asks:

Block-range ? ☐

Type in the numbers of the faulty blocks identified with the BAD BLOCKS command. In some versions of the p-System, you may type individual block numbers, separated by commas. In other versions, you must type the lowest and highest bad block number, separated by a hyphen.

Next press RETURN. The system displays the name of any file that includes bad blocks and asks:

Fix them ? ☐

If you press the N key to answer in the negative, EXAMINE will abort and the FILE prompt will reappear. However, if you press the Y key to answer affirmatively, EXAMINE will execute on each block indicated and tell you it 'may be ok' or it 'is bad'. If there are irreparable blocks, the system will ask:

Mark bad blocks ? ☐

If you answer 'YES' with the Y key, EXAMINE will remove any file from the directory that includes a bad block, and mark the block as BAD. If you answer 'NO' with the N key, none of the bad blocks will be marked and no files will be removed from the directory. Let's try an example.

Example of EXAMINE   We know the volume GAMES has two bad blocks, 25 and 49, and we want to try to fix them. Press the X key to select EXAMINE. Answer the prompt by typing:

Examine blocks on what vol ? **GAMES:**

We will assume here that your version of the p-System permits you to list individual blocks separated by a comma. Answer the prompt by typing:

Block-range ? **25,49**

Block 49 is part of an unused area on the volume. Block 25, however, is part of the file BLKJACK.TEXT, so this message appears:

```
File(s) endangered
BLKJACK.TEXT   22   25
Fix them ? ☐
```

Answer affirmatively by pressing the Y key. EXAMINE then executes and the following messages appear:

```
Block 25 may be ok
Block 49 is bad
Mark bad blocks ? ☐
```

Block 25 has been examined and now seems to be OK. Block 49, however, is beyond repair. Since Block 49 is in an unused area, you can mark it without removing a file. Answer 'YES' to the question 'Mark bad blocks?' by pressing the Y key.

The final EXAMINE operation executes. There is now a new entry in the GAMES directory at block 49, namely:

BAD.00049.BAD

This block is now unavailable for use, and it will not be moved in a KRUNCH operation.

We have now studied all the commands in the FILER but one: the DATE command.

The DATE Command

Recall from Chapter 2 that the DATE command sets the current date, which appears with every file name in a directory and on the welcome message when you boot the system. When you create or update a file, the current date is recorded in the directory. Remember to use the DATE command whenever you begin a day or night's work with the system.

Executing DATE   Recall that to execute DATE, you press the D key to select DATE from the FILER mode. The screen displays:

Date set: <1..31>-<Jan..Dec>-<00..99>
Today is 25-Dec-81
New date ? ☐

where 'DATE' is the current date at the moment you invoke the DATE command. You now have two options. You may:

1. leave the date unchanged by pressing RETURN. The FILER prompt will reappear.

2. type in a new date, and press RETURN. The new date will be set and it will appear under the FILER prompt.

It is possible to change only a part of a date instead of retyping all of it. To change only the day of the month, for example, you type the new day, and press RETURN. Let's consider an example.

Example of DATE   The current date of the system is 11-Nov-80 and we want to change it to 12-Nov-80.

Press the D key to select the DATE command. Answer the prompt by typing only the new day.

```
Date set: <1..31>-<Jan..Dec>-<00..99>
Today is 11-Nov-80
New date ? 12
```

The FILER prompt reappears over a message indicating the new current date.

```
Filer: G(et, S(ave, W(hat, N(ew, L(dir, R(em, C(hng, T(rans, D(ate, Q(uit [C.4]□
Date set: <1..31>-<Jan..Dec>-<00..99>
Today is 11-Nov-80
New date ? 12
The date is 12-Nov-80
```

PART TWO: FILER REFERENCE SUMMARY

This reference summary describes, in alphabetical order (*according to the way they appear on the prompt*), the commands in the FILER mode. Each description includes an example of the prompt, and information and suggestions on how and when to use each command. As before, user responses appear in **UPPERCASE BOLDFACE** type.

BAD BLOCKS

Prompt:

Bad block scan of what vol ? **VOLUMENAME:**)
Scan for 494 blocks ? (Y/N) **Y**☐

Description:

The BAD BLOCKS command scans the blocks on a volume for those with faulty CRC characters (i.e., degraded information) and displays the name and location of any files with bad blocks.

How To Use It:

To perform a BAD BLOCKS scan on a volume: In response to the first prompt, type either a volume name followed by a colon, or a sharp sign (#) followed by a unit number and a colon. Then press RETURN. This causes the system to search for the selected volume and read the length of the volume from the volume's directory. The second prompt then asks you to verify that the number of blocks read from the directory is correct. If you type N to answer 'NO', a third prompt appears:

Scan for how many blocks ? ☐

In response to this prompt, type in the number of blocks that the volume actually contains, and press RETURN. Appendix A contains a list of the numbers of blocks on typical disk volumes.

When To Use It:

Use Bad Blocks whenever you

— put a new disk into your system

— plan to use the KRUNCH command

— suspect disk errors.

The EXAMINE command attempts to fix the bad blocks identified by the BAD BLOCKS command.

CHANGE

Prompts:

Change what file ? **CURRENTNAME**↵
Change to what ? **NEWNAME**↵

Description:

The CHANGE command allows you to rename a file, group of files or a volume.

How To Use It:

To change the name of a file: In response to the first prompt, type the current file name, and press RETURN. Then in response to the second prompt, type the new name, and press RETURN.

To change the name of a group of files: In response to the first prompt, type in a file name including a wild card, specifying a group of files. Then press RETURN. Then in response to the second prompt, type in a file name specifying the names that the files should be changed to. This file name must also contain a wild card. For example, to change the group of files OLDJUNK.TEXT, OLDJUNK.CODE and OLDJUNK.DATA to the new names NEWSTUFF.TEXT, NEWSTUFF.CODE and NEWSTUFF.DATA, you would type the following in response to the prompts:

Change what file ? **OLDJUNK =** ↵
Change to what ? **NEWSTUFF =** ↵

To change the name of a volume: In response to the first prompt, type either the current name of the volume followed by a colon, or type a sharp sign, the unit number, and a colon. Then press RETURN. In response to the second prompt, type the new volume name followed by a colon, and press RETURN.

In all three cases you can combine both responses on one line in response to the first prompt by simply separating the old name from the new name with a comma and then pressing RETURN. For example, you could make the change above as:

Change what file ? **OLDJUNK = ,NEWSTUFF =** ↵

When To Use It:

Use the CHANGE command whenever you need to change the names of files or volumes. For example, use CHANGE to avoid using duplicate names or whenever you want to use more appropriate names.

```
┌─────────────────────┐
│                     │
│     DATE            │
│                     │
└─────────────────────┘
```

Prompt:

Date set: <1..31>-<Jan..Dec>-<00..99>
Today is 25-Dec-81
New date ? ☐

Description:

The DATE command sets the system date. The system date is stored with each file when you create or update it.

How To Use It:

To change the system date: In response to the DATE prompt, type in the current date, using the format shown in the first line of the prompt. Then press RETURN. To keep the date shown in the prompt, simply press RETURN.

It is also possible to change only certain parts of the date without respecifying the entire date. For example, if you type:

3 ⌡	the day of the month will change to 3; the month or year will not change.
1-JAN ⌡	the date will change to January 1; the year will not change.
-JUL ⌡	the month will change to July; the day of the month and the year will not change.
--82 ⌡	the year will change to 1982; the day of the month and the month will not change.

When To Use It:

Use the DATE command whenever you start a new day or night's work on the system, or whenever you work past midnight.

EXTENDED DIRECTORY

Prompt:

Dir listing of what vol ? ☐

Description:

The EXTENDED DIRECTORY command displays information about the files on a particular volume.

How To Use It:

To display information about all the files on a volume: Type in the volume specification, and press RETURN.

To display information about a group of files on a volume: Type in a file name, including a wild card in the file specification, and press RETURN.

To display information about a single file: Type in the file name, and press RETURN.

You can specify the prefix volume with a colon (:), and the root volume with an asterisk (*).

If you want to store the information listed in a file, or to send it to the printer, rather than the console, type a comma and a file name after the first part of the response. For example, to store the information about all the .TEXT files on the volume DEMO: in a file named DEMODIR.TEXT, you would type the following in response to the prompt:

Dir listing of what vol ? **DEMO: = .TEXT,DEMODIR.TEXT**

When To Use It:

Use the EXTENDED DIRECTORY command whenever you want to find out how the free space on a volume is distributed, the type of a file, or the block number where a particular file starts. You can also use the EXTENDED DIRECTORY command to view the names of the files on a volume; however, the LIST DIRECTORY command is slightly faster.

```
┌─────────────────────────┐
│                         │
│          GET            │
│                         │
└─────────────────────────┘
```

Prompt:

Get what file ? □

Description:

The GET command designates a file or a pair of files as the work file.

How To Use It:

To designate a file or a pair of files as the work file: Type in the file name of the file, without the suffix. The corresponding files with .TEXT and .CODE suffixes will then be designated as the work file. If there is an unsaved work file when you execute the GET command, you will be asked if you wish to discard this work file before designating the new work file. The prompt for this question is:

Throw away current workfile ? □

Answering N for 'No' to this question will abort the GET command.

When To Use It:

Before making modifications to a file, you will want to use the GET command to designate the file as the work file.

KRUNCH

Prompt:

Crunch what vol ? ☐
From end of disk (block 493) ? (Y/N) ☐

Description:

The KRUNCH command consolidates all the unused area on a volume into one contiguous space.

How To Use It:

To consolidate all the unused areas on a volume: In response to the first prompt, type the name of the volume to be crunched followed by a colon. Then press RETURN. The second prompt asks you to verify the location on the volume where the unused space will be collected. If you answer Y, for 'YES', the default is the end of the volume. However, if you answer N for 'NO', then you need to specify a location by typing a block number and then pressing RETURN, in response to the following prompt:

From what block ? ☐

When To Use It:

Small scattered unused sections of a volume are of little use. If these small sections are combined into one large unused section, they become useful. Use the KRUNCH command when the unused areas of your volumes are fragmented into small sections.

LIST DIRECTORY

Prompt:

Dir listing of what vol ? ☐

Description:

The LIST DIRECTORY command displays information about the files on a particular volume.

How To Use It:

To display information about all the files on a volume: Type in the volume specification, and press RETURN.

To display information about a group of files on a volume: Type in a file name, including a wild card, and press RETURN.

To display information about a single file: Type in the file name, and press RETURN.

You can specify the prefix volume by typing a colon (:), and the root volume by typing an asterisk (*).

If you want to store the information listed in a file, or to send it to the printer, rather than the console, type a comma and the file name after the first part of the response. For example, to store the information about all the .TEXT files on the volume DEMO: in a file named DEMODIR.TEXT, you would type in response to the prompt:

Dir listing of what vol ? **DEMO: = .TEXT,DEMODIR.TEXT**₁

When To Use It:

Use the LIST DIRECTORY command whenever you want to quickly examine the names of the files on a particular volume. You can obtain more detailed information by using the EXTENDED DIRECTORY command.

MAKE

Prompt:

Make what file ? ☐

Description:

The MAKE command creates a file that contains a specific number of blocks. An entry is created in the directory of the volume reserving the specified number of blocks. The contents of the blocks are unchanged.

How To Use It:

To create a file with a specific number of blocks: In response to the prompt, type a file name followed by a number in square brackets. Then press RETURN. This will create a file of the length specified in the brackets, in the first unused area that is at least as large as the length specified. For example, the response:

Make what file ? **SCRATCH:FOOBAR.DATA[10]**

will create a 10 block file in the first unused area at least 10 blocks long on the volume SCRATCH. If you do not specify a file size, the largest unused area on the volume becomes the new file. If you specify '[*]', then either the second largest unused area or half the largest unused area will be the new file, whichever is the larger.

When To Use It:

The MAKE command is handy for retrieving files that you have inadvertently REMOVE'd, or for reserving disk space for future use.

NEW

Prompt:

There is no prompt for the NEW command.

Description:

The NEW command clears the work file.

How To Use It:

To clear the work file: Type N while in the FILER mode. If a file is designated as the work file, the NEW command will remove that designation. If you have never saved that file, the system will ask:

Throw away current workfile ? ☐

If you answer Y, for 'YES', to this question, then the files SYSTEM.WRK.TEXT and SYSTEM.WRK.CODE will be deleted. If you answer N, for 'NO', no deletion will occur and these files will still be the work file.

When To Use It:

Use the NEW command when you want to create a new program or another text file with the editor.

PREFIX

Prompt:

Prefix is VOLUMENAME:

Prefix titles by ? ☐

Description:

The PREFIX command sets the prefix volume name. The prefix volume name is the default volume name when you do not specify a volume name as part of a file name.

How To Use It:

To set the prefix volume name: In response to the prompt, type the volume name you want to use as the prefix volume name, followed by a colon. Then press RETURN. If you type only a colon and press RETURN, the current prefix volume name will appear. The prefix volume name will become the name of the root volume, if you type an asterisk (*) and press RETURN.

When To Use It:

Set the prefix volume name to the volume that you are currently working with, in order to minimize your typing labors. If you are lucky enough to have two disk drives, however, it is convenient to set the prefix volume to the name of the volume in the second drive. You can then refer to the root volume with an asterisk (*) and to the other volume (the prefix volume) with a colon (:).

QUIT

Prompt:

There is no prompt for the QUIT command.

Description:

The QUIT command terminates the FILER mode and returns you to the COMMAND mode.

How To Use It:

To terminate the FILER mode: Type Q.

When To Use It:

Use the QUIT command to leave the FILER mode.

REMOVE

Prompt:

Remove what file ? ☐

Description:

The REMOVE command deletes file entries in the directory of a volume and marks the blocks of the deleted file as unused. The actual contents of the blocks are unaffected.

How To Use It:

To delete a file from a volume's directory: In response to the prompt, type the file name of the file you wish to delete. Then press RETURN. When the file has been located, the system will ask if the deletion should be made, with the question:

Update Directory ? ☐

Answering Y, for 'YES' will make the deletion. Answering N, for 'NO', will abort the REMOVE command and leave the file intact.

To delete a group of files from a volume's directory: In response to the prompt, type a file name containing a wild card. (See the WILD CARD section of this summary for a description of the use of WILD CARDS.) Then press RETURN. When all of the files to be deleted have been located, the system will ask if the deletions should be made, with the question:

Update Directory ? ☐

Again, answer Y for 'YES' to make the deletions or N for 'NO' to leave the files intact.

When To Use It:

Use the REMOVE command to free up space on a volume taken up by unwanted files.

SAVE

Prompt:

Save as what file ? ☐

Description:

The SAVE command renames or copies the temporary work files, SYSTEM.WRK.TEXT and SYSTEM.WRK.CODE. If you specify to SAVE the work files on the root volume, the command will rename the work files. If you specify some other volume, SAVE will copy the files to that volume and give them the names specified.

How To Use It:

To rename the work file: Type in a file name without a suffix, specifying a file on the root volume. The system will assume the suffixes .TEXT and .CODE for the corresponding files.

To copy the work file to another volume: Type in the volume name and a file name without a suffix. The system will assume the suffixes .TEXT and .CODE for the corresponding files.

The work file will remain as the work file after SAVE has renamed or copied it. You can use the NEW command to remove this designation.

When To Use It:

Use the SAVE command when you have finished with a work file and are ready to designate a new work file.

TRANSFER

Prompt:

Transfer what file ? ☐
To where ? ☐

Description:

The TRANSFER command copies, repositions, prints, and displays files, as well as makes backup copies of entire volumes.

How To Use It:

To copy a file: In response to the first prompt, type the name of the file you want to copy, and press RETURN. In response to the second prompt, specify the name of the file you want to hold the copy. You can use the dollar sign ($) in the second file name as a shorthand notation to represent the same file specification as the first file name. The copy will be placed in the largest unused area on the destination volume.

To reposition a file on a volume: In response to the first prompt, type the name of the file to be repositioned, and press RETURN. In response to the second prompt, type the same file name followed by a length specification in square brackets. The file will be moved to the first unused area that is at least as large as the length specified.

To copy a group of files: In response to the first prompt, type a file name containing a wild card, and press RETURN. In response to the second prompt, type a file name containing a wild card or use the dollar sign shorthand, and press RETURN.

To print a text file: In response to the first prompt, type the name of the file to be printed, and press RETURN. In response to the second prompt, type PRINTER:, and press RETURN.

To display a text file on the console: In response to the first prompt, type the name of the file to be displayed, and press RETURN. In response to the second prompt, type CONSOLE:, and press RETURN.

To make a backup copy of an entire volume: In response to the first prompt, type the name of the volume you want to back up, followed by a colon. Then press RETURN. In response to the second prompt, type the name of the volume to be used as the backup, followed by a colon, or type a sharp sign, the unit number of the disk drive to hold the backup and a colon. Then press RETURN.

The system will then ask:

Transfer 494 blocks ? (Y/N) ☐

where 494 is the number of blocks on this particular volume. Answer Y for 'YES' to this question to backup the entire volume. The system will then examine the directory on the destination volume. If a valid directory is found, the question:

Destroy VOLNAME: ? ☐

will appear. If you answer Y for 'YES', the contents of the backup disk will be overwritten with the contents of the original volume. The entire volume, including directory, volume name, files, bootstrap, and unused areas will be copied. At the conclusion of this operation, you will have two volumes with the same volume name and identical contents. If you answer N for 'NO', the TRANSFER command will be aborted and the two volumes will be unchanged.

When To Use It:

You will use the TRANSFER command whenever you want to shuffle files around, make backup copies of files or volumes, printout files, or display files on the console.

<hr>

VOLUMES

Prompt:

There is no prompt for the VOLUMES command.

Description:

The VOLUMES command displays the volume names and unit numbers of the volumes that are currently on-line. In addition, it displays the prefix volume name and root volume name.

How To Use It:

To display the current volume names: Type V.

When To Use It:

You can use the VOLUMES command to quickly determine the volume name of an unmarked volume.

WHAT

Prompt:

There is no prompt for the WHAT command.

Description:

The WHAT command displays the status of the work file with the following messages:

no workfile	No file has been designated as the work file and neither SYSTEM.WRK.TEXT nor SYSTEM.WRK.CODE exists.
workfile is FILENAME	The file, FILENAME, has been designated as the work file.
not named	The files SYSTEM.WRK.TEXT and SYSTEM.WRK.CODE exist, but have not been named by a previous GET or SAVE command.
not saved	The work file consists of the temporary files SYSTEM.WRK.TEXT or SYSTEM.WRK.CODE.

How To Use It:

To display the status of the work file: Type W.

When To Use It:

Use the WHAT command before invoking the editor to check the status of the work file.

WILD CARDS

Prompts:

Wild cards can be used in response to the prompts for the CHANGE, REMOVE and TRANSFER commands.

Description:

Wild cards specify a group of files. A wild card matches any sequence of characters in a file specification. There are two wild cards in the p-System: the equals sign (=) and the question mark (?).

How To Use It:

To specify a group of files with verification: Type a file name containing the question mark (?) wild card. The system will find all the files that match the file name. Before an operation takes place on each file that matches the file name, you will be asked to verify that the file is correct.

To specify a group of files without verification: Type a file name containing the equals sign (=) wild card. The system will find all the files that match the file name and then perform the specified operation on those files, without requesting verification.

When To Use It:

To be safe, when specifying more than one file, use the question mark wild card, although it is more convenient to use the equals sign wild card: especially when you have several files to TRANSFER, when you are sure that you have not made a mistake in specifying the file name with the wild card, and when you don't want to be bothered with typing Y before TRANSFERing each file.

(X) EXAMINE

Prompt:

Examine blocks on what vol ? ☐
Block-range ? ☐

Description:

The EXAMINE command attempts to recover bad blocks on a volume. This command should be used after a BAD BLOCKS command.

How To Use It:

To attempt to recover bad blocks on a volume: In response to the first prompt, type the name of the volume containing bad blocks, followed by a colon. Then press RETURN. In response to the second prompt, enter the numbers of the blocks found bad by the BAD BLOCKS command. In some versions of the p-System you may enter only a range of block numbers separated by a hyphen. In other versions, you may enter separate block numbers, separated by commas. Check your system's documentation to see what works on your system.

The EXAMINE command will display any files endangered by the bad blocks and request permission to try to fix them by prompting:

Fix them ? ☐

Type Y for 'YES', to attempt to recover the bad blocks. If a block can not be fixed by this procedure, the EXAMINE command will offer the option of marking the block as bad. Once it is marked as bad, it will not be used in any file, and it will not be shifted by a KRUNCH command.

When To Use It:

Use the EXAMINE command whenever the BAD BLOCKS command detects bad blocks on any of your disks.

```
┌─────────────┐
│    ZERO     │
└─────────────┘
```

Prompts:

Zero dir of what vol ? ☐
Destroy VOLNAME: ? ☐
Duplicate dir ? ☐
Are there 494 blocks on the disk ? (Y/N) ☐
New volume name ? ☐
NEWNAME: correct ? ☐

Description:

The ZERO command initializes the directory on a volume. In the p-System, you must ZERO a new disk before you can store files on it. On some systems you must format a new disk before it can be ZEROed. Check your documentation for the requirements of your system.

How To Use It:

To initialize the directory of a volume: In response to the first prompt, type either the name of the volume to be ZEROed followed by a colon (VOLNAME:), or a sharp sign, the unit number of the drive containing the volume to be ZEROed and a colon (#5:). Then press RETURN. If the volume you are ZEROing has never been ZEROed before, it will not have a volume name. In that case, you must use a sharp sign and the unit number.

The 'Destroy VOLNAME: ?' verification will appear if the volume to be ZEROed has a valid directory. Answer Y to continue or N to abort the ZEROing.

Some versions of the p-System support duplicate directories. If your system supports this feature, you may answer Y for 'YES' to the 'Duplicate dir ?' prompt to create a backup directory on your volume. Otherwise answer N for 'NO' and a duplicate directory will not be created.

If the volume has a valid directory, then the system can determine the number of blocks on the volume. This appears for your confirmation in the prompt 'Are there 494 blocks on the disk ? (Y/N)', where 494 is the number of blocks on this particular volume. Answer N to this question, if the number of blocks displayed is not correct.

If there is no directory on the volume, or if the number of blocks is incorrect, then you will be asked to specify the number of blocks on the volume with this prompt:

# of blocks on the disk ? ☐

>Type in the proper number of blocks for the type of disk that you are using (see Appendix A) and press RETURN.
>
>In response to the 'New vol name ?' prompt, type the name for the volume you are ZEROing and a colon. Once you have verified it, by answering Y to the next prompt, the ZEROing process will proceed.

New volume name ? **VOLNAME:** ₎

VOLNAME: correct ? **Y**

>The message

VOLNAME: zeroed

>will signify that ZEROing is complete.

>**When To Use It:**

>All new disks must be ZEROed.

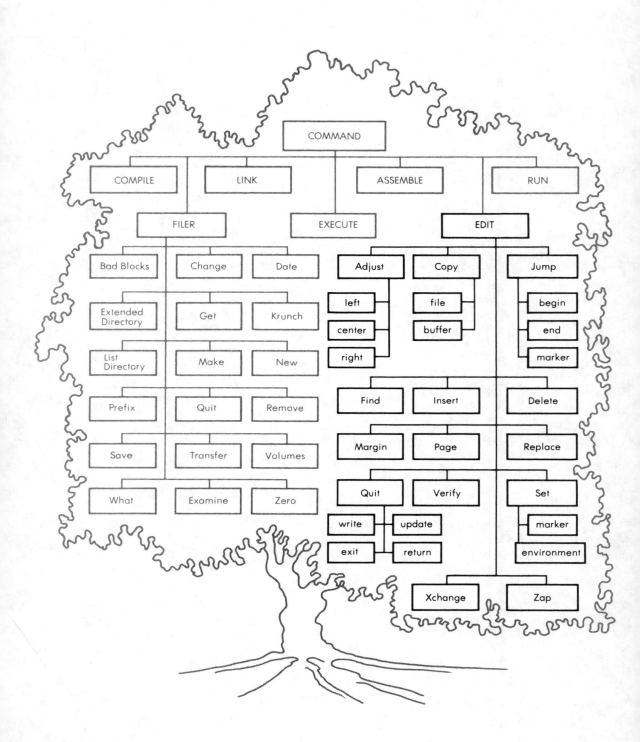

THE EDITOR 4

THIS CHAPTER DISCUSSES the text editor. The text editor is used to create and revise written material. Part One briefly describes the three editors available on the p-System: YALOE, the screen oriented editor, and L2. Parts Two, Three and Four discuss, in detail, the screen oriented editor—the most widely used of the three editors. In particular, Part Two examines the commands available on the screen oriented editor which you can use to write Pascal programs. Part Three looks at the commands for editing natural language (e.g., English) documents. Part Four offers a reference summary of *all* the commands of the screen oriented editor.

PART ONE: THE p-SYSTEM EDITORS

We will now briefly describe the three editors available on the p-System.

YALOE

YALOE (Yet Another Line Oriented Editor) is, as its name indicates, a line oriented editor. A line oriented editor manipulates and displays individual lines of text, a line at a time. For this reason, YALOE is more difficult to use than the other two editors on the p-System. It is normally used only on systems that do not have a CRT screen console.

The Screen Oriented Editor

The *screen oriented editor* can manipulate and display several lines of text at a time. It reads a text file into a section of main memory, called the text buffer, and displays the file on a CRT screen a screenful at a time. As you make changes to the text, they are visible on the screen. Once all the desired changes are in place, you can write the contents of the buffer out to a text file on disk.

The most serious limitation of the screen oriented editor is that the text being edited must fit into the text buffer. The size of the text buffer depends on the amount of main memory in the system and varies between versions of the p-System.

For the text on the console to accurately represent the text in the buffer, a large amount of information must be sent from the system to the console each time you modify the text. Therefore, you need a reasonably fast console and interface between the console and system in order to use the screen oriented editor. (2400 baud or faster should be sufficient.)

The screen oriented editor performs a number of functions to the text on the screen. To use this editor, the CRT console must be able to move the cursor up a line, down a line, one character to the left, one character to the right, and to the home position (upper left corner). It must also be able to erase text from the current cursor position to the end of a line, and from the current cursor position to the end of a screen. Most CRT terminals can perform these functions.

L2

L2 is an experimental (as of this writing), large file version of the screen oriented editor. The L2 editor is designed for editing large pieces of text. Recall that the amount of text the screen oriented editor can handle is limited to the size of the text buffer. The L2 editor does not have this limitation. L2 keeps the entire text in a disk file and only brings a portion at a time into the text buffer. Since L2 is still experimental, it may have a few bugs—beware!

Editor Summary

Your choice of editors is fairly simple. If you do not have a fast CRT screen on your console, you will want to use YALOE. If you are using large files (and feeling brave), then you may want to try L2. Otherwise, you will probably choose the screen oriented editor.

In the rest of this chapter, we will take a close look at the screen oriented editor which, from now on, we will refer to simply as "the editor."

PART TWO: WRITING PASCAL PROGRAMS

We will now write a Pascal program using the editor. Figure 4.1 lists the editor commands in alphabetical order and gives a brief description of each command.

Command	Description
ADJUST	centers, justifies, or moves a line or group of lines.
COPY	copies material from a buffer or a file.
DELETE	deletes characters from the text buffer.
FIND	locates a string of characters in the text buffer.
INSERT	inserts characters into the text buffer.
JUMP	moves the cursor to the beginning or end of the text buffer, or to a marker within it.
MARGIN	resets a paragraph to conform with the margin settings.
PAGE	displays the next "page" of the text buffer.
QUIT	quits the editor and permits various options for storing the text in a file.
REPLACE	replaces a string of characters with a new string.
SET	permits the establishment of markers in a text, or control of certain editor features such as AUTO-INDENT.
VERIFY	displays the part of the text buffer centered around the cursor on the screen.
XCHANGE	replaces characters on a line, character by character.
ZAP	deletes a certain portion of the text buffer.

Figure 4.1: The Editor Commands

We will use these commands and learn how to:

— enter the editor from the COMMAND mode

— move the cursor

— insert, exchange, and delete text

— adjust line position

— quit the editor

— find and replace character strings.

Entering The Editor: The EDIT Command

To enter the editor, select the EDIT command from the COMMAND mode by pressing the E key. This causes the system to enter the EDIT mode, load the work file and display it on the screen. If the system does not have a work file, a prompt appears. Let's discuss each case in more detail.

Work File Present

A work file is present in the system if the root volume has a file named SYSTEM.WRK.TEXT, or if some other file has been designated as the work file, with the GET command. When the system enters the EDIT mode, the work file is automatically loaded into the text buffer and displayed on the screen. (You can clear the current work file from the system using the NEW command in the FILER.)

No Work File Present

If there is no file named SYSTEM.WRK.TEXT on the root volume, or if no other file has been designated as the work file, then pressing the E key causes the system to display the following prompt:

```
>Edit:
No workfile is present. File? (<ret> for no file <esc-ret> to exit)
: ▢
```

You now have three options. You may:

1. Type in a file name without suffix, and press RETURN. The file specified will be loaded into the text buffer and appear on the screen. It is not necessary to type the .TEXT suffix with the file name because the system automatically appends it. In fact, typing .TEXT will only confuse the system, as it will then try to find: '(file name).TEXT.TEXT.' As an example, if you specify the file name GAMES:KENO, the system will look for the file KENO.TEXT on the volume GAMES. Of course, if a file is on the prefix volume, you can omit the volume name and colon before the file specification. If you misspell a file name, or if there is no such file, the message 'NOT PRESENT' will appear.

2. Press RETURN. This allows you to create a new file. You will enter the EDIT mode, but no file will be loaded into the text buffer. The EDIT prompt will appear over a blank screen.

3. Press the ESC key and then press RETURN. This aborts the EDIT mode and returns you to the COMMAND mode. You might use this option if you select EDIT by mistake.

The EDIT Prompt

Once you specify the file (if any) to be loaded into the text buffer and enter the EDIT mode, the prompt for the EDIT mode appears over the contents (if any) of the text buffer:

>Edit: A(djst C(py D(lete F(ind I(nsrt J(mp R(place Q(uit X(chng Z(ap [E.6g]

The EDIT prompt lists the various editor commands that you can select by pressing the appropriate letter key; for example, A for ADJUST, I for IN-SERT, etc. Some commands (i.e., VERIFY and PAGE) do not appear on the EDIT prompt, but you can still invoke them whenever the EDIT prompt is on screen.

Setting Up

We are now ready to examine the various features of the editor. The best way to learn these features is to actually try them. In other words, by putting some text on your screen and duplicating the examples as they are presented, you will quickly become fluent in using the editor.

We will use the text of the SUM program, presented at the end of

Chapter 2, to demonstrate the EDITOR commands. If you don't have the SUM text already in your system, turn on your system and boot the p-System. Then, invoke the EDIT command from the COMMAND mode. Press the RETURN key (option 2 above) to set up an empty text buffer and enter the EDIT mode. Next, select the INSERT command and type in the following text:

```
>Edit: A(djst C(py D(lete F(ind I(nsrt J(mp R(place  Q(uit X(chng Z(ap [E.6g]
PROGRAM SUM;
VAR A, B, TOTAL: INTEGER;
BEGIN
    WRITELN ('ENTER TWO NUMBERS TO BE ADDED... ');
    READ (A,B);
    TOTAL: = A + B;
    WRITELN ('THE SUM OF ',A,' AND ',B,' IS ',TOTAL)
END.
```

Use the backspace key to erase any typing mistakes. When the program is complete, end the insertion by striking the ETX key. The EDIT prompt will reappear as you leave the INSERT mode and return to the EDIT mode. You are now ready to practice the cursor moves and other editor commands.

Cursor Moves

We will begin our discussion of the EDIT commands by considering the commands that move the cursor. This is a humble but vital operation. You cannot insert, delete, or exchange text unless the cursor is positioned properly on the screen.

Whenever you are in the EDIT mode with the prompt for the EDIT mode displayed, the cursor will move over the screen without affecting text, i.e., it will move non-destructively. You can move the cursor non-destructively using any one of the following keys or commands:

- the arrow keys
- the spacebar
- the backspace key

- the RETURN key

- the TAB key

- the JUMP command

- the PAGE command

- the EQUALS (=) command

We will consider each of these possibilities in turn, using standard p-System terminology. That is, we will refer to the up-arrow key, even though some keyboards do not have one. Some keyboards may, however, have an equivalent key. If necessary, you should refer to the documentation for your system to learn your keyboard equivalents.

Arrow Keys

The left-arrow, right-arrow, up-arrow and down-arrow keys invoke commands that move the cursor left or right one space, or up or down one line, respectively. If you type a number before striking an arrow key, you can perform multiple commands with a single key stroke. We will begin by examining each arrow key individually, and then we will consider multiple arrow commands.

Left-Arrow   The left-arrow key moves the cursor one space to the left. If the cursor is at the beginning of a text line, however, the left-arrow key will move it to the end of the previous line. Let's try out the left-arrow command on our SUM program.

Assuming you have just entered the SUM program into the text buffer, the cursor is now sitting at the end of the text buffer:

```
>Edit: A(djst C(py D(lete F(ind I(nsrt J(mp R(place Q(uit X(chng Z(ap [E.6g]
PROGRAM SUM;
VAR A, B, TOTAL: INTEGER;
BEGIN
    WRITELN ('ENTER TWO NUMBERS TO BE ADDED...');
    READ (A,B);
    TOTAL: = A + B;
    WRITELN ('THE SUM OF ',A,' AND ',B,' IS ',TOTAL)
END.□
```

Press the left-arrow key four times. The cursor moves to the beginning of the last line:

```
>Edit: A(djst C(py D(lete F(ind I(nsrt J(mp R(place Q(uit X(chng Z(ap [E.6g]
PROGRAM SUM;
VAR A, B, TOTAL: INTEGER;
BEGIN
    WRITELN ('ENTER TWO NUMBERS TO BE ADDED...');
    READ (A,B);
    TOTAL:= A + B;
    WRITELN ('THE SUM OF ',A,' AND ',B,' IS ',TOTAL)
[E]ND.
```

Press the left-arrow key once again. The cursor moves to the end of the next-to-last line:

```
>Edit: A(djst C(py D(lete F(ind I(nsrt J(mp R(place Q(uit X(chng Z(ap [E.6g]
PROGRAM SUM;
VAR A, B, TOTAL: INTEGER;
BEGIN
    WRITELN ('ENTER TWO NUMBERS TO BE ADDED...');
    READ (A,B);
    TOTAL:= A + B;
    WRITELN ('THE SUM OF ',A,' AND ',B,' IS ',TOTAL)□
END.
```

Finally, press the left-arrow key three more times. The cursor moves to the 'A' of 'TOTAL':

```
>Edit: A(djst C(py D(lete F(ind I(nsrt J(mp R(place Q(uit X(chng Z(ap [E.6g]
PROGRAM SUM;
VAR A, B, TOTAL: INTEGER;
BEGIN
    WRITELN ('ENTER TWO NUMBERS TO BE ADDED...');
    READ (A,B);
    TOTAL:= A + B;
    WRITELN ('THE SUM OF ',A,' AND ',B,' IS ',TOT[A]L)
END.
```

Right-Arrow   The right-arrow key moves the cursor one space to the right each time you press it. At the end of a text line, however, the cursor will not continue out onto the screen. Instead, it will jump to the first non-blank character of the next line. Let's experiment with the right-arrow key.

The cursor is on the 'A' of 'TOTAL' in the next-to-last line. Press the right-arrow key three times. The cursor moves to the end of the line:

WRITELN ('THE SUM OF ',A,' AND ',B,' IS ',TOTAL)☐

Press the right-arrow key once more. The cursor moves to the beginning of the next line:

WRITELN ('THE SUM OF ',A,' AND ',B,' IS ',TOTAL)
[E]ND.

Up-Arrow   The up-arrow key moves the cursor up one line. With this key (and with the down-arrow key), it is possible to move the cursor onto the screen outside of the text. This is only its apparent position, however. If you then press the right-arrow or left-arrow key, the cursor will move back into the text. Let's see how this works.

The cursor is on the 'E' of 'END' in the last line:

```
>Edit: A(djst C(py D(lete F(ind I(nsrt J(mp R(place Q(uit X(chng Z(ap [E.6g]
PROGRAM SUM;
VAR A, B, TOTAL: INTEGER;
BEGIN
    WRITELN ('ENTER TWO NUMBERS TO BE ADDED...');
    READ (A,B);
    TOTAL:= A + B;
    WRITELN ('THE SUM OF ',A,' AND ',B,' IS ',TOTAL)
[E]ND.
```

Press the up-arrow key once. The cursor appears to move up one line and to be outside the text:

```
>Edit: A(djst C(py D(lete F(ind I(nsrt J(mp R(place Q(uit X(chng Z(ap [E.6g]
PROGRAM SUM;
VAR A, B, TOTAL: INTEGER;
BEGIN
    WRITELN ('ENTER TWO NUMBERS TO BE ADDED...');
    READ (A,B);
    TOTAL:= A + B;
☐   WRITELN ('THE SUM OF ',A,' AND ',B,' IS ',TOTAL)
END.
```

Press the right-arrow key once. The cursor jumps to the 'R' of 'WRITELN':

W⬚ITELN ('THE SUM OF ',A,' AND ',B,' IS ',TOTAL)
END.

Down-Arrow   The down-arrow key moves the cursor down one line. It is possible to use the down-arrow and up-arrow keys to scroll the text across the screen, but we will not describe this operation until later. Now let's try the down-arrow key.

The cursor is on the 'R' of 'WRITELN' in the next-to-last line:

W⬚ITELN ('THE SUM OF ',A,' AND ',B,' IS ',TOTAL)
END.

Press the down-arrow once. The cursor moves down to the end of the last line:

WRITELN ('THE SUM OF ',A,' AND ',B,' IS ',TOTAL)
END.☐

Multiple Cursor Moves   There are two ways you can move the cursor some distance with the arrow keys. You can press the arrow key several times, moving the cursor one line or character at a time. (Some terminals have a repeat key or an auto-repeat feature that makes this method easier on the fingers and the keys.) Alternatively, you can type a number before you press the arrow key. This will move the cursor a number of characters or lines in one bound.

Numerical Arguments   In formal terms, we say an arrow key can accept numerical arguments. For example, if you type the number 9 and then press the right-arrow key, the cursor will move 9 spaces to the right. Similarly, if you type the number 5 and then press the down-arrow key, the cursor will move down 5 lines. As you will soon see, not only arrow keys but also other cursor commands accept numerical arguments. Try this example.

The cursor is at the end of the last line of the 'SUM' program. Type the number 5 and then press the up-arrow key once. The cursor jumps to the 'N' of 'BEGIN' in the third line:

```
>Edit: A(djst C(py D(lete F(ind I(nsrt J(mp R(place Q(uit X(chng Z(ap [E.6g]
PROGRAM SUM;
VAR A, B, TOTAL: INTEGER;
BEGI N
    WRITELN ('ENTER TWO NUMBERS TO BE ADDED...');
    READ (A,B);
    TOTAL: = A + B;
    WRITELN ('THE SUM OF ',A,' AND ',B,' IS ',TOTAL)
END.
```

The Direction Marker

The "arrow-head" character (>) at the beginning of the EDIT prompt is the direction marker. It determines the direction the cursor will move in response to certain commands. When the direction marker is pointing right (>), the cursor will move forward, toward the end of the text. When it is pointing left (<), the cursor will move backward, toward the beginning of the text.

The spacebar, TAB, RETURN, and PAGE commands are all sensitive to the direction marker. For example, when the direction marker is forward (>), the spacebar moves the cursor one space to the right; when the marker is backward (<), it moves the cursor one space to the left. Note that arrow keys are *not* sensitive to the direction marker.

You may change the direction marker only when you are in the EDIT or DELETE mode. To set the direction marker backward, type the less than symbol (<), the comma (,), or the minus character (−). The new direction marker (<) will then appear at the top of the screen. To set the direction marker forward, type the greater than symbol (>), the period (.), or the plus (+) character. Let's do a quick example.

The direction marker is currently forward (>):

>Edit: A(djst C(py D(lete F(ind I(nsrt J(mp R(place Q(uit X(chng Z(ap [E.6g]

Press the < key. The direction marker is now set backward:

<Edit: A(djst C(py D(lete F(ind I(nsrt J(mp R(place Q(uit X(chng Z(ap [E.6g]

The Spacebar

The spacebar moves the cursor one space left or right, depending on the setting of the direction marker. The spacebar command accepts numerical arguments. For example, if you type the number 3, and then press the spacebar, the cursor will move three spaces. Let's try it.

The cursor is on the 'N' of 'BEGIN' in the third line. The direction marker is currently set backward:

```
<Edit: A(djst C(py D(lete F(ind I(nsrt J(mp R(place Q(uit X(chng Z(ap [E.6g]
PROGRAM SUM;
VAR A, B, TOTAL: INTEGER;
BEGI[N]
    WRITELN ('ENTER TWO NUMBERS TO BE ADDED...');
    READ (A,B);
    TOTAL:= A + B;
    WRITELN ('THE SUM OF ',A,' AND ',B,' IS ',TOTAL)
END.
```

Press the spacebar four times. The cursor moves to the 'B' of 'BEGIN':

```
<Edit: A(djst C(py D(lete F(ind I(nsrt J(mp R(place Q(uit X(chng Z(ap [E.6g]
PROGRAM SUM;
VAR A, B, TOTAL: INTEGER;
[B]EGIN
    WRITELN ('ENTER TWO NUMBERS TO BE ADDED...');
    READ (A,B);
    TOTAL:= A + B;
    WRITELN ('THE SUM OF ',A,' AND ',B,' IS ',TOTAL)
END.
```

Then, press the spacebar three more times. The cursor moves to the 'R' of 'INTEGER' in the second line:

```
PROGRAM SUM;
VAR A, B, TOTAL: INTEGE[R];
BEGIN
```

The RETURN Key

The RETURN key moves the cursor to the first non-blank character on the preceding or following line, depending on the setting of the direction marker. The RETURN key takes numerical arguments. For example, if you type the number 7 and press RETURN, the cursor will jump seven lines. Here's an example.

The cursor is on the 'R' of 'INTEGER' in the second line. The direction marker is pointing backward:

```
<Edit: A(djst C(py D(lete F(ind I(nsrt J(mp R(place Q(uit X(chng Z(ap [E.6g]
PROGRAM SUM;
VAR A, B, TOTAL: INTEGE[R];
```

Press RETURN once. The cursor jumps to the beginning of the previous line (i.e., the 'P' of 'PROGRAM'):

```
<Edit: A(djst C(py D(lete F(ind I(nsrt J(mp R(place Q(uit X(chng Z(ap [E.6g]
[P]ROGRAM SUM;
VAR A, B, TOTAL: INTEGER;
```

Now press the > key to switch the direction marker so that it is pointing forward:

```
>Edit: A(djst C(py D(lete F(ind I(nsrt J(mp R(place Q(uit X(chng Z(ap [E.6g]
[P]ROGRAM SUM;
VAR A, B, TOTAL: INTEGER;
```

Type the number 4 and then press RETURN. The cursor moves to the beginning of the fifth line (i.e., to the 'R' of 'READ'):

```
>Edit: A(djst C(py D(lete F(ind I(nsrt J(mp R(place Q(uit X(chng Z(ap [E.6g]
PROGRAM SUM;
VAR A, B, TOTAL: INTEGER;
BEGIN
    WRITELN ('ENTER TWO NUMBERS TO BE ADDED...');
    [R]EAD (A,B);
    TOTAL: = A + B;
    WRITELN ('THE SUM OF ',A,' AND ',B,' IS ',TOTAL)
END.
```

The TAB Key

The TAB key moves the cursor forward or backward, depending on the setting of the direction marker, to the next tab setting. Tab settings occur every 8 spaces on the screen at screen columns 1, 9, 17, 25, . . . , etc. Tab settings are not related to the text on the screen. You can use the TAB key with a numerical argument. Let's try it.

The cursor is on the 'R' of 'READ' in the fifth line. The direction marker is forward:

[R]EAD (A,B);

Press the TAB key once. The cursor moves to the left parenthesis. Notice that this is in the ninth screen column:

READ [(]A,B);

Now let's examine two EDIT commands that change the position of the cursor: JUMP and PAGE.

The JUMP Command (In Part)

The JUMP command places the cursor either at the beginning of the text buffer, at the end of the text buffer, or at a marker that has been previously set somewhere within the text buffer. You will use JUMP whenever you want to move quickly to the beginning or end of the text buffer, or to a marker within it. The JUMP command doesn't accept numerical arguments. Here is the way JUMP is executed.

Select the JUMP command from the EDIT mode by pressing the J key. The JUMP prompt replaces the EDIT prompt at the top of the screen:

>JUMP: B(eginning E(nd M(arker   <esc>

As shown on this prompt, you now have four options:

- B)EGINNING   Press the B key to put the cursor at the beginning of the text buffer. The EDIT prompt will reappear.

- E)ND   Press the E key to place the cursor at the end of the text buffer. The EDIT prompt will reappear.

- M)ARKER   Press the M key to move the cursor to a designated marker somewhere in the text buffer. This option is described in detail later in this chapter.

- ESC   Press the ESC key to terminate the JUMP command and to redisplay the EDIT prompt. The cursor will not move.

Now let's consider an example.

The cursor is on the left parenthesis in the fifth line of the program:

```
>Edit: A(djst C(py D(lete F(ind I(nsrt J(mp R(place Q(uit X(chng Z(ap [E.6g]
PROGRAM SUM;
VAR A, B, TOTAL: INTEGER;
BEGIN
    WRITELN ('ENTER TWO NUMBERS TO BE ADDED...');
    READ [|(A,B);
    TOTAL: = A + B;
    WRITELN ('THE SUM OF ',A,' AND ',B,' IS ',TOTAL)
END.
```

Press the J key selecting the JUMP comand. The JUMP prompt appears on screen:

>JUMP: B(eginning E(nd M(arker   <esc>

Press the B key selecting the BEGINNING option. The cursor moves to the first character in the text (i.e., the 'P' of 'PROGRAM'). The EDIT prompt reappears:

```
>Edit: A(djst C(py D(lete F(ind I(nsrt J(mp R(place Q(uit X(chng Z(ap [E.6g]
[P]ROGRAM SUM;
VAR A, B, TOTAL: INTEGER;
BEGIN
    WRITELN ('ENTER TWO NUMBERS TO BE ADDED...');
    READ (A,B);
    TOTAL: = A + B;
    WRITELN ('THE SUM OF ',A,' AND ',B,' IS ',TOTAL)
END.
```

The PAGE Command

The PAGE command moves the cursor to the next 'page' of the text buffer. The absolute position of the cursor on the screen doesn't change. Alternatively, we can say the PAGE command displays the next page of the text on the screen. The PAGE command accepts numerical arguments and is sensitive to the direction marker.

A screen can only display a certain number of lines of text at one time. If your text is long, the screen acts as a moving window through which you may view various parts of the material in the text buffer. Depending on the direction marker, the PAGE command moves this "window" one screenful (or page) at a time toward the beginning or end of the text buffer. The PAGE command is very useful when you have a large amount of text in active memory and want to move to a particular region. The PAGE command does not appear on the prompt for the EDIT mode, but you must be in the EDIT mode before you can use it.

Execute the PAGE command by pressing the P key. There is no PAGE prompt. The screen will move a page forward or backward, according to the current direction marker.

To use a numerical argument, type a number before pressing the P key. For example, if you press the 6 key and then the P key, the screen will move six pages. Figure 4.2 contains a diagram showing how the PAGE command works.

The movement of text across the screen is termed *scrolling*. We say the PAGE command "scrolls by page." We will now look at ways to scroll by line.

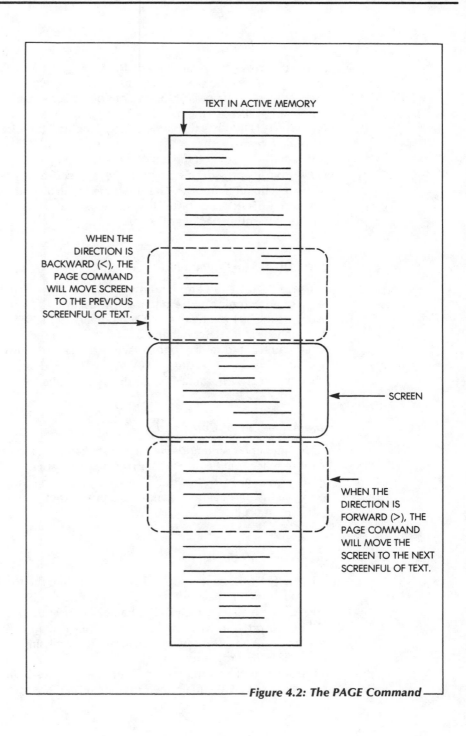

TEXT IN ACTIVE MEMORY

WHEN THE DIRECTION IS BACKWARD (<), THE PAGE COMMAND WILL MOVE SCREEN TO THE PREVIOUS SCREENFUL OF TEXT.

SCREEN

WHEN THE DIRECTION IS FORWARD (>), THE PAGE COMMAND WILL MOVE THE SCREEN TO THE NEXT SCREENFUL OF TEXT.

Figure 4.2: The PAGE Command

Scrolling By Line

The up-arrow, down-arrow, and RETURN keys all scroll by line. That is, these keys move the screen "window" up or down one or more lines of text. When the cursor is at the bottom of the screen, pressing the down-arrow key will cause the next line of the text buffer to appear on screen. Pressing RETURN has the same effect, provided the direction marker is pointing forward (>).

When the cursor is at the top of the screen (i.e., immediately under the EDIT prompt), pressing the up-arrow key will cause the previous half-page of the text buffer to appear. The cursor will be in the middle of the screen. Pressing RETURN performs the same operation when the direction marker is pointing backward (<).

The EQUALS (=) Command

The EQUALS (=) command moves the cursor from anywhere in the text to the beginning of the material you last inserted, found, or replaced, using the INSERT mode, the FIND command, or the REPLACE command. Although the EQUALS command is not frequently used, it can be very handy when you want to return to the place in the text buffer where you made the last correction. Execute the EQUALS command by pressing the = key while in the EDIT mode. EQUALS does not appear on the EDIT prompt.

Summary—Cursor Commands

The keys and commands we have just examined move the cursor one or more spaces or lines at a time, to the beginning or end of the text buffer, or to a new page in the text buffer. Before continuing, you should practice using the cursor keys and commands. When they feel familiar, read on, and learn more about the editor.

The INSERT Mode

The INSERT mode lets you type characters into the text buffer without disturbing anything already there. You can use INSERT to create a new piece of text. You used INSERT in Chapter 2 when you wrote the text of the GREETING program. You can also use INSERT to add new characters to existing files. You did this when you inserted the missing quote mark (') into the GREETING program.

The amount of new material inserted is ultimately limited by the size of the system's available main memory. The ENVIRONMENT option of the

SET command displays the number of bytes in use in the text buffer and the number still available.

Selecting INSERT To use INSERT, place the cursor at the location where you wish to make the insertion. Then press the I key. The INSERT prompt appears:

>Insert: Text {<bs> a char,<del> a line} [<etx> accepts, <esc> escapes]

Any character key you now type will be entered into the text buffer and appear on the screen to the left of the cursor.

As indicated on the prompt, there are two options that you can use to correct mistakes during insertion, and two options to terminate INSERT. They are:

- BACKSPACE Press the BACKSPACE key to erase an incorrect character. The cursor will move back one space and erase the character you just inserted.

- DEL Press the DEL (delete) key to erase to the end of the previous inserted line. The DEL key, however, will not erase the first inserted line, since there is no previous inserted line.

and

- ETX Press the ETX key to terminate an insertion and "officially" put the text you typed into the text buffer. We say that the ETX key "accepts" the insertion. The accepted text is also stored in the copy buffer, which you can use with the COPY command (as we will see later in this chapter).

- ESC Press the ESC key to terminate an insertion and return the text buffer to the condition it was in before entering the INSERT mode. The system will erase the material you typed from the screen.

Let's look at an example.

Example of INSERT We will use the INSERT mode to perform a common operation—putting a new line of code into a program. We will insert a 'WRITELN' into the SUM program in order to format the output more attractively.

First, move the cursor to the letter 'W' in the word 'WRITELN' on the line before 'END':

```
>Edit: A(djst C(py D(lete F(ind I(nsrt J(mp R(place Q(uit X(chng Z(ap [E.6g]
PROGRAM SUM;
VAR A, B, TOTAL: INTEGER;
BEGIN
    WRITELN ('ENTER TWO NUMBERS TO BE ADDED...');
    READ (A,B);
    TOTAL:= A + B;
    WRITELN ('THE SUM OF ',A,' AND ',B,' IS ',TOTAL)
END.
```

Press the I key to enter the INSERT mode. The cursor doesn't move, but the entire next-to-last line does. It is set flush against the right margin of the screen:

```
>Insert: Text {<bs> a char,<del> a line} [<etx> accepts, <esc> escapes]
PROGRAM SUM;
VAR A, B, TOTAL: INTEGER;
BEGIN
    WRITELN ('ENTER TWO NUMBERS TO BE ADDED...');
    READ (A,B);
    TOTAL:= A + B;
    □                        WRITELN ('THE SUM OF ',A,' AND ',B,' IS ',TOTAL)
END.
```

Now, type in the new line, but intentionally include some mistakes:

```
>Insert: Text {<bs> a char,<del> a line} [<etx> accepts, <esc> escapes]
PROGRAM SUM;
VAR A, B, TOTAL: INTEGER;
BEGIN
    WRITELN ('ENTER TWO NUMBERS TO BE ADDED...');
    READ (A,B);
    TOTAL:= A + B;
    WRITXCXC□                WRITELN ('THE SUM OF ',A,' AND ',B,' IS ',TOTAL)
END.
```

Use the BACKSPACE key to erase the incorrect characters:

```
>Insert: Text {<bs> a char,<del> a line} [<etx> accepts, <esc> escapes]
PROGRAM SUM;
VAR A, B, TOTAL: INTEGER;
BEGIN
    WRITELN ('ENTER TWO NUMBERS TO BE ADDED...');
    READ (A,B);
    TOTAL:= A + B;
    WRIT□              WRITELN ('THE SUM OF ',A,' AND ',B,' IS ',TOTAL)
END.
```

Retype the insertion correctly:

```
>Insert: Text {<bs> a char,<del> a line} [<etx> accepts, <esc> escapes]
PROGRAM SUM;
VAR A, B, TOTAL: INTEGER;
BEGIN
    WRITELN ('ENTER TWO NUMBERS TO BE ADDED...');
    READ (A,B);
    TOTAL:= A + B;
    WRITELN;□            WRITELN ('THE SUM OF ',A,' AND ',B,' IS ',TOTAL)
END.
```

Insert a carriage return by pressing RETURN. The line against the right screen margin moves down one line and the last line disappears. (Don't worry, it hasn't been lost.)

```
>Insert: Text {<bs> a char,<del> a line} [<etx> accepts, <esc> escapes]
PROGRAM SUM;
VAR A, B, TOTAL: INTEGER;
BEGIN
    WRITELN ('ENTER TWO NUMBERS TO BE ADDED...');
    READ (A,B);
    TOTAL:= A + B;
    WRITELN;
    □                  WRITELN ('THE SUM OF ',A,' AND ',B,' IS ',TOTAL)
```

Finally, press the ETX key to accept the insertion. The new line becomes part of the text buffer. The line against the right margin and the last line are placed under the new line. The EDIT prompt reappears:

```
>Edit: A(djst C(py D(lete F(ind I(nsrt J(mp R(place Q(uit X(chng Z(ap [E.6g]
PROGRAM SUM;
VAR A, B, TOTAL: INTEGER;
BEGIN
    WRITELN ('ENTER TWO NUMBERS TO BE ADDED...');
    READ (A,B);
    TOTAL: = A + B;
    WRITELN;
    W̲RITELN ('THE SUM OF ',A,' AND ',B,' IS ',TOTAL)
END.
```

Auto-Indent   The Auto-Indent feature controls the behavior of the cursor when you press RETURN in the INSERT mode. The editor normally operates with Auto-Indent 'ON' (or 'TRUE'). This means that when you press RETURN the cursor will line up under the first non-blank character of the line it came from. In other words, the same indentation will be maintained for a series of lines—a great convenience when you are writing Pascal programs.

Of course, you can change the indentation of a new line after pressing a RETURN by using the backspace, tab, or spacebar keys to move the cursor left or right on the screen.

Later in this chapter, we will explain how you can turn the Auto-Indent feature 'OFF'.

Overflow   It is possible to insert a line of characters beyond the right screen margin. The line, however, will "overflow" the margin. You are warned of this condition by the exclamation character (!), which appears as the last character next to the screen margin.

You can move the part of the line beyond the screen to a new line by first accepting the insertion with the ETX key and then placing the cursor on the offending line near the right screen margin. By entering the INSERT mode again, pressing RETURN, and accepting the inserted carriage return with the ETX key, the invisible end of the line will appear on screen.

So far we have studied the INSERT mode, the Auto-Indent facility, and screen overflow. We will continue with a discussion of the EXCHANGE mode, which allows you to change material in the text buffer.

The EXCHANGE Mode

The EXCHANGE mode lets you replace material in the text buffer, character by character. The EXCHANGE mode is handy when you need to fix a small typing error that escaped your attention previously. In the EXCHANGE mode, however, you cannot exchange material beyond the end of a line, nor can you replace a text character with a carriage return.

Entering EXCHANGE   To enter the EXCHANGE mode, first, place the cursor on the character you wish to replace. Then, select the EXCHANGE mode by pressing the X key. The EXCHANGE prompt replaces the EDIT prompt at the top of the screen:

>eXchange: TEXT {<bs> a char} [<esc> escapes; <etx> accepts]

Any character key you now type, except RETURN, will replace the character on which the cursor is positioned. As noted on the prompt, there is *one* option you can use for correcting incorrect typing and *two* options for terminating EXCHANGE. They are:

- BACKSPACE   Press the BACKSPACE key if you type the wrong letter. The cursor will move back one space and the original character will reappear.

- ETX   Press the ETX key to leave the EXCHANGE mode and to accept the changes you have made into the text buffer. The EDIT prompt will reappear.

- ESC   Press the ESC key to leave the EXCHANGE mode and to disregard whatever you have just typed. The text buffer will remain unchanged. The characters you typed will be erased from the screen and the original characters will reappear. The EDIT prompt will also reappear at the top of the screen.

Here's an example.

Example of EXCHANGE   In this example, we will use the EXCHANGE mode to change the name of the SUM program to ADD. We will then change our minds and return to the status quo.

Place the cursor on the 'S' of 'SUM':

```
>Edit: A(djst C(py D(lete F(ind I(nsrt J(mp R(place Q(uit X(chng Z(ap [E.6g]
PROGRAM [S]UM;
VAR A, B, TOTAL: INTEGER;
BEGIN
    WRITELN ('ENTER TWO NUMBERS TO BE ADDED...');
    READ (A,B);
    TOTAL:= A + B;
    WRITELN;
    WRITELN ('THE SUM OF ',A,' AND ',B,' IS ',TOTAL)
END.
```

Select the EXCHANGE mode by pressing the X key. The EXCHANGE prompt appears:

```
>eXchange: TEXT {<bs> a char} [<esc> escapes; <etx> accepts]
PROGRAM [S]UM;
VAR A, B, TOTAL: INTEGER;
BEGIN
    WRITELN ('ENTER TWO NUMBERS TO BE ADDED...');
    READ (A,B);
    TOTAL:= A + B;
    WRITELN;
    WRITELN ('THE SUM OF ',A,' AND ',B,' IS ',TOTAL)
END.
```

Type the letters ADX.

```
>eXchange: TEXT {<bs> a char} [<esc> escapes; <etx> accepts]
PROGRAM ADX[;]
VAR A, B, TOTAL: INTEGER;
BEGIN
    WRITELN ('ENTER TWO NUMBERS TO BE ADDED...');
    READ (A,B);
    TOTAL:= A + B;
    WRITELN;
    WRITELN ('THE SUM OF ',A,' AND ',B,' IS ',TOTAL)
END.
```

Use the BACKSPACE key to recover from the mistake (the X). Notice how the original character ('M') reappears.

```
>eXchange: TEXT {<bs> a char} [<esc> escapes; <etx> accepts]
PROGRAM ADM;
VAR A, B, TOTAL: INTEGER;
BEGIN
    WRITELN ('ENTER TWO NUMBERS TO BE ADDED...');
    READ (A,B);
    TOTAL: = A + B;
    WRITELN;
    WRITELN ('THE SUM OF ',A,' AND ',B,' IS ',TOTAL)
END.
```

Now, retype the second 'D'.

```
>eXchange: TEXT {<bs> a char} [<esc> escapes; <etx> accepts]
PROGRAM ADD
VAR A, B, TOTAL: INTEGER;
BEGIN
    WRITELN ('ENTER TWO NUMBERS TO BE ADDED...');
    READ (A,B);
    TOTAL: = A + B;
    WRITELN;
    WRITELN ('THE SUM OF ',A,' AND ',B,' IS ',TOTAL)
END.
```

However, at this point you decide you prefer the original name. Simply, press the ESC key. The system disregards the exchange. The EDIT prompt reappears over the initial text:

```
>Edit: A(djst C(py D(lete F(ind I(nsrt J(mp R(place Q(uit X(chng Z(ap [E.6g]
PROGRAM [S]UM;
VAR A, B, TOTAL: INTEGER;
BEGIN
    WRITELN ('ENTER TWO NUMBERS TO BE ADDED...');
    READ (A,B);
    TOTAL: = A + B;
    WRITELN;
    WRITELN ('THE SUM OF ',A,' AND ',B,' IS ',TOTAL)
END.
```

We have now looked at two modes (INSERT and EXCHANGE) that allow the insertion of new characters into the text buffer. Next, we will consider the DELETE mode, which, not surprisingly, allows the deletion of characters.

The DELETE Mode

The DELETE mode lets you remove material from the text buffer. After entering DELETE, you can make the deletion by moving the cursor forward or backward from its initial position. As the cursor moves over the characters, the characters are erased from the screen. The characters are not actually deleted from the text buffer, however, until you terminate DELETE with the ETX key. You may change the setting of the direction marker while you are in DELETE.

Entering DELETE   To enter the DELETE mode, move the cursor to the text you wish to delete. Then press the D key. The DELETE prompt appears:

>Delete: < > <Moving commands> {<etx> to delete, <esc> to abort}

Now, whenever you move the cursor, you will erase characters from the screen. However, if you move the cursor back towards its initial position, the original characters will reappear.

You can move the cursor using the arrow keys, the spacebar, the TAB key, the backspace key or the RETURN key. You cannot use the PAGE,

JUMP, or EQUALS commands, however. The direction marker determines the direction the cursor will move in response to the spacebar, the TAB key, and RETURN; you can set it either forward or backward.

In DELETE, all the cursor moving commands accept numerical arguments. So it is possible to erase several lines of characters with only a few key strokes.

As the prompt indicates, there are two ways to leave the DELETE mode:

- ETX   Press the ETX key to "accept" the deletion. The characters you have erased from the screen will disappear from the text buffer. The EDIT prompt will reappear.

- ESC   Press the ESC key to disregard the deletion. This causes the system to ignore whatever you've just done in the DELETE mode. The characters in the text buffer will remain unchanged and will reappear on your screen together with the EDIT prompt.

After an ETX or ESC command, the text you erased from the screen is actually still available. It is stored in the copy buffer in the system's main memory. You have access to it with the COPY command. Let's look at an example of DELETE.

Example of DELETE   In this example, we will delete the line of Pascal source code we recently inserted into the SUM program. (Deleting one or more lines is something you will do frequently as you rewrite your Pascal programs.)

Move the cursor so that it is on the 'W' of 'WRITELN' in the line you inserted. The direction marker is forward (>):

```
>Edit: A(djst C(py D(lete F(ind I(nsrt J(mp R(place Q(uit X(chng Z(ap [E.6g]
PROGRAM SUM;
VAR A, B, TOTAL: INTEGER;
BEGIN
    WRITELN ('ENTER TWO NUMBERS TO BE ADDED...');
    READ (A,B);
    TOTAL: = A + B;
    [W]RITELN;
    WRITELN ('THE SUM OF ',A,' AND ',B,' IS ',TOTAL)
END.
```

Now, press the D key, selecting the DELETE mode. The DELETE prompt appears:

>Delete: < > <Moving commands> {<etx> to delete, <esc> to abort}

Press the right-arrow key three times. The 'WRI' of 'WRITELN' is erased:

```
>Delete: < > <Moving commands> {<etx> to delete, <esc> to abort}
PROGRAM SUM;
VAR A, B, TOTAL: INTEGER;
BEGIN
    WRITELN ('ENTER TWO NUMBERS TO BE ADDED...');
    READ (A,B);
    TOTAL:= A + B;
        [T]ELN;
    WRITELN ('THE SUM OF ',A,' AND ',B,' IS ',TOTAL)
END.
```

Press the backspace key three times. The 'WRI' characters reappear:

```
>Delete: < > <Moving commands> {<etx> to delete, <esc> to abort}
PROGRAM SUM;
VAR A, B, TOTAL: INTEGER;
BEGIN
    WRITELN ('ENTER TWO NUMBERS TO BE ADDED...');
    READ (A,B);
    TOTAL:= A + B;
    [W]RITELN;
    WRITELN ('THE SUM OF ',A,' AND ',B,' IS ',TOTAL)
END.
```

Now erase the entire line by pressing RETURN. The inserted line is erased, and the cursor moves to the beginning of the next line:

```
>Delete: < > <Moving commands> {<etx> to delete, <esc> to abort}
PROGRAM SUM;
VAR A, B, TOTAL: INTEGER;
BEGIN
    WRITELN ('ENTER TWO NUMBERS TO BE ADDED...');
    READ (A,B);
    TOTAL:= A + B;

    ⬛RITELN ('THE SUM OF ',A,' AND ',B,' IS ',TOTAL)
END.
```

Make the deletion from the text buffer final by pressing the ETX key. The text is now rearranged to fill in the deleted line. The EDIT prompt reappears:

```
>Edit: A(djst C(py D(lete F(ind I(nsrt J(mp R(place Q(uit X(chng Z(ap [E.6g]
PROGRAM SUM;
VAR A, B, TOTAL: INTEGER;
BEGIN
    WRITELN ('ENTER TWO NUMBERS TO BE ADDED...');
    READ (A,B);
    TOTAL:= A + B;
    ⬛RITELN ('THE SUM OF ',A,' AND ',B,' IS ',TOTAL)
END.
```

You can delete several lines at one time by using a numerical argument with RETURN. You might want to experiment with that idea, and with other cursor moves in the DELETE mode. Go ahead. Simply finish with the ESC command, so that the actual text of SUM is unchanged.

We have seen how to use DELETE to remove text from active memory. We will now discuss the COPY command, which we can combine with DELETE or INSERT to duplicate or move text.

The COPY Command

The COPY command lets you duplicate or move text in active memory. It also lets you copy all or part of a file into the text buffer. The COPY command can save a great deal of retyping.

Executing COPY   To execute COPY, first move the cursor to the position in the text where you wish the copied material to appear. Then, select COPY by pressing the C key. This produces the COPY prompt:

>Copy: B(uffer F(rom file   <esc>□

You now have three options:

- ESC   Press the ESC key to abort the COPY command and return to the EDIT mode. The text buffer will be unchanged.

- FROM FILE   Press the F key to copy all or part of a disk file. We will explain the operation of this option in detail in Part Three of this chapter.

- BUFFER   Press the B key to copy the material in the copy buffer to the immediate left of the cursor. This buffer is loaded with characters whenever you terminate the DELETE mode with the ETX or ESC commands, or whenever you conclude an INSERT operation with the ETX command. The buffer contains only the most recent characters of an INSERT or DELETE operation.

In practice, you may insert material and then immediately duplicate it elsewhere using the BUFFER option. Alternatively, you can erase some characters from the screen in the DELETE mode, use the ESC key to disregard the erasure, and then replicate the characters you "erased" elsewhere. Finally, you can delete some characters with the ETX key, and then restore these characters in a new position (i.e., move them) using the BUFFER option. Let's consider an example.

Example of COPY   We will use the DELETE command and the BUFFER option of the COPY command to move two lines of the SUM program to a new position.

Place the cursor on the 'R' of 'READ' in the fifth line:

```
>Edit: A(djst C(py D(lete F(ind I(nsrt J(mp R(place Q(uit X(chng Z(ap [E.6g]
PROGRAM SUM;
VAR A, B, TOTAL: INTEGER;
BEGIN
    WRITELN ('ENTER TWO NUMBERS TO BE ADDED...');
    READ (A,B);
    TOTAL: = A + B;
    WRITELN ('THE SUM OF ',A,' AND ',B,' IS ',TOTAL)
END.
```

Press the D key to enter the DELETE mode. The DELETE prompt appears. Then press RETURN twice to erase the fifth and sixth lines:

```
>Delete: < > <Moving commands> {<etx> to delete, <esc> to abort}
PROGRAM SUM;
VAR A, B, TOTAL: INTEGER;
BEGIN
    WRITELN ('ENTER TWO NUMBERS TO BE ADDED...');


    WRITELN ('THE SUM OF ',A,' AND ',B,' IS ',TOTAL)
END.
```

Press the ETX key to accept the deletion. The EDIT prompt reappears.

The deleted lines are now stored in the Copy buffer. We can use the BUFFER option to place them anywhere in the text. We will put them, inappropriately, between the second and third lines.

Move the cursor to the 'B' of 'BEGIN' in the third line:

```
>Edit: A(djst C(py D(lete F(ind I(nsrt J(mp R(place Q(uit X(chng Z(ap [E.6g]
PROGRAM SUM;
VAR A, B, TOTAL: INTEGER;
BEGIN
    WRITELN ('ENTER TWO NUMBERS TO BE ADDED...');
    WRITELN ('THE SUM OF ',A,' AND ',B,' IS ',TOTAL)
END.
```

Press the C key to select the COPY command and the B key to select the BUFFER option. The buffer contents are copied to the left of the cursor. The EDIT prompt reappears:

```
>Edit: A(djst C(py D(lete F(ind I(nsrt J(mp R(place Q(uit X(chng Z(ap [E.6g]
PROGRAM SUM;
VAR A, B, TOTAL: INTEGER;
    READ (A,B);
    TOTAL: = A + B;
BEGIN
    WRITELN ('ENTER TWO NUMBERS TO BE ADDED...');
    WRITELN ('THE SUM OF ',A,' AND ',B,' IS ',TOTAL)
END.
```

Now we will use the BUFFER option of the COPY command again to unscramble the text of SUM.

Place the cursor on the 'W' of 'WRITELN' in the next-to-last line:

```
>Edit: A(djst C(py D(lete F(ind I(nsrt J(mp R(place Q(uit X(chng Z(ap [E.6g]
PROGRAM SUM;
VAR A, B, TOTAL: INTEGER;
    READ (A,B);
    TOTAL:= A + B;
BEGIN
    WRITELN ('ENTER TWO NUMBERS TO BE ADDED...');
    ▮W▮RITELN ('THE SUM OF ',A,' AND ',B,' IS ',TOTAL)
END.
```

Select the COPY command by pressing the C key. Then choose the BUFFER option by pressing the B key. The two lines reappear:

```
>Edit: A(djst C(py D(lete F(ind I(nsrt J(mp R(place Q(uit X(chng Z(ap [E.6g]
PROGRAM SUM;
VAR A, B, TOTAL: INTEGER;
    READ (A,B);
    TOTAL:= A + B;
BEGIN
    WRITELN ('ENTER TWO NUMBERS TO BE ADDED...');
    ▮R▮EAD (A,B);
    TOTAL:= A + B;
    WRITELN ('THE SUM OF ',A,' AND ',B,' IS ',TOTAL)
END.
```

Finally, use DELETE to remove the misplaced lines and return the text of SUM to its initial form. You may now want to experiment and duplicate parts of the SUM program. Do so by all means. Use the DELETE mode terminated by the ESC key. Then copy from the buffer.

We will next look at the ADJUST command—a very useful tool for rewriting Pascal programs.

The ADJUST Command

The ADJUST command moves the entire line on which the cursor is sitting. You simply press the right-arrow or left-arrow key. You may then similarly adjust adjacent lines by using the up-arrow or down-arrow keys. There are also ADJUST options that allow you to place a line against the left or right margin or to center a line between the margins.

Proper indentation makes Pascal programs more readable. The ADJUST command is very useful for re-indenting a group of Pascal lines.

Executing ADJUST   To execute the ADJUST command, move the cursor to the line you wish to adjust. Then press the A key selecting the ADJUST command. The ADJUST prompt appears:

>Adjust: L(just R(just C(enter <left,right,up,down-arrows> {<etx> to leave}

You now have several options available for adjusting the line on which the cursor is positioned.

- L(JUST (Left Justify)   Press the L key to set the line against the left margin. You may then use the up-arrow or down-arrow keys to similarly adjust the lines above or below.

- R(JUST (Right Justify)   Press the R key to set the line against the right margin. Again, the up-arrow or down-arrow keys will right justify the lines above or below.

- C(ENTER   Press the C key to center the line between the margins. The up-arrow or down-arrow keys will function as above.

- ARROW KEYS   Press the left-arrow or right-arrow key to move the line one space to the left or right. Numerical arguments are acceptable. For example, typing 3 and then pressing the right-arrow key will move the line 3 spaces to the right. The up-arrow or down-arrow keys adjust the lines above or below in the same way that the initial line was adjusted. Furthermore, the up- and down-arrow keys accept numerical arguments. This means that you can re-indent the first of a series of Pascal lines, type the appropriate number, and then strike the up- or down-arrow key once. The entire group of lines will then have the same indentation.

- ETX   Press the ETX key when you are satisfied with the indentation of the text on your screen. This will accept the adjustment. The EDIT prompt will reappear.

Note that there is no ESC option with the ADJUST command that will return the text to its original form. Let's consider an example.

Example of ADJUST   We will use the ADJUST command to adjust the indentation of several lines in the SUM program.

Place the cursor at the beginning of the fifth line:

```
>Edit: A(djst C(py D(lete F(ind I(nsrt J(mp R(place Q(uit X(chng Z(ap [E.6g]
PROGRAM SUM;
VAR A, B, TOTAL: INTEGER;
BEGIN
    WRITELN ('ENTER TWO NUMBERS TO BE ADDED...');
    [R]EAD (A,B);
    TOTAL: = A + B;
    WRITELN ('THE SUM OF ',A,' AND ',B,' IS ',TOTAL)
END.
```

Press the A key selecting the ADJUST command. The ADJUST prompt appears:

```
>Adjust: L(just R(just C(enter <left,right,up,down-arrows> {<etx> to leave}
PROGRAM SUM;
VAR A, B, TOTAL: INTEGER;
BEGIN
    WRITELN ('ENTER TWO NUMBERS TO BE ADDED...');
    [R]EAD (A,B);
    TOTAL: = A + B;
    WRITELN ('THE SUM OF ',A,' AND ',B,' IS ',TOTAL)
END.
```

Press the right-arrow key three times. The line moves three spaces to the right:

```
>Adjust: L(just R(just C(enter <left,right,up,down-arrows> {<etx> to leave}
PROGRAM SUM;
VAR A, B, TOTAL: INTEGER;
BEGIN
    WRITELN ('ENTER TWO NUMBERS TO BE ADDED...');
        [R]EAD (A,B);
    TOTAL: = A + B;
    WRITELN ('THE SUM OF ',A,' AND ',B,' IS ',TOTAL)
END.
```

Type the number 2 and then press the down-arrow key. The next two lines are adjusted three spaces rightward:

```
>Adjust: L(just R(just C(enter <left,right,up,down-arrows> {<etx> to leave}
PROGRAM SUM;
VAR A, B, TOTAL: INTEGER;
BEGIN
    WRITELN ('ENTER TWO NUMBERS TO BE ADDED...');
        READ (A,B);
        TOTAL:= A + B;
        [W]RITELN ('THE SUM OF ',A,' AND ',B,' IS ',TOTAL)
END.
```

Press the ETX key to accept the adjustment. The EDIT prompt reappears.

The SUM program is now badly indented. Use the ADJUST command again to restore it to its original form.

Thus far, we have looked at a variety of EDITOR commands. We will now conclude Part Two with a discussion of the QUIT command, and the FIND and REPLACE commands. Before you go on, however, you may want to review the material presented so far. You could rewrite the SUM program, so that it adds three numbers instead of two. This will give you a chance to practice most of the commands we have discussed. Here is an example of an extended SUM program:

```
>Edit: A(djst C(py D(lete F(ind I(nsrt J(mp R(place Q(uit X(chng Z(ap [E.6g]
PROGRAM NEWSUM; (*ADDS THREE INTEGERS*)
VAR A, B, C, TOTAL: INTEGER;
BEGIN
    WRITELN; (*SPACE*)
    WRITELN ('PLEASE ENTER THREE NUMBERS TO BE ADDED...');
    READ (A,B,C);
    TOTAL:= A + B + C;
    WRITELN; (*SPACE*)
    WRITELN ('THE SUM OF ',A,' AND ',B,' AND ',C,' IS ',TOTAL);
END.
```

The QUIT Command

The QUIT command terminates the EDIT command and returns you to the COMMAND prompt. There are four ways of using QUIT.

1. You can store the material in the text buffer as the file SYSTEM.WRK.TEXT on the root volume.

2. You can store it as a file (named by you) on any volume.

3. You can discard the material in the text buffer and return to the COMMAND mode without writing to any file.

4. You can return to the EDIT mode and continue using the editor without writing to any file.

Executing QUIT   To execute QUIT, select the QUIT command while in the EDIT mode, by pressing the Q key. This causes the text and EDIT prompt to vanish and the QUIT prompt to appear:

```
>QUIT:
      U(pdate the workfile and leave
      E(xit without updating
      R(eturn to the editor without updating
      W(rite to a file name and return
```

QUIT offers four options:

- U)PDATE   Press the U key to store the material in the text buffer on the root volume under the file name SYSTEM.WRK.TXT. A minimum of four blocks are required for this file. If there isn't room on the disk, the following message will appear:

'ERROR: Writing out the file. Please press <spacebar> to continue'.

You must press the spacebar and choose another option.

If the root volume already has a file SYSTEM.WRK.TEXT, that file will be replaced by the new file. If the root volume contains a file SYSTEM.WRK.CODE at the moment you select the UPDATE option, this file will be erased from the directory.

As the characters in the text buffer are being written to the file, the message 'WRITING...' appears on the screen. When the process is complete, another message will indicate the number of bytes in the file. During a long editing session, you should use the UPDATE option frequently. That way you won't lose any work if there is a power failure or some other accident.

- E(XIT Press the E key to disregard the contents of the text buffer and to return to the COMMAND mode. No file will be created, and nothing already in a file will be changed. Use the EXIT option when you want to throw out unsatisfactory editorial changes.

- R)ETURN Press the R key to abort the QUIT command and to return to the EDIT mode with the contents of the text buffer unchanged. Use this option if you strike the Q key inadvertently.

- W)RITE Press the W key to store the contents of the text buffer under a file name you select. The screen will then display this prompt:

Quit:
Name of output file (<cr> to return) --> ☐

Now type in a file name without suffix and hit RETURN. The .TEXT suffix isn't necessary because the system will supply it. Since the total number of characters in a file specification must not exceed 15, the file specification part of the file name you type (without a suffix) should not exceed 10 characters. For example, to store the contents of the text buffer as the file BOGGLE.TEXT on the volume GAMES, you would type:

GAMES:BOGGLE ⏎

If you want to store the file on the prefix volume, you may omit the volume specification part of the file name. For example, to store the contents of the text buffer on the prefix volume as the file TEST.TEXT, you would type:

TEST ⏎

If a file already exists with the same file name you have specified, it will be erased from the directory. In some versions of the p-System, the system checks to make sure you really want to do this before it performs the WRITE option.

The file will be written into the largest unused area on the volume unless you specify otherwise. You may type a number, n, in square brackets ([ ]) after the file name. The system will then write the file in the first available area on the volume that has n or more blocks. For example, to put the BOGGLE.TEXT file in the first unused area on the GAMES volume that is 10 or more blocks in size, you would type:

GAMES:BOGGLE[10] ⟍

As the WRITE option is executing, the message 'Writing...' appears on screen. When the process is finished, the system tells you the number of bytes written and asks if you wish to E(xit to the COMMAND mode or R(eturn to the contents of the text buffer and the EDIT mode.

You may abort the WRITE option by pressing RETURN before typing anything. This takes you back to the contents of the text buffer and the EDIT mode.

In some versions of the p-System, the QUIT command also has a SAVE option that allows you to avoid the typing required by the WRITE option. The SAVE option "saves" the contents of the text buffer under its original file name.

The FIND And REPLACE Commands

We will introduce the FIND and REPLACE commands together because they are closely related. REPLACE, in fact, is an extension of FIND.

The FIND command looks through the text buffer for one or more occurrences of a string of characters and places the cursor after the last occurrence. The FIND command enables you to locate a particular spot in a long file, if you can remember a word or two of text.

The REPLACE command looks through the text buffer for one or more occurrences of a string of characters and replaces it with a substitute string. The REPLACE command is very useful when you want to change the name of a variable or some other identifier in a Pascal program.

Both the FIND and REPLACE commands operate from the current position of the cursor. Both can work forward toward the end of the text buffer or backward toward the beginning, depending on the setting of the direction marker.

Before we discuss FIND and REPLACE in detail, we should first examine some new concepts.

Numerical Arguments With FIND And REPLACE   Both the FIND and REPLACE commands accept numerical arguments in the same manner as the cursor moving commands. In other words, you can use a number, n, with these commands to find the nth occurrence of a string or to replace n occurrences of a string. The number is always typed before the command is selected (i.e., before the F or R key is hit). The number will then appear in the FIND or REPLACE prompt in square brackets ([n]). If you don't type a number, the system will automatically set the numerical argument to 1. This is the default setting.

You can use the slash character (/) as the numerical argument. In this case, the FIND or REPLACE commands will operate from the location of the cursor all the way through the text buffer. For example, if you use the slash argument when the cursor is positioned at the beginning of the text buffer and the direction marker is forward (>), the FIND command will locate the last occurrence of the string. In a similar case, the REPLACE command will replace all the designated strings in the text buffer.

Targets And Substitutes   The string you are searching for is the *target string*. The string you want to replace it with is the *substitute string*. You specify both strings by typing them in response to the FIND or REPLACE prompts.

Delimiters   When typing in the target or substitute strings on the FIND or REPLACE prompt lines, you must use a *delimiter* at both the beginning and end of each string. A delimiter is any character that is not a number or a letter. The slash is a popular choice, but you can use any character that does not appear in your string. For example:

/PASCAL/

is a correctly delimited string. But

/BASIC)

is not, as you must use the same delimiter at the beginning and end of the string. You cannot use the blank character as a delimiter.

Upper And Lower Case Letters   If your system permits upper and lower case letters, you must remember to type your target string accordingly. In other words, the target /Pascal/ will not match the word PASCAL in the text.

The TOKEN And LITERAL Modes   The FIND and REPLACE commands operate in the TOKEN or LITERAL modes. In the TOKEN mode, the system searches for an "isolated" occurrence of the target string in the text buffer. If the string is not isolated, it will not match the target. A string is isolated if it is set off by any combination of delimiters, including blanks. Also, in the TOKEN mode, the system will treat sequences of blanks within the target or substitute strings you type at the keyboard, as a single separator. Thus, the target

/Pascal lives/

will match a sequence of characters in the second line of the following example, but it will not match any sequence of characters in the first line:

Pascal livestock
Pascal   lives   on

In the LITERAL mode, on the other hand, the system matches the target string and the text exactly. So the target

/pro/

occurs twice in the sentence

You're a programming pro.

In the TOKEN mode it would occur only once.

FIND and REPLACE normally operate in the TOKEN mode. You can set the default mode with the ENVIRONMENT option of the SET command. (This is described in Part Three of this chapter.) Furthermore, you can switch modes from the FIND or REPLACE prompt. In general, the TOKEN mode is better for writing Pascal programs.

We will now look at FIND and REPLACE, in detail.

The FIND Command

The FIND command places the cursor after the n'th occurrence of the target string. FIND is very useful when you want to move to a particular region in the text buffer and you can recall one or two words to use as the target.

Executing FIND   To execute FIND, place the cursor at the point you wish to begin the search. Check the setting of the direction marker. It will determine the direction of the search. If you want to find the first occurrence of a target, select the FIND command directly by simply pressing the F key. Otherwise, type a number, n, or the slash (/), and then invoke FIND. When the TOKEN mode is set, the FIND prompt looks like this:

>Find [n]: L(it <target> => □

where n is the numerical argument. Before you type in the target, there are three options to consider.

- L(IT   Press the L key to change the mode to LITERAL. If the LITERAL mode has been established by the ENVIRONMENT option of the SET command the FIND prompt will present a T(OK option instead of L(IT. This allows you to switch to the TOKEN mode by pressing the T key.

- ESC   Press the ESC key to abort the FIND command and to return to the EDIT prompt.

- SAME   Press the S key, instead of typing the target. This causes the system to use the current contents of a target buffer for the search. The most recent target typed is kept in this buffer. No delimiters are necessary when you choose the SAME option.

You may view the current contents of the target buffer by using the EN-VIRONMENT option of the SET command. When you type the second delimiter of the target, or press the S key to use the SAME option, the FIND command will execute immediately. If the system can't match anything in the text with the target, the following error message will appear:

ERROR: Pattern not in the file. Please press <spacebar> to continue.

Let's look at an example.

Example of FIND   We want to find the third occurrence of the variable B from the beginning of the SUM program.

Place the cursor at the beginning of the text with the JUMP command, making sure the direction marker is forward (>):

```
>Edit: A(djst C(py D(lete F(ind I(nsrt J(mp R(place Q(uit X(chng Z(ap [E.6g]
[P]ROGRAM SUM;
VAR A, B, TOTAL: INTEGER;
BEGIN
    WRITELN ('ENTER TWO NUMBERS TO BE ADDED...');
    READ (A,B);
    TOTAL: = A + B;
    WRITELN ('THE SUM OF ',A,' AND ',B,' IS ',TOTAL)
END.
```

Type the number 3, selecting the numerical argument. Then press the F key, selecting the FIND command. The 3 will appear in square brackets on the FIND prompt:

```
>Find[3]: L(it <target> =>□
PROGRAM SUM;
VAR A, B, TOTAL: INTEGER;
BEGIN
    WRITELN ('ENTER TWO NUMBERS TO BE ADDED...');
    READ (A,B);
    TOTAL: = A + B;
    WRITELN ('THE SUM OF ',A,' AND ',B,' IS ',TOTAL)
END.
```

Using the slash (/) as the delimiter, type the target, except for the final /:

```
>Find[3]: L(it <target> =>/B□
PROGRAM SUM;
VAR A, B, TOTAL: INTEGER;
BEGIN
    WRITELN ('ENTER TWO NUMBERS TO BE ADDED...');
    READ (A,B);
    TOTAL:= A + B;
    WRITELN ('THE SUM OF ',A,' AND ',B,' IS ',TOTAL)
END.
```

Now type the second delimiter. FIND executes immediately. The cursor is positioned after the third 'B' in the text. The EDIT prompt reappears:

```
>Edit: A(djst C(py D(lete F(ind I(nsrt J(mp R(place Q(uit X(chng Z(ap [E.6g]
PROGRAM SUM;
VAR A, B, TOTAL: INTEGER;
BEGIN
    WRITELN ('ENTER TWO NUMBERS TO BE ADDED...');
    READ (A,B);
    TOTAL:= A + B□
    WRITELN ('THE SUM OF ',A,' AND ',B,' IS ',TOTAL)
END.
```

The target buffer now contains the target B.

The REPLACE Command

The REPLACE command finds n occurrences of a target and replaces each occurrence with a substitute string. You will find REPLACE extremely handy when you want to change the name of an identifier in a Pascal program.

Executing REPLACE   To execute REPLACE, place the cursor at the point where you want the search and replacement to begin. Then, check the direction marker that determines the direction of the search. If you only want to replace the first occurrence of a string, select the REPLACE command directly by pressing the R key. Otherwise, type a number, n, or a slash (/) as the numerical argument, then press the R key. When the TOKEN mode is set, pressing the R key will produce the following prompt:

>Replace[n]: L(it V(fy <targ> <sub> =>□

where n is the numerical argument. There are four options to consider before you type the target and substrings:

- ESC   Press the ESC key to abort the REPLACE command and return to the EDIT mode.

- L(IT   Press the L key to switch to the LITERAL mode. If the LITERAL mode is already set, a T(OK option replaces L(IT on the REPLACE prompt. You can then press the T key to switch to the TOKEN mode.

- V(FY   Press the V key to instruct the system to verify each replacement before it is made. The cursor will be placed at the end of a string matching the target, and the following prompt will appear:

>Replace[n]: <esc> aborts, 'R' replaces, ' ' doesn't □

You may then:

1. Press the ESC key to abort the REPLACE command and return to the EDIT mode.

2. Press the R key to instruct the system to make the replacement. The cursor will move to the next string to be replaced, if any.

3. Press the spacebar to skip the replacement. The cursor will move to the next string to be replaced, if there is one.

You may select the VERIFY option before typing the target or before typing the substitute.

- SAME   Press the S key to use the contents of the target buffer or the substitute-buffer for the target or substitute. No delimiters are required.

Two buffers store the most recent target and substitute strings typed at the keyboard. You can use the ENVIRONMENT option of the SET command to display the contents of these buffers.

After considering these options, type in the target and substitute strings on the REPLACE prompt line. Both must be delimited. For example, if you want to replace TWO with THREE, you could type:

>Replace[n]: L(it V(fy <targ> <sub> =>**/TWO//THREE/**

The moment you type the final delimiter or press the S key to use the sub buffer, the REPLACE command will execute. Here's an example.

Example of REPLACE   We want to change the variable name 'TOTAL' to the name 'RESULT' throughout the SUM program. You might make this sort of change frequently, as you develop Pascal programs and revise your identifiers.

Place the cursor at the beginning of the SUM program. Make sure the direction marker is forward (>):

```
>Edit: A(djst C(py D(lete F(ind I(nsrt J(mp R(place Q(uit X(chng Z(ap [E.6g]
PROGRAM SUM;
VAR A, B, TOTAL: INTEGER;
BEGIN
    WRITELN ('ENTER TWO NUMBERS TO BE ADDED...');
    READ (A,B);
    TOTAL: = A + B;
    WRITELN ('THE SUM OF ',A,' AND ',B,' IS ',TOTAL)
END.
```

Type the slash (/) so that REPLACE will work all the way through the text of SUM. Then press the R key selecting the REPLACE command. The slash will appear in the square brackets:

```
>Replace[/]: L(it V(fy <targ> <sub> =>□
PROGRAM SUM;
VAR A, B, TOTAL: INTEGER;
BEGIN
    WRITELN ('ENTER TWO NUMBERS TO BE ADDED...');
    READ (A,B);
    TOTAL: = A + B;
    WRITELN ('THE SUM OF ',A,' AND ',B,' IS ',TOTAL)
END.
```

Type in the target and substring except for the final delimiter:

```
>Replace[/]: L(it V(fy <targ> <sub> =>/TOTAL//RESULT☐
PROGRAM SUM;
VAR A, B, TOTAL: INTEGER;
BEGIN
    WRITELN ('ENTER TWO NUMBERS TO BE ADDED...');
    READ (A,B);
    TOTAL:= A + B;
    WRITELN ('THE SUM OF ',A,' AND ',B,' IS ',TOTAL)
END.
```

Now type the last delimiter. REPLACE executes. 'TOTAL' becomes 'RESULT' everywhere in the text. The EDIT prompt reappears:

```
>Edit: A(djst C(py D(lete F(ind I(nsrt J(mp R(place Q(uit X(chng Z(ap [E.6g]
PROGRAM SUM;
VAR A, B, RESULT: INTEGER;
BEGIN
    WRITELN ('ENTER TWO NUMBERS TO BE ADDED...');
    READ (A,B);
    RESULT:= A + B;
    WRITELN ('THE SUM OF ',A,' AND ',B,' IS ',RESULT☐)
END.
```

The target buffer now contains the string TOTAL; the substitute buffer has the string RESULT. If you wish, use REPLACE once more to restore TOTAL as the variable name.

We have now learned to use the editor to write and revise Pascal programs. Let's proceed to Part Three, and use the editor with natural language material.

PART THREE: WRITING NATURAL LANGUAGE TEXT

Recall that text editors have two main uses. They are used to prepare programs (as we discussed in Part Two) and to prepare documents in a natural language.

Natural Language Commands

In this section we will examine several useful commands for preparing documents in a natural language. In particular, we will examine the ENVIRONMENT option of the SET command, which controls features such as AUTO-INDENT and FILLING. We will also study the MARGIN command. Additionally, we will look at the MARKER option of the SET command, which allows you to put a marker somewhere in the text buffer. Finally, we will discuss two miscellaneous commands: ZAP and VERIFY. Let's begin by examining the SET command.

The SET Command

The SET command offers two options: ENVIRONMENT and MARKER. Each option has a different purpose. We will now execute SET and examine the options.

Executing SET   To execute SET, select the SET command from the EDIT mode by hitting the S key. This produces the SET prompt:

>Set: E(nvironment M(arker <esc> ☐

The SET command is not listed on the EDIT prompt.

You may now press ESC to abort the SET command and return to the EDIT mode, or select either the ENVIRONMENT or MARKER option.

The ENVIRONMENT Option   The ENVIRONMENT option produces a display that lists certain features that are used to control the behavior of the editor. It also displays other useful information, which we will describe later.

You will use the ENVIRONMENT option when you want to configure the editor for writing natural language texts, or when you want to check various items of information.

Selecting ENVIRONMENT   You can select the ENVIRONMENT option from the SET prompt by pressing the E key. This produces the ENVIRONMENT display. Here is a sample display:

```
>Environment: {options} <etx> or <sp> to leave☐
     A(uto indent          True
     F(illing              False
     L(eft margin          0
     R(ight margin         78
     P(ara margin          5
     C(ommand ch           ^
     T(oken def            True


     187 bytes used, 18757 available.


     Patterns:
       <target> = 'TOTAL', <subst> = 'RESULT'


     Markers:
       LAST


     Date Created: 11-25-80    Last Used 11-28-80
```

The top half of this display lists seven features that control the operation of the editor. It also lists the settings for those features. The bottom half presents other useful information. Let's begin by considering the first seven features.

- AUTO INDENT   When this feature is 'TRUE', pressing RETURN while in the INSERT mode will indent the next line so that it matches the indentation of the previous line. When it is 'FALSE', the next line is placed against the left margin.
- FILLING   When this feature is 'TRUE', the system scans the right margin as you insert material.

  When a word exceeds that margin, it is automatically placed on the next line. In other words, you don't have to use RETURN to start a new line. Filling will also break words at hyphens.

  When Filling is 'FALSE', the right margin is ignored. You can actually type beyond the screen. The system will warn you of this 'overflow' condition with an exclamation mark (!) next to the right margin.
- LEFT MARGIN   This feature sets the left margin. However, the system only "obeys" this setting when Auto Indent is 'FALSE' and

Filling is 'TRUE'. All margin settings require whole numbers of no more than 4 digits without a plus (+) or minus (−) sign.

- RIGHT MARGIN   This feature determines the right margin. Like Left Margin, it is only valid when Auto-Indent is 'FALSE' and Filling is 'TRUE'.

- PARA MARGIN   This feature sets the indentation for the first line of a paragraph. Again, it doesn't work unless Auto Indent is 'FALSE' and Filling is 'TRUE'.

- COMMAND CHARACTER   This feature establishes the command character used with a p-System formatting program that is not yet available. The default setting is the caret (^). The MARGIN command will not affect a line of text preceded by the command character.

- TOKEN DEFAULT   This feature controls the default setting for the TOKEN and LITERAL modes used by the FIND and REPLACE commands. If the setting is 'TRUE', both commands will operate in the TOKEN mode. Their prompts, however, allow you to switch to the LITERAL mode. If TOKEN DEFAULT is 'FALSE', FIND and REPLACE will work in the LITERAL mode and their prompts will allow you to switch to the TOKEN mode.

Changing The ENVIRONMENT Display   Setting the features in the ENVIRONMENT display involves several steps. Here's how you do it:

- Press the code letter key for the feature you want to change. For example, press the F key for the Filling feature. This causes the cursor to move to the setting column for the feature selected.

- If the setting is the TRUE/FALSE type, press the T or F keys. The feature is set to 'TRUE' or 'FALSE' and the cursor returns to the ENVIRONMENT prompt line.

- If the value requires a number (e.g., Left Margin) or a character, type in the number or character. Then press RETURN or the spacebar. The value is set according to the entry you typed. The cursor returns to the ENVIRONMENT prompt.

Once you are satisfied with the values selected for the ENVIRONMENT features, you may return to the EDIT prompt by pressing the ETX key, the spacebar, or RETURN. All three options will accept the current values of the features.

Later we will present an example showing how to change the values of the ENVIRONMENT features.

An Important Note When you write the contents of the text buffer to a file, the ENVIRONMENT settings are also stored as part of the file. Then when the file is loaded back into the text buffer, these settings are "remembered" by the system. You don't have to establish them again.

Let us now take a look at the information displayed on screen when the ENVIRONMENT option is selected.

- BYTES The first line under the TOKEN DEFAULT option tells you the number of bytes used by the text in the text buffer and the number of bytes in the text buffer still available. In our sample display, 187 bytes are used and 18757 are available. When you are creating or editing a long file, obviously, this information can help you stay within the limits of your system.

- PATTERNS: TARGETS AND SUBSTITUTES If you have used the FIND or REPLACE commands since last invoking the editor, the latest target and substitute strings typed will appear here. These strings may be used by the SAME option. In the sample display above, the user has most recently "found" the string 'TOTAL'. The substitute string most recently used is 'RESULT'.

- MARKERS When you create a marker in the text buffer, the name of the marker is stored in the text buffer and displayed here. Only the name of the marker appears, not its position. In our sample display the text contains one marker named LAST.

- DATE Finally, the date on which you created the file and the date on which you last updated it appear at the bottom of the screen. The sample display shows that the file was created on 11-25-80 and last updated on 11-28-80.

We will now consider the practical importance of the first five features on the ENVIRONMENT display.

TEXT Mode Versus PROGRAM Mode

Most of the time you will probably use the screen oriented editor to write and revise Pascal programs. Therefore, the editor is automatically set in the PROGRAM mode whenever you invoke it without reading in an existing file. Sometimes, however, you may wish to write something in ordinary English (or some other natural language). In that case, you will want to change several of the ENVIRONMENT features, so that the editor is operating in the TEXT mode. These two modes are defined as follows:

— The PROGRAM mode means that Auto Indent is 'TRUE' and Filling is 'FALSE'.

— The TEXT mode means that Auto Indent is 'FALSE' and Filling is 'TRUE'.

All the examples in this book have, thus far, been performed in the PRO-GRAM mode. We will now switch to the TEXT mode and examine the difference.

Switching To TEXT Mode   We will create an entirely new piece of text using the TEXT mode. But, first, if you have a work file, save it with the SAVE command, and then clear it with the NEW command. Next, QUIT the FILER and select the EDIT command from the COMMAND prompt. Now, when you have this prompt:

```
>Edit:
No workfile is present. File ? ( <ret> for no file <esc-ret> to exit )
: ▢
```

press RETURN to enter the editor with an empty text buffer.

Select the SET command by pressing the S key. Then press the E key to choose the ENVIRONMENT option. Notice the default settings for the PROGRAM mode:

```
>Environment: {options} <etx> or <sp> to leave▢
    A(uto indent        True
    F(illing            False
    L(eft margin        0
    R(ight margin       78
    P(ara margin        5
    C(ommand ch         ^
    T(oken def          True


    2 bytes used, 18942 available.


    Date Created: 11-25-80   Last Used 11-28-80
```

Press the A key, moving the cursor to the Auto Indent value:

```
>Environment: {options} <etx> or <sp> to leave
        A(uto indent          ☐
        F(illing              False
        L(eft margin          0
        R(ight margin         78
        P(ara margin          5
        C(ommand ch           ^
        T(oken def            True


        2 bytes used, 18942 available.


        Date Created: 11-25-80   Last Used 11-28-80
```

Press the F key. This sets Auto Indent to 'FALSE' and returns the cursor to the ENVIRONMENT prompt:

```
>Environment: {options} <etx> or <sp> to leave ☐
        A(uto indent          **False**
        F(illing              False
        L(eft margin          0
        R(ight margin         78
        P(ara margin          5
        C(ommand ch           ^
        T(oken def            True


        2 bytes used, 18942 available.


        Date Created: 11-25-80   Last Used 11-28-80
```

Press the F key, moving the cursor to the Filling feature:

>Environment: {options} <etx> or <sp> to leave

A(uto indent	False
F(illing	☐
L(eft margin	0
R(ight margin	78
P(ara margin	5
C(ommand ch	^
T(oken def	True

2 bytes used, 18942 available.

Date Created: 11-25-80   Last Used 11-28-80

Press the T key, setting Filling 'TRUE' and returning the cursor to the EN-
VIRONMENT prompt. The TEXT mode is now established.

>Environment: {options} <etx> or <sp> to leave ☐

A(uto indent	False
F(illing	**True**
L(eft margin	0
R(ight margin	78
P(ara margin	5
C(ommand ch	^
T(oken def	True

2 bytes used, 18942 available.

Date Created: 11-25-80   Last Used 11-28-80

The Left, Right and Para margin features are activated. In other words,
the system now follows the values you set for these options. The Left or

Right margins bind the text on the screen. The Paragraph margin sets the indentation for the first line of a paragraph. It is always calculated from the left margin of the screen. Note that when you leave a line entirely blank, and press RETURN, the cursor will be placed on the following line in the location designated by the current value of the Para margin feature.

We will continue by setting the margins for a 40-character-wide screen. We will set the Left, Right, and Para margins to 5, 38, and 8, respectively. Press the L key. This moves the cursor to the Left margin feature.

```
>Environment: {options} <etx> or <sp> to leave
      A(uto indent           False
      F(illing               True
      L(eft margin           ▢
      R(ight margin          78
      P(ara margin           5
      C(ommand ch            ^
      T(oken def             True


      2 bytes used, 18942 available.


      Date Created: 11-25-80    Last Used 11-28-80
```

Now type the number 5 and then press RETURN. The Left margin value is set to 5 and the cursor returns to the ENVIRONMENT prompt:

```
>Environment: {options} <etx> or <sp> to leave▢
      A(uto indent           False
      F(illing               True
      L(eft margin           5
      R(ight margin          78
      P(ara margin           5
      C(ommand ch            ^
      T(oken def             True


      2 bytes used, 18942 available.


      Date Created: 11-25-80    Last Used 11-28-80
```

Press the R key, which moves the cursor to the Right margin feature:

```
>Environment: {options} <etx> or <sp> to leave
    A(uto indent          False
    F(illing              True
    L(eft margin          5
    R(ight margin         ☐
    P(ara margin          5
    C(ommand ch           ^
    T(oken def            True

    2 bytes used, 18942 available.

    Date Created: 11-25-80    Last Used 11-28-80
```

Then type the number 38 and press RETURN. The Right margin is set to 38 and the cursor returns to the ENVIRONMENT prompt:

```
>Environment: {options} <etx> or <sp> to leave☐
    A(uto indent          False
    F(illing              True
    L(eft margin          5
    R(ight margin         38 ﹜
    P(ara margin          5
    C(ommand ch           ^
    T(oken def            True

    2 bytes used, 18942 available.

    Date Created: 11-25-80    Last Used 11-28-80
```

Next press the P key, moving the cursor to the Para margin option:

```
>Environment: {options} <etx> or <sp> to leave
    A(uto indent          False
    F(illing              True
    L(eft margin          5
    R(ight margin         38
    P(ara margin          ☐
    C(ommand ch           ^
    T(oken def            True


    2 bytes used, 18942 available.


    Date Created: 11-25-80    Last Used 11-28-80
```

Now type the number 8, and press the spacebar. The Para margin feature is set to 8. Our paragraphs will be indented 3 spaces from the left margin. Remember, the Para margin is calculated from the left screen margin, not the value of the Left margin setting.

```
>Environment: {options} <etx> or <sp> to leave☐
    A(uto indent          False
    F(illing              True
    L(eft margin          5
    R(ight margin         38
    P(ara margin          8
    C(ommand ch           ^
    T(oken def            True


    2 bytes used, 18942 available.


    Date Created: 11-25-80    Last Used 11-28-80
```

Now press the spacebar or RETURN once more. This returns you to the EDIT mode with the current values of the ENVIRONMENT features in force. Let us now see how the TEXT mode affects the editor.

Press the I key to enter the INSERT mode. The cursor is now flush against the left screen margin:

>Insert: Text {<bs> a char,<del> a line} [<ext> accepts, <esc> escapes]
□

Press RETURN. This leaves the first line of the text blank and delimits the first paragraph. The cursor moves 8 spaces in on the second screen line.

>Insert: Text {<bs> a char,<del> a line} [<ext> accepts, <esc> escapes]

□

Type in the following text without using RETURN at the end of a line.

>Insert: Text {<bs> a char,<del> a line} [<ext> accepts, <esc> escapes]

**THIS IS AN EXAMPLE OF THE
TEXT MODE. IT IS NOT NECESSARY
TO USE THE RETURN KEY AT THE END
OF A LINE. THE FILLING OPTION
IS NOW TRUE.**

**NOTICE HOW THE FILLING OPTION
CAN BREAK WORDS AT A HYPHEN. IF
YOU FIND YOURSELF TYPING A LONG
WORD AS YOU APPROACH THE RIGHT
MARGIN, PUT IN A HYPHEN AND CON-
TINUE TYPING.**□

Finally, press the ETX key to accept the inserted text. The EDIT prompt returns.

Insert And Delete In The TEXT Mode   When you use the editor in the TEXT mode, inserting new material into a paragraph causes the portion of the paragraph following the insertion to be reformatted according to the settings of the margin options. When you delete material, however, the paragraph will not be rearranged. In that case, you can use the MARGIN command (discussed in the next section.)

Let's continue with our example. We will now insert the words 'OF THE SCREEN' after 'RIGHT MARGIN' in the second paragraph.

Place the cursor on the comma after the word 'MARGIN':

>Edit: A(djst C(py D(lete F(ind I(nsrt J(mp R(place Q(uit X(chng Z(ap [E.6g]

    THIS IS AN EXAMPLE OF THE
    TEXT MODE. IT IS NOT NECESSARY
    TO USE THE RETURN KEY AT THE END
    OF A LINE. THE FILLING OPTION
    IS NOW TRUE.

    NOTICE HOW THE FILLING OPTION
    CAN BREAK WORDS AT A HYPHEN. IF
    YOU FIND YOURSELF TYPING A LONG
    WORD AS YOU APPROACH THE RIGHT
    MARGIN☐PUT IN A HYPHEN AND CON-
    TINUE TYPING.

Press the I key, selecting the INSERT mode. Then type in a blank followed by the words 'OF THE SCREEN'.

>Insert: Text {<bs> a char,<del> a line} [<etx> accepts, <esc> escapes]

    THIS IS AN EXAMPLE OF THE
    TEXT MODE. IT IS NOT NECESSARY
    TO USE THE RETURN KEY AT THE END
    OF A LINE. THE FILLING OPTION
    IS NOW TRUE.

    NOTICE HOW THE FILLING OPTION
    CAN BREAK WORDS AT A HYPHEN. IF
    YOU FIND YOURSELF TYPING A LONG
    WORD AS YOU APPROACH THE RIGHT
    MARGIN **OF THE SCREEN**☐   , PUT IN A HYPHEN AND CON-
    TINUE TYPING.

Press the ETX key, accepting the insertion. Notice how the paragraph is reformatted.

>Edit: A(djst C(py D(lete F(ind I(nsrt J(mp R(place Q(uit X(chng Z(ap [E.6g]

    ˙   THIS IS AN EXAMPLE OF THE
    TEXT MODE. IT IS NOT NECESSARY
    TO USE THE RETURN KEY AT THE END
    OF A LINE. THE FILLING OPTION
    IS NOW TRUE.

    NOTICE HOW THE FILLING OPTION
    CAN BREAK WORDS AT A HYPHEN. IF
    YOU FIND YOURSELF TYPING A LONG
    WORD AS YOU APPROACH THE RIGHT
    MARGIN OF THE SCREEN☐ PUT IN A
    HYPHEN AND CON- TINUE TYPING.

As you can see, the hyphen in 'CONTINUE' is no longer appropriate. We will use the DELETE mode to get rid of it.
    Put the cursor on the hyphen in the last line:

>Delete: < > <Moving commands> {<etx> to delete, <esc> to abort}

```
    THIS IS AN EXAMPLE OF THE
    TEXT MODE. IT IS NOT NECESSARY
    TO USE THE RETURN KEY AT THE END
    OF A LINE. THE FILLING OPTION
    IS NOW TRUE.

    NOTICE HOW THE FILLING OPTION
    CAN BREAK WORDS AT A HYPHEN. IF
    YOU FIND YOURSELF TYPING A LONG
    WORD AS YOU APPROACH THE RIGHT
    MARGIN OF THE SCREEN, PUT IN A
    HYPHEN AND CON[-] TINUE TYPING.
```

Now press the D key, selecting the DELETE mode. Then press the right-arrow key twice, erasing the hyphen and the space from the screen.

Use the ETX key to accept the deletion. In this case, the deletion leaves the paragraph correctly formatted:

>Edit: A(djst C(py D(lete F(ind I(nsrt J(mp R(place Q(uit X(chng Z(ap [E.6g]

```
    THIS IS AN EXAMPLE OF THE
    TEXT MODE. IT IS NOT NECESSARY
    TO USE THE RETURN KEY AT THE END
    OF A LINE. THE FILLING OPTION
    IS NOW TRUE.

    NOTICE HOW THE FILLING OPTION
    CAN BREAK WORDS AT A HYPHEN. IF
    YOU FIND YOURSELF TYPING A LONG
    WORD AS YOU APPROACH THE RIGHT
    MARGIN OF THE SCREEN, PUT IN A
    HYPHEN AND CON[T]INUE TYPING.
```

However, we now decide to delete the words 'OF THE SCREEN'.
Put the cursor on the blank after the word MARGIN, and press the D key again, selecting DELETE:

>Delete: < > <Moving commands> {<etx> to delete, <esc> to abort}

THIS IS AN EXAMPLE OF THE
TEXT MODE. IT IS NOT NECESSARY
TO USE THE RETURN KEY AT THE END
OF A LINE. THE FILLING OPTION
IS NOW TRUE.

NOTICE HOW THE FILLING OPTION
CAN BREAK WORDS AT A HYPHEN. IF
YOU FIND YOURSELF TYPING A LONG
WORD AS YOU APPROACH THE RIGHT
MARGIN☐ OF THE SCREEN, PUT IN A
HYPHEN AND CONTINUE TYPING.

Erase the text by moving the cursor 14 spaces to the right, up to the comma:

>Delete: < > <Moving commands> {<etx> to delete, <esc> to abort}

THIS IS AN EXAMPLE OF THE
TEXT MODE. IT IS NOT NECESSARY
TO USE THE RETURN KEY AT THE END
OF A LINE. THE FILLING OPTION
IS NOW TRUE.

NOTICE HOW THE FILLING OPTION
CAN BREAK WORDS AT A HYPHEN. IF
YOU FIND YOURSELF TYPING A LONG
WORD AS YOU APPROACH THE RIGHT
MARGIN   ☐ PUT IN A
HYPHEN AND CONTINUE TYPING.

Then press the ETX key, accepting the deletion. The second paragraph of text now requires reformatting. To do this, you can use the MARGIN command.

>Edit: A(djst C(py D(lete F(ind I(nsrt J(mp R(place Q(uit X(chng Z(ap [E.6g]

    THIS IS AN EXAMPLE OF THE
    TEXT MODE. IT IS NOT NECESSARY
    TO USE THE RETURN KEY AT THE END
    OF A LINE. THE FILLING OPTION
    IS NOW TRUE.

    NOTICE HOW THE FILLING OPTION
    CAN BREAK WORDS AT A HYPHEN. IF
    YOU FIND YOURSELF TYPING A LONG
    WORD AS YOU APPROACH THE RIGHT
    MARGIN☐ PUT IN A
    HYPHEN AND CONTINUE TYPING.

The MARGIN Command

The MARGIN command reformats a particular paragraph according to the current values of the right, left, and paragraph margins. The MARGIN command only works when the TEXT mode is set (i.e., when Auto Indent is 'FALSE' and Filling is 'TRUE'). Also, it only affects the paragraph containing the cursor.

Use the MARGIN command when a paragraph written in the TEXT mode has to be reformatted. Alternatively, you can use MARGIN to format a particular paragraph in a way that is different from the rest of the text.

You execute MARGIN by placing the cursor somewhere in the paragraph you want to format, and then pressing the M key. There is no MARGIN prompt and the command is not listed on the EDIT prompt.

Let's go on with the example on the screen. We will use the MARGIN command to reformat the second paragraph. Since the cursor is already placed somewhere in the second paragraph, press the M key to invoke the MARGIN command. The paragraph is immediately reformatted:

>Edit: A(djst C(py D(lete F(ind I(nsrt J(mp R(place Q(uit X(chng Z(ap [E.6g]

    THIS IS AN EXAMPLE OF THE
    TEXT MODE. IT IS NOT NECESSARY
    TO USE THE RETURN KEY AT THE END
    OF A LINE. THE FILLING OPTION
    IS NOW TRUE.

    NOTICE HOW THE FILLING OPTION
    CAN BREAK WORDS AT A HYPHEN. IF
    YOU FIND YOURSELF TYPING A LONG
    WORD AS YOU APPROACH THE RIGHT
    MARGIN☐ PUT IN A HYPHEN AND
    CONTINUE TYPING.

If you wish, insert the hyphen in 'CONTINUE' and then repeat the MARGIN command. This will reformat the paragraph to its initial form.

We have now explored the practical uses of the features listed by the ENVIRONMENT option of the SET command. We will now examine the MARKER option.

The MARKER Option

The MARKER option of the SET command allows you to place up to ten invisible markers anywhere in the text buffer. The JUMP and COPY commands can then refer to these markers by name. Marker names may be numbers or identifiers of up to eight characters. Identifiers can be more descriptive (INTRO, PARA5, CONCL, etc.) than numbers, but they are also more laborious to type.

A marker is a permanent part of the text. It is stored in the file just like the settings for AUTO INDENT, FILLING and the margins. You can always check the names of the markers in the text buffer by using the Environment display of the SET command.

Executing The MARKER Option   To execute the MARKER option, first place the cursor at the location in the text you wish to mark. Then select the SET command from the EDIT mode by pressing the S key. Next, choose the MARKER option by pressing the M key. The MARKER prompt appears:

Set what marker? ☐

Type in the name of the marker, and press RETURN. The EDIT prompt reappears. The text is now marked at the current cursor position.

Moving A Marker   You can move a marker elsewhere in the text buffer by placing the cursor at a new position and retyping the name in response to the MARKER prompt.

Deleting Marked Text   If you delete text containing a marker, you do not delete the marker. It will no longer indicate the same text and, therefore, you should consider moving it.

Marker Overflow   If you try to put more than ten markers in a text, the system will present this message:

```
Marker ovflw. Which one to replace?
0) name 1
1) name 2
...
...
9) name 10
```

where 'name 1' is the name of the first marker, 'name 2' is the name of the second marker, etc.

You select the marker you want to replace by typing its list number. Then, you type in the new marker name, and press RETURN. Your new marker will now be established at the current cursor position in the text buffer. Let's consider an example.

Example of MARKER   We will place a marker at the beginning of the second paragraph of the sample text.

Place the cursor on the 'N' of 'NOTICE' at the start of the second paragraph:

>Edit: A(djst C(py D(lete F(ind I(nsrt J(mp R(place Q(uit X(chng Z(ap [E.6g]

        THIS IS AN EXAMPLE OF THE
    TEXT MODE. IT IS NOT NECESSARY
    TO USE THE RETURN KEY AT THE END
    OF A LINE. THE FILLING OPTION
    IS NOW TRUE.

        [N]OTICE HOW THE FILLING OPTION
    CAN BREAK WORDS AT A HYPHEN. IF
    YOU FIND YOURSELF TYPING A LONG
    WORD AS YOU APPROACH THE RIGHT
    MARGIN, PUT IN A HYPHEN AND CON-
    TINUE TYPING.

Press the S key, selecting the SET command. Then press the M key, choosing the MARKER option from the SET prompt. The MARKER prompt appears.

Set what marker? ☐

        THIS IS AN EXAMPLE OF THE
TEXT MODE. IT IS NOT NECESSARY
TO USE THE RETURN KEY AT THE END
OF A LINE. THE FILLING OPTION
IS NOW TRUE.

        NOTICE HOW THE FILLING OPTION
CAN BREAK WORDS AT A HYPHEN. IF
YOU FIND YOURSELF TYPING A LONG
WORD AS YOU APPROACH THE RIGHT
MARGIN, PUT IN A HYPHEN AND CON-
TINUE TYPING.

Type in the marker name, 2ND, and press RETURN.

Set what marker? **2ND**⌋

    The cursor returns to its initial position. The EDIT prompt reappears. Although we can't see the marker in the text, it *is* really there. We can use the JUMP command to prove it.

The JUMP Command: MARKER Option

    When the JUMP command is selected, the JUMP prompt presents three options: BEGINNING, END and MARKER. We have already looked at the first two. The third, MARKER, is selected by pressing the M key. This produces the prompt:

Jump to what marker? ☐

    You type in the name of a marker in the text, and press RETURN. The cursor will move to the marker specified. The EDIT prompt reappears. Let's try this operation with our sample text and the marker ('2ND') we have placed in it.

Put the cursor anywhere in the text, except on the 'N' at the beginning of the second paragraph. Press the J key, selecting the JUMP command. Then press the M key, choosing the MARKER option from the JUMP prompt. A new prompt will appear. Type in '2ND' and press RETURN.

Jump to what marker? **2ND**」

The JUMP command executes immediately. The cursor is placed on the 'N' of 'NOTICE'— the marked position in the text.

The COPY Command: Marker Option

When the COPY command is selected, the COPY prompt offers two options: BUFFER and FROM FILE. We previously discussed the BUFFER option. Let's now look at the FROM FILE option.

FROM FILE lets you copy all or part of a file into the text buffer. To use FROM FILE, first place the cursor where you want the copied material to appear. Then, invoke the COPY command, and select the FROM FILE option by pressing the F key. This will produce the prompt:

>Copy: From what file[marker,marker]? ☐

Type in the name of the file you wish to copy into the text buffer and press RETURN. Note that if you don't type anything after the file name, the system will copy all of the file into the text buffer. If you use marker names in square brackets after the file name, the system will copy only part of the file into the text buffer. Here are the ways marker names specify parts of the file:

[ALPHA,OMEGA]	copies the part of the file between the markers ALPHA and OMEGA.
[,ALPHA]	copies the part of the file from the beginning of the file to the marker ALPHA.
[ALPHA,]	copies the part of the file from the marker ALPHA to the end of the file.

We have now seen how markers may be set in the text buffer and used with the JUMP and COPY commands. We will conclude Part Three by looking at two miscellaneous editor commands: ZAP and VERIFY.

The ZAP Command

The ZAP command deletes all the text between the cursor and the first character of the text that was most recently found, replaced or inserted. The ZAP command is normally used immediately after the termination of a FIND, REPLACE or INSERT command. If you haven't moved the cursor or invoked another command, ZAP will delete the inserted text, the last target string located by the FIND command, or the last substring placed in the text by the REPLACE command. A word of warning: use ZAP cautiously.

Executing ZAP   To execute ZAP, simply check the cursor position, then invoke ZAP by pressing the Z key. There is no ZAP prompt. If the ZAP command deletes more than 80 characters, you will be warned with this prompt:

>WARNING! You are about to zap more than 80 chars, do you wish to zap? (Y/N)☐

You must respond by typing the Y key to execute the ZAP. Any other key will abort the ZAP command without deleting any characters.

The VERIFY Command

The VERIFY command redisplays the contents of the text buffer on the screen. The cursor will be centered in the display unless it is on the first page of the text buffer. If you've made several changes and are not sure if the text on the screen is a valid representation of that portion of the text buffer, VERIFY will show you the actual contents of the text buffer.

VERIFY is not listed on the EDIT prompt. You can execute it by pressing the V key. There is no VERIFY prompt.

PART FOUR: REFERENCE SUMMARY

The Reference Summary presented here is a compilation of the essential information from Parts Two and Three of this chapter. It presents an alphabetical listing of the commands in the EDIT mode and a brief description of each one.

ADJUST

Prompt:

>Adjust: L(just R(just C(enter <left,right,up,down-arrows> {<etx> to leave}

Description:

The ADJUST command moves an entire line of text (designated by the cursor) according to the option selected.

Options:

L(JUST	sets the line against the left margin.
R(JUST	sets the line against the right margin.
C(ENTER	centers the line between the left and right margins.
Left (←) arrow key	moves the line one space left.
Right (→) arrow key	moves the line one space right.
Down (↓) arrow key	applies most recently selected ADJUST option to the next line.
Up (↑) arrow key	applies most recently selected ADJUST option to the prior line.
Backspace key	moves the line one space left.
ETX key	accepts adjustments made and returns the EDIT prompt. There is no ESC option to disregard adjustments.

When To Use It:

The ADJUST command can assist you in indenting your Pascal programs properly, especially as you rewrite them. Use numerical arguments with the up- or down-arrow keys to re-indent entire Pascal blocks quickly. The other options are useful for formatting natural-language texts.

COPY

Prompt:

>Copy: B(uffer F(rom file <esc>

Description:

The COPY command copies text from a file or the copy buffer into the text buffer, placing it to the immediate left of the cursor.

Options:

B(UFFER	copies material from a buffer in active memory. This buffer is loaded with the text from the most recent Delete operation (which was terminated with ETX or ESC), Insert operation (which was terminated with ETX), or ZAP command.
F(ROM FILE	copies material from a file into the text buffer. A complete file may be copied or, if marker names are used, then you can copy part of a file.
ESC	aborts the COPY command and returns to the EDIT mode.

When To Use It:

You can use the COPY command to move material from one place in the text buffer to another. First, delete the material by using the DELETE mode, and terminating it with the ETX key. Then place the cursor in the new position and copy from the buffer.

You can also duplicate material in a text by using the COPY command. First, erase the material by using the DELETE mode terminated by the ESC key. Then move the cursor to the desired spot and copy from the buffer. Similarly, you can duplicate the material just inserted.

CURSOR KEYS

Description:

The cursor keys move the cursor in various ways. All cursor keys accept numerical arguments. Some are sensitive to the direction marker, as indicated below. Certain keys may not appear on your keyboard, but your system will probably have equivalent ones to replace them. Consult your system's documentation. (*Note:* The JUMP, PAGE and EQUALS commands, which affect the cursor position, are listed separately in this Reference Summary.)

The Keys:

Left-arrow (←)	moves the cursor one space leftward.
Right-arrow (→)	moves the cursor one space rightward.
Up-arrow (↑)	moves the cursor one line upward.
Down-arrow (↓)	moves the cursor one line downward.
Spacebar	moves the cursor one space left or right.
Backspace	moves the cursor one space leftward.
RETURN	moves the cursor to the beginning of the subsequent or preceding line.
TAB	moves the cursor left or right to the nearest tab setting.

The Direction Marker:

The DIRECTION MARKER determines the direction that the cursor moves when the spacebar, RETURN, or TAB keys are used. The DIRECTION MARKER also affects the PAGE command.

The DIRECTION MARKER appears before all the prompts in the Editor. It may only be changed when the EDIT or DELETE prompts are on screen. The DIRECTION MARKER is set forward by typing the greater-than symbol (>), the period (.), or the plus (+) character. It is set backward by typing the less-than symbol (<), the comma (,) or the minus (−) character.

> . +	set direction forward
< , −	set direction backward

Numerical Arguments:

All cursor keys (and the PAGE command) accept numerical arguments. They are entered by typing a number (n) before pressing a cursor command key. The command you type then executes n number of times. For example, if you type 3 and press the right-arrow key, the cursor will move three spaces to the right.

When To Use Them:

The cursor keys allow you to place the cursor anywhere in the text buffer. The position of the cursor is crucial to many EDIT mode commands.

DELETE

Prompt:

>Delete: < > <moving commands> {<etx> to delete, <esc> to abort}

Description:

The DELETE mode lets you delete material from the text buffer. The deletion can be made forward or backward from the initial cursor position by using the cursor keys.

Options:

Cursor moves	erase characters from the screen. Any cursor command is valid, except PAGE, JUMP or EQUALS. Returning the cursor toward its initial position restores erased characters.
ETX	terminates the DELETE mode and removes the erased characters from the text buffer.
ESC	terminates the DELETE mode and restores any erased characters to the screen. The text buffer remains unchanged.

When To Use It:

You can use the DELETE mode to remove unwanted characters. Also, you can use it in conjunction with the COPY command to move or duplicate material.

ENVIRONMENT OPTION (SET command)

Prompt:

>Environment: {options} <etx> or <sp> to leave

A(uto indent	(current values)
F(illing	"
L(eft margin	"
R(ight margin	"
P(ara margin	"
C(ommand ch	"
T(oken def	"
Bytes	(information)
Patterns	"
Markers	"
Dates	"

Description:

The ENVIRONMENT option of the SET command permits the control of seven features listed at the top of the screen and the viewing of four information items listed at the bottom.

Features:

AUTO INDENT controls the position of the cursor after the RETURN key is used in the INSERT mode. If Auto Indent is 'TRUE', the cursor aligns with the first non-blank character of the line it came from. This preserves the same indentation for a series of lines. If Auto Indent is 'FALSE', then the cursor moves to the left margin.

FILLING controls the filling of lines with words to the right margin. When Filling is 'TRUE', any word exceeding the right margin is placed on the next line. When it is 'FALSE', the right margin is ignored.

LEFT MARGIN	sets the value of the left margin. This option and the Right and Para margin options only work when Filling is 'TRUE' and Auto Indent is 'FALSE'.
RIGHT MARGIN	sets the value of the right margin.
PARA MARGIN	sets the indentation for the first line of a paragraph. Note that the margin is calculated from the left screen margin, not the setting of the Left margin option. Paragraphs must be delimited by blank lines.
COMMAND CH	sets the value of a command character for use in a text formatting program currently not available. Also disables Filling for any line starting with this character.
TOKEN DEF	controls the default search mode for the FIND and REPLACE commands. When this option is 'TRUE', the TOKEN mode is established for FIND and REPLACE. When it is 'FALSE', the LITERAL mode is set.

Information:

BYTES	displays the number of bytes used in the text buffer, and the number still available.
PATTERNS	displays the contents, if any, of the Target and Substitute buffers created by the FIND or REPLACE commands.
MARKERS	displays the names of all the markers that are currently part of the text buffer.
DATES	displays the date the file was created and the most recent update.

You may quit the ENVIRONMENT option and accept the current values of the features in one of two ways:

ETX	leaves the ENVIRONMENT display and returns to the EDIT prompt with the current values of the features in effect.
Spacebar	does the same as the ETX key.

When To Use It:

To set an option on the ENVIRONMENT display, press the appropriate letter key (e.g., F for Filling). Then enter a setting and press RETURN, or simply press the T or F keys to establish TRUE or FALSE settings.

When Auto Indent is 'FALSE' and Filling is 'TRUE', the editor is in the TEXT mode. When Auto Indent is 'TRUE' and Filling is 'FALSE', it is in the PROGRAM mode. Use the PROGRAM mode when you write Pascal programs and the TEXT mode when you write something in English or some other natural language.

```
┌──────────────────────┐
│                      │
│   EQUALS             │
│                      │
└──────────────────────┘
```

Prompt:

There is no EQUALS prompt.

Description:

The EQUALS command—executed by typing the equals character (=)—moves the cursor from its present location to the beginning of the text most recently inserted, found or replaced, using the INSERT mode, the FIND command, or the REPLACE command.

Options:

There are no EQUALS options.

When To Use It:

You can use the EQUALS command to return to your original location after you have used the PAGE or JUMP commands to look at some other part of the text buffer.

EXCHANGE

Prompt:

>eXchange: TEXT {<bs> a char} [<esc> escapes; <ext> accepts]

Description:

The EXCHANGE mode—selected by pressing the X key—lets you replace material on the screen, character-by-character.

Options:

BACKSPACE	moves the cursor to the left and restores the original material to the screen.
ESC	terminates the EXCHANGE mode, disregarding all changes that have been made. The text buffer remains unchanged.
ETX	terminates the EXCHANGE mode and puts any newly typed material into the text buffer.
ANY OTHER CHARACTER	replaces the character at the cursor and advances the cursor one character position.

When To Use It:

Use EXCHANGE when you want to correct small typing mistakes on a single line.

```
┌─────────────────┐
│                 │
│      FIND       │
│                 │
└─────────────────┘
```

Prompts:

>Find[n]: L(it <target> =>□

  or

>Find[n]: T(ok <target> =>□

where n is the numerical argument.

Description:

The FIND command searches the text buffer for one or more occurrences of a string that matches the delimited target string. The search is conducted from the current cursor position, forward or backward in the text buffer, depending on the setting of the direction marker. FIND searches in the TOKEN or LITERAL modes. If the search is successful, the cursor is placed in the text buffer after the "found" string.

Definition of Terms:

Delimited—beginning and ending with a character that is not a number, letter or space. For example, /PASCAL/ is a delimited string.

Target—the delimited string typed by the user in response to the FIND prompt. This is the string that will be searched for.

Numerical argument—a number typed before the FIND command that causes the nth occurrence of the target to be found. This number appears in square brackets on the FIND prompt. The default value is 1. The slash (/) indicates a search to the end of the text.

LITERAL mode—the system searches the text for a string that exactly matches the target, character-for-character.

TOKEN mode—the system searches the text for a delimited string that matches the target, whose blanks, if any, are treated as separators.

Options:

L(IT	changes the search mode to LITERAL. This option only appears when the Token Default feature in the Set Environment display is 'TRUE'.
T(OK	changes the search mode to TOKEN. This option only appears when the Token Default feature in the Set Environment display is 'FALSE'.
S(AME	permits the use of the contents of the Target buffer as the target string. The Environment option of the SET command displays the current contents of this buffer.

When To Use It:

The FIND command can help you place the cursor in a long file. If you remember one or two words, you can easily locate the region you want to edit. Remember, FIND operates from the cursor and is sensitive to the direction marker.

INSERT

Prompt:

>Insert: Text {<bs> a char <del> a line} [<etx> accepts, <esc> escapes]

Description:

The INSERT mode permits the insertion of characters into the text buffer. The amount of material inserted is only limited by the size of main memory.

Options:

BACKSPACE	moves the cursor back one space and erases the character just inserted.
DEL	deletes an entire inserted line.
ETX	terminates the INSERT mode and puts the text typed into the text buffer.
ESC	terminates the INSERT mode and discards all the inserted material. The initial contents of the text buffer remain unchanged.

When To Use It:

You use the INSERT mode when you want to add characters to a new or established file. When you terminate INSERT with the ETX key, the material inserted is stored in a buffer and may be duplicated using the COPY command.

JUMP

Prompt:

>Jump: B(eginning E(nd M(arker <esc>

Description:

The JUMP command moves the cursor to the beginning or end of the text buffer. It can also move it to a designated marker.

Options:

BEGINNING	jumps the cursor to the beginning of the text buffer.
END	jumps the cursor to the end of the text buffer.
MARKER	jumps the cursor to a user-designated marker somewhere in the text buffer. Markers are established using the MARKER option of the SET command.
ESC	aborts the JUMP command without moving the cursor.

When To Use It:

The JUMP command is convenient for moving the cursor quickly to the beginning or end of the text buffer or to frequently used sections of the text buffer that you have marked.

MARGIN

Prompt:

There is no MARGIN prompt.

Description:

The MARGIN command operates on the paragraph containing the cursor and reformats it according to the margin settings in the ENVIRONMENT option of the SET command.

The MARGIN command only works when the editor is set in the TEXT mode, i.e., when the Auto-Indent feature is 'FALSE' and the Filling feature is 'TRUE'. These features are controlled by the ENVIRONMENT option of the SET command.

Options:

There are no MARGIN options.

When To Use It:

The MARGIN command lets you format a paragraph differently from other paragraphs in the text. Additionally, you may use it after a Delete operation in the TEXT mode to reformat a paragraph. You can also use the MARGIN command to format paragraphs that were INSERTed while the editor was not in the TEXT mode.

MARKER Option (SET Command)

Prompt:

Set what marker? □

Description:

The MARKER option of the SET command establishes a named, invisible marker anywhere in the text buffer. The marker name must be no longer than eight characters. Up to ten markers may be put in the text buffer. The ENVIRONMENT option of the SET command displays the names of all current markers in the text buffer.

Options:

There are no MARKER options.

When To Use It:

Once you have a marker in a text, you may move the cursor to it using the MARKER option of the JUMP command. Also, the COPY command permits reference to markers in a file, so that you can copy all or part of a file, into the text buffer.

```
┌─────────────────────┐
│                     │
│      PAGE           │
│                     │
└─────────────────────┘
```

Prompt:

There is no PAGE prompt.

Description:

The PAGE command moves the screen forward or backward one "page" through the text buffer. Or, from a different perspective, it scrolls one page of the text buffer across the screen.

The PAGE command takes numerical arguments and is sensitive to the direction marker.

Options:

Numerical arguments	determine the number of 'pages' scrolled. You type a number (n) before selecting the PAGE command, and the PAGE command then executes n times.
Direction marker	determines the effective direction of the PAGE command, i.e., forward (>) or backward (<) in the text.

When To Use It:

The PAGE command is useful when there is a long file in the text buffer and you wish to move to a particular region of text. Don't forget that the PAGE command is sensitive to the direction marker.

QUIT

Prompt:

>Quit:

    U(pdate the workfile and leave

    E(xit without updating

    R(eturn to the editor without updating

    W(rite to a file name and return

Description:

The QUIT command causes the p-System to leave the EDIT mode and return to the COMMAND mode.

Options:

UPDATE	writes the current contents of the text buffer to a file under the file name SYSTEM.WRK.TEXT. This is the default file which appears on screen automatically when the EDIT mode is invoked.
EXIT	disregards the contents of the text buffer and returns to the COMMAND mode.
RETURN	returns to the EDIT mode with the text buffer unchanged.
WRITE	writes the contents of the text buffer under a file name typed in by the user.

When To Use It:

It is wise practice, during a long editing session, to frequently use the QUIT command with the UPDATE or WRITE option. Then, if there is a power failure or an accidental rebooting of the system, your work will not be lost.

REPLACE

Prompt:

> Replace[n]: L(it V(fy <targ> <sub> =>

> or

>Replace[n]: T(ok V(fy <targ> <sub> =>

where n is the numerical argument.

Description:

The REPLACE command searches the text buffer for one or more occurrences of a target string. The target string is replaced with a substitute string. The REPLACE command operates from the cursor toward the beginning or end of the text, depending on the setting of the direction marker. The REPLACE command can function in the TOKEN or LITERAL modes. The user must type properly delimited target and substitute strings on the REPLACE prompt line.

Refer to the Reference Summary entry for the FIND command for definitions of delimiters and the TOKEN and LITERAL modes.

Options:

L(IT	changes the mode to LITERAL. This option is only available when Token Default is 'TRUE'. Token Default is an option on the ENVIRONMENT display of the SET command.
T(OK	changes the mode to TOKEN. This option is only available when Token Default is 'FALSE'.
V(FY	causes the system to ask for user verification for each replacement.
S(AME	permits the user to designate the contents of the Target and/or Sub-buffers as the target or substrings by typing the letter S without delimiters. These buffers are displayed by the ENVIRONMENT option of the SET command.

Numerical arguments — allows the user to specify the number of times the replacement will be made. The default value is 1. The slash (/) indicates replacement to the end of the text. The numerical argument appears in square brackets on the REPLACE prompt.

When To Use It:

The REPLACE command is most useful when you wish to change the name of a variable everywhere in a Pascal program. In this case, be careful to put the cursor in the appropriate place (i.e., the beginning), to set the direction marker forward, and to use the global numerical argument: the slash (/).

```
SET
```

Prompt:

>Set: E(nvironment M(arker <esc>

Description:

The SET command permits control of a variety of important editor features with the ENVIRONMENT option, as well as the setting of markers in a text with the MARKER option.

Options:

ENVIRONMENT   presents a display of seven options and miscellaneous system information.

MARKER   permits the creation of markers in a text, which may then be used by the JUMP or COPY commands.

The ENVIRONMENT and MARKER options appear as independent entries in this Reference Summary.

VERIFY

Prompt:

There is no VERIFY prompt.

Description:

The VERIFY command displays the portion of the text buffer that is centered around the position of the cursor.

Options:

There are no VERIFY options.

When To Use It:

If you wish to display a specific section of the text buffer on the screen while editing, then you can position the cursor in the center of this section and use the VERIFY command.

ZAP

Prompt:

There is no ZAP prompt.

Description:

The ZAP command deletes all of the text positioned between the cursor and the beginning of the text most recently inserted, found, or replaced, using the INSERT mode, the FIND command, or the REPLACE command.

Options:

There are no ZAP options.

When To Use It:

To delete a large portion of text conveniently, FIND the beginning, move the cursor to the end, and use ZAP to do the deletion. If the cursor has not been moved since the last FIND, REPLACE, or INSERT, then ZAP is a convenient way to delete the last change that you have made.

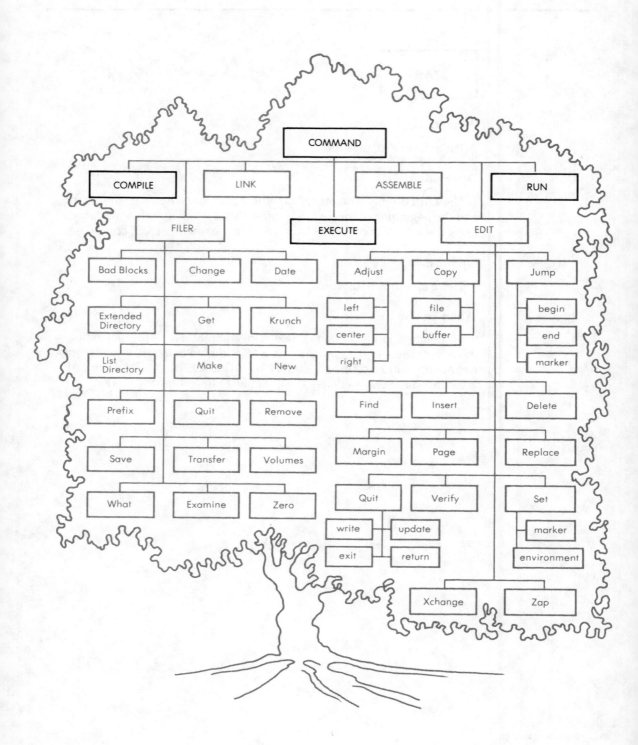

CREATING SHORT PASCAL PROGRAMS 5

THIS CHAPTER EXPLORES those features of the p-System that let you compile, correct, and run short Pascal programs. Part One discusses the COMPILE, RUN, and EXECUTE commands, which are used to develop, test, and run short programs. Part Two describes aspects of the UCSD Pascal compiler.

Although the examples are written in Pascal, the information presented in Part One is useful for other languages supported by the p-System.

PART ONE: COMPILE, RUN, AND EXECUTE

The COMPILE, RUN, and EXECUTE commands are available from the COMMAND mode, and appear in the prompt for that mode:

Command: E(dit, R(un, F(ile, C(omp, L(ink, X(ecute, A(ssem, D(ebug,? [II.0] ☐

Other commands available from the COMMAND mode include EDIT, FILER, ASSEMBLE, DEBUG, and LINK. The EDIT command was discussed in detail in Chapter 4; the FILER command was discussed in Chapter 3. The ASSEMBLE command invokes the p-System Assembler, which translates an assembly-language program into machine code. The DEBUG command is intended to call up a debugging program; this program however, is not yet commercially available. The LINK command invokes the p-System linker, which combines parts of programs. This command will be discussed in detail in Chapter 6.

Some versions of the p-System have additional commands available from the COMMAND mode, including USER RESTART, INITIALIZE, HALT, and SWAP. Refer to your documentation for a description of the commands available on your system.

The COMPILE Command

The COMPILE command calls up the UCSD Pascal compiler, which translates the source code of a Pascal program into the P-code understood by the interpreter. You will use COMPILE when you have written the source code for a Pascal program and want to translate it into P-code for execution.

The COMPILE command looks for the work file and attempts to compile it. If the compiler detects an error during compilation, it stops and displays an error message. You then have the option of continuing compilation, aborting compilation, or invoking the editor and fixing the mistake. If compilation is successful (i.e., there are no errors), the COMPILE command creates a new file SYSTEM.WRK.CODE on the root volume. This file contains the executable P-code.

If there is no work file when you select the COMPILE command, the system will prompt you for the name of the text file you want compiled. It will also ask for the name of the file where the P-code will be stored.

Executing COMPILE   To execute COMPILE, select the COMPILE command from the COMMAND mode by pressing the C key. The message

Compiling...

appears on the screen immediately. The compiler will process the work file.

On the other hand, if there is no work file, the system asks:

Compile what text ? ☐

Type in the name of a file without a suffix, and press RETURN. If the file is on the prefix volume, you may, of course, omit the volume specification part of the file name. The system will automatically append a .TEXT suffix to the file name you have typed. In other words, if you type SUM and press RETURN, it will look for the file SUM.TEXT on the prefix volume and try to compile it.

In some versions of the p-System, it is possible to compile the contents of a file, even though the name does not have the .TEXT suffix. You can do this by including a period (.) after the file name. For example, if you type

SUM.

the system will look for the file SUM, not SUM.TEXT.

After you specify the text file and press RETURN, the system asks:

To what codefile ? ☐

That is, where do you want the compiled code stored? You now have four options. You may:

1. Press the ESC key. This will abort the COMPILE command and return you to the COMMAND mode.

2. Press RETURN. The compiled code will be stored in the file SYSTEM.WRK.CODE on the root volume. You might choose this option when you are going to run and then revise a program several times in succession.

3. Type a dollar sign ($) and press RETURN. The compiled code will be kept in a file with the same name as the text file containing the source program, but the .CODE suffix will replace the .TEXT suffix. In other words, if you specified the file SUM as the text file, the system will store the P-code in the file SUM.CODE.

    This is a useful option. It means the text file and compiled program file will have identical names, except for the suffixes. The $ option also "remembers" any volume name you typed with the text file name, so you don't have to retype it.

4. Type in a file name without a suffix, and press RETURN. The system will use the name you have typed and append a .CODE suffix. If you want the compiled code on the prefix volume, you may, of course, omit the volume specification.

    In some versions of the p-System, you can prevent the system from appending the .CODE suffix by putting a period immediately after the name you type. For example, if you enter TEST. in response to the prompt:

To what codefile ? **TEST.**⟩

the file containing the compiled code will be named TEST, not TEST.CODE.

Let's look at an example.

Example of COMPILE   Suppose we have just revised a program in the file GAME.TEXT on the volume SYBEX and that GAME.TEXT has not been designated as the work file. We now want to compile the program as the file GAME.CODE.

Press the C key, selecting the COMPILE command. Then in response to the first question, type the volume name, a colon, and the file name without a suffix:

Compile what text ? **SYBEX:GAME**⟩

Answer the next question by typing the dollar sign and pressing RETURN:

To what codefile ? **$**⟩

The compiler will process the contents of the file GAME.TEXT on the volume, SYBEX, and, if the process is successful, store the resulting P-code on the volume SYBEX under the file name GAME.CODE.

The system will normally put the P-code file in the largest unused area on a disk. You can change this by typing a number, n, in square brackets after the file name. The P-code file will then be written into the first unused area, n or more blocks in size. For example, to put compiled code in the file DEMO.CODE in the first 10 block unused area of the prefix volume, you would type the following in response to the prompt:

To what codefile ? **DEMO[10]**

The COMPILE Display   As the compiler translates source code into P-code, your screen will display information about this process. In particular, it will tell you the number of text lines already compiled, the name of the procedure being compiled, and the space available in main memory. When compilation is finished, the screen will indicate the total number of source lines processed and the smallest space available in memory during compilation. Perhaps there is not much information in this display which is immediately useful to the beginning Pascal programmer. Understanding it from the outset, however, will minimize mystification.

Let's see what sort of display is produced when we compile a sample Pascal program. Here is a slightly modified version of the GREETING program from Chapter 1:

```
PROGRAM GREETING;

PROCEDURE SPACE;
   BEGIN
      WRITELN;
   END;

BEGIN
   SPACE;
   WRITELN ('HI THERE!');
   SPACE
END.
```

This modest program includes the equally modest procedure SPACE, which inserts a blank line in the output. SPACE is called twice from the main program. (If your knowledge of the Pascal language doesn't yet include procedures, read on. You should be able to understand the sample COMPILE display in any case.)

When it is compiled, this version of GREETING produces the following display on the screen:

```
PASCAL COMPILER [II.0.A.1]
<  0>....
SPACE [2095 words]
<  4>....
GREETING   [2106 words]
<  8>...
11 lines
smallest available space = 2095 words
```

The numbers 0, 4, and 8 in "angle brackets" (<>) are the numbers of the source lines already compiled. A dot appears after each number as the subsequent lines are processed. For example, after line four is compiled, the compiler displays "<4>" on the screen. As each of the following lines (5th, 6th, 7th, and 8th) are compiled, the compiler displays an additional dot after the "<4>". A blank line, by the way, is counted as a source line.

The names of the procedures, functions, and the main program appear when the compiler starts to compile the executable statements in that part of the program. For example, the identifier 'SPACE' appears when the compiler reaches line 5 of the source program ('WRITELN;'). This is the first, and only, executable statement in the procedure 'SPACE'. The identifier 'GREETING' appears when the compiler starts processing line 9 ('SPACE;'), the first executable statement in the main body of the program.

The number in square brackets ([ ]) after an identifier indicates the number of 16-bit words available in main memory at that point in the compilation. In our sample, there are 2106 words available when the compiler starts translating the executable portion of the main program (line 9).

If the amount of available memory is ever less than 550 words, the compiler will stop. Recovery from this difficulty is usually possible by using the SWAP compiler directive described in Chapter 6.

The bottom two lines of the display indicate the total number of source lines compiled and the smallest available memory during the process. In our example, there were 11 source lines, including blank lines. The smallest available space during compilation was 2095 words.

When the last two lines appear on screen, compilation is complete. The compiled code is now stored in a file. You can test it with the RUN or EXECUTE commands.

Syntax Errors

It is a fact of computing life that most programs won't compile flawlessly the first time around. Obvious or not-so-obvious errors will occur. It isn't hard, as you no doubt know, to forget a semicolon or a quote mark.

The UCSD Pascal compiler is designed to help you repair errors quickly and easily. When the compiler detects an error, it stops and displays the source line where it "thinks" the error has occurred. You can then abort compilation, continue compilation, or invoke the editor and fix the problem.

On the screen, four "arrowheads" (<<<<) point to the offending part of the source. A message then gives the number of the source line with the mistake, the error number, and the three options available. The UCSD Pascal error messages and their associated numbers appear in Appendix C.

When an error message appears on screen, you have three options. You may:

1. Press the ESC key to abort-compilation and return to the COMMAND mode.
2. Press the spacebar to continue compilation. You might choose this option if you want to see if there are other errors in the program. Note, however, that one error can create others. The compiler might lose its way and produce a cascade of spurious error messages.
3. Press the E key to select the editor to fix the error. The system quits the COMPILE command, invokes EDIT, loads SYSTEM.WRK.TEXT into the text buffer, and displays it on screen under a description of the error message. Then press the spacebar. The EDIT prompt appears and the cursor is positioned next to the line where, supposedly, the mistake occurs. If, however, you are compiling a file other than SYSTEM.WRK.TEXT, press the E key, and type in the name of the text file that was being processed. Then press RETURN.

The third option is automatically selected if you are in the "student" mode of the p-System. The student mode is established at system configuration time with the program SETUP.CODE. The student mode is not particularly useful, since there is no reason that a "student" should not be able to choose one of the first two options. Now let's try an example.

An Example of the EDIT Option We have revised the enhanced GREETING program by deleting the second quote mark in line 9. The

GREETING program is now designated as the work file and looks like this:

```
PROGRAM GREETING;

PROCEDURE SPACE;
   BEGIN
      WRITELN;
   END;

BEGIN
   SPACE;
   WRITELN ('HI THERE!);
   SPACE
END.
```

When this program is compiled, the compiler stops at line 9 and displays the following message:

```
PASCAL Compiler [II.0.A.1]
<  0>....
SPACE [2095 words]
<  4>....
GREETING [2106 words]
<  8>.
SPACE;
WRITELN ('HI THERE!); <<<<
Line 9, error 202: <sp> (continue), <esc> (terminate), E(dit
```

The display tells us that error 202 occurs in line 9, which appears on screen with the preceding line 8.

We select the EDIT option by pressing the E key. Since the GREETING program was in the work file, the system enters the editor and displays the GREETING program under the error message:

String constant must not exceed source line. Type <sp>
PROGRAM GREETING;

PROCEDURE SPACE;
   BEGIN
      WRITELN;
   END;

BEGIN
   SPACE;
   WRITELN ('HI THERE!');
   SPACE
END.

Press the spacebar. The EDIT prompt appears and the cursor is positioned next to line 9. You can move the cursor and use the INSERT mode to add the missing quote mark.

The description of the error message comes from the file SYSTEM.SYNTAX, which occupies 14 blocks on the root volume. If this file is unavailable, only the error number will appear over the program. If you are in an extreme squeeze for disk space, you can print the contents of the file SYSTEM.SYNTAX and then transfer it off the root volume. However, when an error occurs, you will have to look up the error number on your printout, instead of simply reading the description from the screen.

The compiler will not always stop at the line that actually contains the error. It is possible that the mistake may have occurred several lines previously. Furthermore, the error message may not always describe the mistake accurately. We will consider these possibilities in Part Two of this chapter.

Once a program is successfully compiled, it is time to test it. If it is in the work file, use the RUN command; if it isn't, then employ EXECUTE.

The RUN Command

The RUN command loads the file SYSTEM.WRK.CODE, or the code file designated as the work file, into main memory and executes it. If there is no code file part of the work file, then the COMPILE command is invoked and operates as described previously. If compilation is successful, the new machine code is executed immediately. RUN also automatically invokes the LINK command (described in Chapter 6), if necessary. You will normally use RUN to execute the work file after it has been successfully compiled.

Executing RUN   To execute RUN, select RUN from the COMMAND mode by pressing the R key. The message 'RUNNING...' will appear on screen. There is no RUN prompt. During the operation of RUN, the system may return momentarily to the COMMAND mode. For this reason, the root volume should remain on line. Let's consider an example.

Example of RUN   Now that we have repaired the syntax error in GREETING by inserting the missing quote mark, we will update the program and establish the file SYSTEM.WRK.TEXT on the root volume. We will then successfully compile it, and thus create the P-code file SYSTEM.WRK.CODE.

To test the GREETING program, press the R key selecting the RUN command. The screen displays:

```
RUNNING....


HI THERE!
```

The program executes satisfactorily.

The COMPILE And RUN Commands

How do you normally use COMPILE and RUN? Suppose you have a short Pascal program you want to write, compile, and execute. Here is the sequence of operations you might follow:

1. Invoke EDIT from the COMMAND mode. Use the INSERT mode to write the source code for the program.

2. QUIT EDIT with the UPDATE option. This creates the file SYSTEM.WRK.TEXT on the root volume.

3. Select the COMPILE command. The contents of SYSTEM.WRK.TEXT will be compiled. If there is an error, use the EDIT option to fix the problem.

4. Select COMPILE again, if necessary. When compilation is successful, the system stores the P-code in the file SYSTEM.WRK.CODE on the root volume.

5. Use the RUN command to execute the P-code SYSTEM.WRK.CODE.

If your program doesn't work as expected, or if you want to enhance it, or if there is a run-time error, repeat the series of steps just outlined.

On the other hand, if the program works and you don't want to fuss with it, enter the FILER and use the SAVE command to rename the SYSTEM.WRK files appropriately. Then clear the work file with the NEW command and go on to something else. Recall that we followed a similar sequence of steps in Chapter 2, when we wrote, compiled, corrected, recompiled, executed, and saved the program GREETING.

The EXECUTE Command

The EXECUTE command loads the P-code for a Pascal program into main memory and executes it. You will use this command when you want to execute a code file that is not the current work file.

Executing EXECUTE   To execute EXECUTE, select the EXECUTE command from the COMMAND mode by pressing the X key. The system asks:

Execute what file ? □

Type in a file name without suffix and press RETURN. EXECUTE will then execute. Of course, if the file is on the prefix volume, you may omit the volume specification part of the file name.

Since compiled code is usually stored in a file with the .CODE suffix, the system will assume that it should append this suffix to the name you typed. In other words, if you type the name TEST, the system will look for the file TEST.CODE. A message will tell you if the search is unsuccessful. In some versions of the p-System, you can get around this requirement for the .CODE suffix by simply typing a period (.) after the file name. The system will then look for a file with the exact name you have specified. For example, if you type

TEST.⌡

the system will search for the file 'TEST' and execute it. Let's consider an example.

Example of EXECUTE   Suppose we have stored the compiled code for the program 'SUM' in the file SUM.CODE on the volume SYBEX. SUM.CODE is not designated as the work file.

To execute the 'SUM' program, select EXECUTE by pressing the X key. Answer the prompt by typing:

Execute what file ? **SYBEX:SUM** ⌡

The file SUM.CODE is loaded into main memory and executed.

PART TWO: THE UCSD PASCAL COMPILER

We will now turn our attention to the UCSD Pascal compiler. In particular, we will look at compiler directives, especially the LIST directive.

Compiler Directives

Compiler directives are commands which control the behavior of the compiler. You embed these commands in appropriate places in the source code of a Pascal program. As the compiler is processing source code, it encounters the directive and responds accordingly.

Compiler directives provide a variety of possibilities. For example, the QUIET directive suppresses the screen display during compilation; the INCLUDE directive takes material from another file and includes it in the program being compiled; the SWAP directive moves material in and out of main memory so that larger programs can be compiled.

Compiler directives are similar to Pascal comments. Recall that in Pascal, comments are enclosed either by braces { } or by parentheses and asterisks (* *). A compiler directive begins with a dollar sign ($) placed immediately after the left brace or parenthesis-asterisk, followed by the actual directive. The following are two examples of the form of a compiler directive:

{$directive}

or

(*$directive*)

Directives are abbreviated with a single letter and are, usually, turned 'ON' and 'OFF' with a plus (+) or minus (−) character. There must be no space between the letter representing the directive and the dollar sign. For example, to activate the QUIET option somewhere in a Pascal program, you would write in your program:

(*$Q+*)

To deactivate QUIET, you would write:

(*$Q−*)

You can insert some compiler directives, like QUIET, anywhere in the text of a Pascal program; others must be placed in particular positions. Also, you can list several directives, separated by commas (,), within one pair of braces or parentheses-asterisks.

We will now look carefully at the LIST directive.

The LIST Directive

The LIST directive instructs the compiler to produce a listing of the program it is processing. The listing contains a numbered list of each line in the program, together with certain useful information (described below). You can display the listing on screen, print it, or put it into a separate disk file. You will use the LIST directive when you are developing and testing a program. The listing will help you locate errors.

Selecting LIST   There are several ways you can specify the LIST directive. You can write:

   (*$L + *)

to put the listing in a file SYSTEM.LST.TEXT on the root volume. Or you can write:

   (*$L CONSOLE:*)

to display the listing on the screen. Or you can write:

   (*$L PRINTER:*)

to print the listing on the system line printer. Or you can write:

   (*$L filename*)

to store the listing in a disk file.

If the file name starts with the plus (+) or minus (−) characters, be careful to leave a space between the L and the file name. Otherwise, a space isn't necessary.

To "turn off" the LIST directive, write:

   (*$L − *)

This is the default setting. In other words, unless you instruct it differently, the compiler will not automatically produce a listing of the program it is compiling. Let's consider some examples.

Examples of LIST   To print a listing of the GREETING program, write the directive (*$L PRINTER:*) at the beginning of the program. GREETING should now look like this:

```
(*$L PRINTER:*)
PROGRAM GREETING;

PROCEDURE SPACE;
   BEGIN
      WRITELN;
   END;

BEGIN
   SPACE;
   WRITELN ('HI THERE!');
   SPACE
END.
```

When this program is compiled, the listing will be printed on the line printer.

There is nothing to prevent you from listing only part of a program. For example, to list only the procedure SPACE to the printer, the GREETING text should look like this:

```
PROGRAM GREETING;

(*$L PRINTER:*)
PROCEDURE SPACE;
   BEGIN
      WRITELN;
   END;
(*$L — *)

BEGIN
   SPACE;
   WRITELN ('HI THERE!');
   SPACE
END.
```

Alternatively, to store the listing of GREETING in a file named LSTGREET.TEXT on the volume BIG, the directive would look like this:

(*$L BIG:LSTGREET.TEXT*)

Let us now consider the information on the listing produced by the LIST directive.

Information From LIST   What does the listing tell us? As an example, consider this listing for the extended GREETING program:

```
 1    1   1:D    1    (*$L LSTGREET.TEXT*)
 2    1   1:D    1
 3    1   1:D    1    PROGRAM GREETING;
 4    1   1:D    3
 5    1   2:D    1    PROCEDURE SPACE;
 6    1   2:0    0      BEGIN
 7    1   2:1    0        WRITELN;
 8    1   2:0    8      END;
 9    1   2:0   20
10    1   1:0    0    BEGIN
11    1   1:1    0      SPACE;
12    1   1:1    4      WRITELN ('HI THERE!');
13    1   1:1   33      SPACE
14    1   1:0   33    END.
```

On the right side of the listing, the source code of the GREETING program appears as we wrote it. On the top line, we instructed the compiler to put the listing in the file LSTGREET.TEXT on the prefix volume. (After compilation, we can use the filer command TRANSFER to display the contents of LSTGREET.TEXT on the screen.)

On the left, five columns of information appear. Let's look at each column in turn.

- The first column indicates the number of the text line in the program. Altogether, there are 14 lines (including blank lines) in the GREETING program.

- The second column shows the segment number. You can ignore this number until you are writing long Pascal programs that must be broken into segments (see Chapter 6). The short GREETING program only has one segment.

- The third column indicates the procedure number. The main program is always the first "procedure." In our example, SPACE is procedure number 2. Notice how the procedure number changes to 1 when the body of the main program starts at line 10.

- The fourth column is separated from the third by a colon. If the letter D appears here, it indicates that a line of text is blank or part of the declaration section of a procedure. Lines 1 through 5 in the GREETING program are marked D. On the other hand, if a number appears in the fourth column, the line of text is an executable statement. Furthermore, this number shows the nesting level of the statement. Nesting levels range from 0 to 9. A statement at level n is controlled by a statement at level n — 1. In the GREETING program, for example, line 10 of text ('BEGIN') is level 0; the next three lines are level 1, and the last line of text ('END.') returns to level 0.

- The fifth column indicates the offset. If a line is part of a declaration (i.e., marked D in column four), the offset is the number of 2-byte words already allocated to variables in the procedure. If a line is an executable statement, the offset is the number of bytes of P-code compiled for the procedure so far. In our example, text line 4 (a blank line) has the number 3.in the fifth column. This means three 2-byte words had been allocated when the compiler reached the beginning of line 4. At the beginning of text line 13 ('SPACE'), on the other hand, the compiler had issued 33 bytes of executable code.

Using The Information   How can we use the information presented by the LIST directive? There are two major types of errors in programs: compile-time and run-time errors. Compile-time errors, as we have seen, occur during the process of compilation when the compiler tries to process source code which is not legal in Pascal. Run-time errors occur when the compiled code for a program is being executed. A listing can help us locate both types of problems.

Finding Compile-Time Errors   Many times, the compiler will correctly identify the line of the source where a compile-time error occurs and display the appropriate error number and message. Sometimes, however, the compiler will stop at a line that is several lines beyond the actual error. Furthermore, it is possible that the error number and message may not be helpful. In such cases, the information in columns 4 and 5 of the listing can assist in locating the problem.

A frequent error is the omission of a 'BEGIN' or 'END' from a BEGIN-END pair. Let's look at an example.

Example of Compile-Time Errors   We modify the GREETING program by deleting line 8. The 'END' that matches the 'BEGIN' for the procedure SPACE is now missing. We also modify the LIST directive, so that the listing appears on the screen. We add Q (the Quiet directive) to make the display easier to read. The text of GREETING now looks like this:

```
(*$Q,L CONSOLE:*)
PROGRAM GREETING;

PROCEDURE SPACE;
  BEGIN
    WRITELN;

BEGIN
  SPACE;
  WRITELN ('HI THERE!');
  SPACE
END.
```

When we compile GREETING, this display appears on screen:

```
<  0>  1   1   1:D       1  (*$Q,L CONSOLE:*)
       2   1   1:D       1
       3   1   1:D       1  PROGRAM GREETING;
       4   1   1:D       3
       5   1   2:D       1  PROCEDURE SPACE;
       6   1   2:0       0    BEGIN
       7   1   2:1       0      WRITELN;
       8   1   2:1      20
       9   1   2:1      20  BEGIN
      10   1   2:2      20    SPACE;
      11   1   2:2      24    WRITELN ('HI THERE!');
      12   1   2:2      53    SPACE
      13   1   2:1      53  END.
>>>>>>    Error #6
```

The compiler has stopped. The arrows occuring after line 13 indicate that the compiler detected a problem at line 13. We know, of course, the error is really at line 7. The error number is 6. The text for this error is:

Illegal symbol (terminator expected)

which doesn't really describe the problem.

We now use the information in the listing to "locate" the problem. Look at columns 3 and 5, the procedure number and the offset. (Don't be confused by the indentation of the first line, it is displayed before the Quiet directive takes effect.) Note that procedure 2 starts at line 5. However, when the main body of the program starts at line 9, the procedure number doesn't change. It is still 2. The compiler "thinks" the main program is part of the 'SPACE' procedure.

Also notice the offset in the fifth column. At line 9 ('BEGIN'), the offset is 20 bytes. However, since 'BEGIN' in line 9 is the first executable statement for the main program (i.e., procedure 1), the offset should be 0. Again, the evidence shows the compiler is, erroneously, still processing the 'SPACE' procedure.

Both pieces of information together indicate that the 'SPACE' procedure has not been syntactically concluded. We inspect the text for SPACE and "discover" the missing 'END.'

There is a moral to this tale. If the compiler indicates an error in a line of text that seems correct, check the listing. Look carefully at the way the procedure numbers change from one part of the program to the next. Similarly, review the byte offset: at the beginning of the executable part of a procedure it should return to 0.

There are other common syntax errors that may be hard to find without the information in the listing. For example, an unclosed comment (i.e., forgetting the final brace or asterisk-parenthesis) often causes the byte offset to fail to increment or to continue incrementing when it should be reset to 0. Another potential trouble spot is a series of nested if-statements. In this case, the nesting level number in column four can help untangle any problems.

Run-Time Errors   Run-time errors occur when a program attempts an illegal operation. For example, if you try to divide the variable X by the variable Y, and if Y happens to have the value of zero, then, division is illegal, execution stops and an error message appears.

The run-time error message has three lines. The first line describes the error. (Appendix D lists all the run-time errors recognized by the p-System.) The second line displays the segment number, procedure number, and offset where the error occurred. These numbers correspond to columns 2, 3, and 5 in the listing. The third line instructs you to press the spacebar. When you do, execution is aborted and the COMMAND prompt will reappear.

When a program stops because of a run-time error, you should first jot down the error number and the information in the second line. Then press the spacebar to move to the COMMAND prompt. Next, look at the program listing to find the line with the mistake. Finally, invoke EDIT and make the necessary repairs. Let's look at an example.

Example of a Run-Time Error Suppose that the program, BOMB, compiles successfully, but includes a common programming difficulty: a range error. That is, a certain variable is restricted to a range of values in the declaration section. In the execution section, however, the program attempts to exceed the restrictions. This produces a run-time error. Here is the text of BOMB:

```
1    1    1:D    1    (*$L BOMBLIST.TEXT*)
2    1    1:D    1
3    1    1:D    1    PROGRAM BOMB (INPUT, OUTPUT);
4    1    1:D    3
5    1    1:D    3    VAR
6    1    1:D    3        FUSE : ARRAY [1..3] OF INTEGER;
7    1    1:D    6        TIMER : INTEGER;
8    1    1:D    7
9    1    1:0    0    BEGIN
10   1    1:1    0        FOR TIMER : = 1 TO 4
11   1    1:1    5            DO
12   1    1:2   13               BEGIN
13   1    1:3   13                   FUSE [TIMER] : = TIMER;
14   1    1:3   25                   WRITELN ( TIMER );
15   1    1:2   43               END
16   1    1:0   43    END.
```

The array FUSE is indexed by the numbers 1, 2, and 3. Since TIMER is assigned the value of 4, the array FUSE will exceed its index limit after the third repetition of the FOR loop. At that point, BOMB will "blow up."

We test BOMB with the EXECUTE command. The program executes the FOR loop three times and then fails. The screen looks like this:

Execute what file? **BOMB** ⌋

1

2

3

Value range error
S# 1, P# 1, I# 19
Type <space> to continue

We jot down the error message and the numbers, and then press the spacebar. This aborts execution and returns us to the COMMAND mode. We can then use the information from the error message to locate the source line where the program failed.

In our example, the first line ('Value range error') describes the error. The second line indicates that it occurred in segment 1, procedure 1, when the offset was 19 bytes. If we check the Bomb listing, we find text line 13 is in segment 1 and procedure 1. It's offset is 13. Since the offset of the next line is 25, the 19th compiled byte occurred in line 13. Execution failed at this byte when the program tried to use the value 4 to index the Fuse array.

In summary, the three numbers on the second line of the error message serve as locators. You should first find the segment indicated, the procedure, and then the line with the error offset. That's the line where the run-time error occurred.

Range error is not the only common run-time problem. Others include division by zero, stack overflow (i.e., insufficient memory), and integer overflow (i.e., using an integer larger than the maximum permitted by a 2-byte memory word).

We have now looked closely at the LIST directive and some of the ways you can use it to locate non-obvious compile-time and run-time errors. We will now conclude this chapter by briefly describing other compiler directives.

Other Directives

The UCSD Pascal compiler includes the following compiler directives, many of which will not be of interest to the beginning programmer:

INCLUDE	takes a file and includes it in the source being compiled (see Chapter 6).
QUIET	suppresses the console display during compilation.
SWAP	moves parts of compiler in and out of memory to maximize space for source code (see Chapter 6).
GOTO	allows GOTO statements.
IOCHECK	controls checking of the errors on input and output in a program.
RANGE CHECK	performs value range checking.
USER	establishes application or systems programming mode.
USES	accesses UNITS (see Chapter 6).
COMMENT	permits the establishment of copyright on a file.
PAGE	causes a new page when a listing is being printed.

Some versions of the p-System include compiler directives, such as NO LOAD, RESIDENT, or FLIP. Refer to the documentation for your system to learn the details of these and other directives.

SUMMARY

In this chapter we have learned how to compile and run short Pascal programs. We have also learned how to use the listing produced by the UCSD Pascal compiler to find programming errors.

In the next chapter, we will discuss the SWAP, INCLUDE, and USES directives. These directives can prove important when writing large and more complicated Pascal programs.

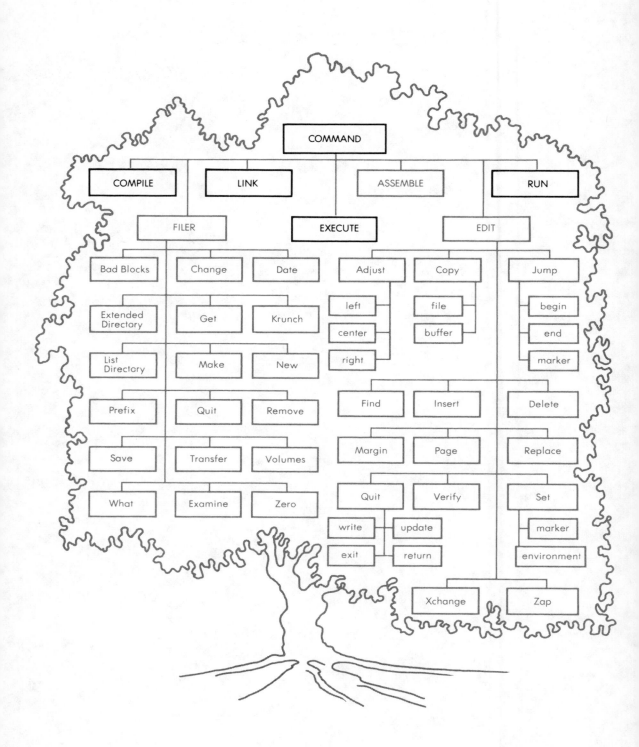

PREPARING LARGE PASCAL PROGRAMS 6

THIS CHAPTER HELPS YOU create and run large Pascal programs. Generally, the larger the program, the more difficult it is to run. On the p-System, because main memory is limited, you create a large program by dividing it into independent program sections. Often, you can reuse these independent sections in other programs. Gradually, you will build a library of independent program sections that you can use over and over again.

It is frequently only possible to keep one program section in main memory at a time. Therefore, there must be ways to combine these sections and the main program after they have been created and modified. In this chapter, we will discuss the techniques available on the p-System for combining independent program sections, compiling a large program, and for fitting large programs into main memory at run-time.

Part One describes the two methods available for managing large source programs and for using the library features of the p-System: INCLUDE files and UNITs. Part Two discusses the techniques used for compiling large programs, including SWAPPING and program restructuring. Part Three examines the two methods available for fitting large programs into main memory at run-time: SEGMENTs and local variables.

PART ONE: MANAGING LARGE SOURCE PROGRAMS

In this section, we will use the screen oriented editor to create and modify example programs. Since all text being edited with this editor must fit into main memory *with the editor,* there is often not enough room in main memory for a large program as a single file. For this reason, we must divide a large program into a group of smaller files that we create and modify individually.

Combining Multiple Source Files

The p-System offers two methods for combining multiple source files into one program: INCLUDE files and UNITs.

The INCLUDE file

The INCLUDE file lets you combine sections of a source program, that have been created as separate files, into one large program. Using INCLUDE files, you can divide a large program into separate files without changing the meaning of the program.

The INCLUDE Directive The INCLUDE directive tells the compiler which INCLUDE file to use and where to include it in the main program. The INCLUDE directive follows the standard form for compiler directives in the Pascal language: a comment that begins with a dollar sign, followed by the letter I, an optional space, and the name of the file to be INCLUDEd. Here are two examples of INCLUDE directives:

(*$I MYFILE*)

{$I YOURFILE}

These directives tell the compiler to include the files MYFILE and YOUR-FILE on the prefix volume.

When the compiler comes across an INCLUDE directive, it searches for the named file. If it does not find that file, it appends the suffix .TEXT to the file name, and searches for that file. When it locates the INCLUDE file, the compiler compiles its contents at the point in the main program where the INCLUDE directive appears. Let's look at an example.

Example of INCLUDE   In this example, we will create a program, called MAIN.TEXT, that will use an INCLUDE file, called PROC.TEXT. We will use an INCLUDE directive in MAIN.TEXT that will specify that PROC.TEXT is to be compiled with the MAIN.TEXT source file.

We will begin by creating PROC.TEXT. The sample program here is short, but it demonstrates how INCLUDE works with programs of any size.

Press the E key while in the COMMAND mode to invoke the editor. Then, in response to the file prompt, press RETURN to specify that no file is to be read in. Next, press the I key to enter the INSERT mode. Type in the following INCLUDE file:

```
FUNCTION FACTORIAL ( N : INTEGER ) : INTEGER;

BEGIN
    IF N = 0
        THEN
            FACTORIAL := 1
        ELSE
            FACTORIAL := N * FACTORIAL ( N - 1 )
END;
```

Now, press the Q key to select the QUIT command. Then, press the W key to select the WRITE option. Type in the file name PROC, and press RETURN. This writes the file out to the disk as the file PROC.TEXT. Press the E key to return to the COMMAND mode.

We now have a file named PROC.TEXT. Let's create the main program, MAIN.TEXT.

Press the E key to enter the editor again. In response to the file prompt, press RETURN, so that no file is read in. Now press the I key to enter the INSERT mode. Type in the following program:

```
(*$L LISTING.TEXT*)

PROGRAM PRINTFACTORIAL ( INPUT, OUTPUT );

VAR
   NUMBER : INTEGER;

(*$I PROC*)

BEGIN
   REPEAT
     WRITE ( 'INPUT A NUMBER: ' );
     READLN ( NUMBER );
     WRITELN ( NUMBER, ' FACTORIAL IS ', FACTORIAL ( NUMBER ) );
   UNTIL NUMBER = 0
END.
```

Next, press the Q key to select the QUIT command. Then press the W key to select the WRITE option. Type in the file name MAIN, and press RETURN. This writes the main program out to the text file MAIN.TEXT. Finally, press the E key to return to the COMMAND mode.

Now let's see how the INCLUDE directive works. We will compile the main program file, MAIN.TEXT, with the INCLUDEd file, PROC.TEXT. Note that we have included a listing directive in the main program. This directive tells the compiler to produce a listing file and store it as LISTING.TEXT.

Press the C key to select the COMPILE command from the COMMAND mode. Answer each prompt from the compiler by typing the file name MAIN, and pressing RETURN:

Compile what text ? **MAIN**
To what code file ? **MAIN**

This produces the file MAIN.CODE, which contains the executable version of the program. It also produces the listing file, LISTING.TEXT. Let's examine this listing file to see how the INCLUDE file was combined with the main program:

```
 1 1  1:D    1     (*$L LISTING.TEXT*)
 2 1  1:D    1
 3 1  1:D    1     PROGRAM PRINTFACTORIAL ( INPUT, OUTPUT );
 4 1  1:D    3
 5 1  1:D    3     VAR
 6 1  1:D    3        NUMBER : INTEGER;
 7 1  1:D    4
 7 1  1:D    4     (*$I PROC*)
 8 1  2:D    3     FUNCTION FACTORIAL ( N : INTEGER ) : INTEGER;
 9 1  2:D    4
10 1  2:0    0     BEGIN
11 1  2:1    0        IF N = 0
12 1  2:1    1        THEN
13 1  2:2    5           FACTORIAL := 1
14 1  2:1    5        ELSE
15 1  2:2   10           FACTORIAL := N * FACTORIAL ( N – 1 )
16 1  2:0   14     END;
17 1  2:0   34
18 1  2:0   34     (*$I PROC*)
19 1  2:0   34
20 1  1:0    0     BEGIN
21 1  1:1    0        REPEAT
22 1  1:2    2           WRITE ( 'INPUT A NUMBER: ' );
23 1  1:2   30           READLN ( NUMBER );
24 1  1:2   48           WRITELN ( NUMBER, ' FACTORIAL IS ', FACTORIAL ( NUMBER ) );
25 1  1:1  106        UNTIL NUMBER = 0
26 1  1:0  107     END.
```

The listing begins with the first seven lines of the MAIN.TEXT file—up to the INCLUDE directive. The INCLUDE directive is then followed by the contents of the INCLUDE file, PROC.TEXT. The INCLUDE directive is then repeated (to signal the end of the INCLUDE file), and the remainder of the MAIN.TEXT file continues.

Nesting INCLUDE files   Some versions of UCSD Pascal allow INCLUDE files to be *nested*. This means that an INCLUDE file can contain other

INCLUDE directives. Figure 6.1 illustrates the nesting of INCLUDE files.

(*Note:* Version IV.0 of USCD Pascal allows you to nest INCLUDE files to a depth of three (as shown below). Previous versions, however, support only one level.)

INCLUDE File Summary

We have now learned to use INCLUDE files to create and edit large programs. INCLUDE files are a convenient tool, but they do have one major drawback: If even one file in the program is modified, all the files (even those that did not change) must be recompiled, in order to produce a modified version of the object code. However, UCSD Pascal does provide a mechanism for avoiding this inefficiency: the UNIT.

The UNIT

A *UNIT* is a collection of Pascal procedures, functions and declarations that form an independent section of a program. A feature of the UCSD Pascal language, the UNIT enables the separate compilation of sections of Pascal code. Thus, several main programs can use a UNIT without recompiling it. All items within a UNIT are either defined within that UNIT or passed in as parameters. A UNIT does not rely on any definition or declaration in the main program.

UNITs are useful when compiling large programs. Each UNIT is first compiled separately; then, through a process called LINKING, the object code from all the UNITs and the object code from the main program are

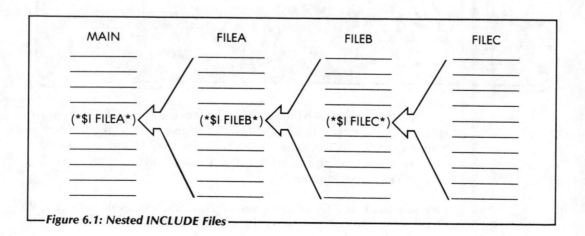

Figure 6.1: Nested INCLUDE Files

combined into an executable file. LINKING occurs when you select either the LINK or RUN command from the COMMAND mode.

If you modify a large program that uses UNITs, you need only recompile the part that contains the modification. Even though you must relink the object codes from all the UNITs and the main program to form the modified executable program, it is much faster to relink than to recompile an entire program. Let's look at an example of a UNIT.

Example of a UNIT We will now modify the INCLUDE file in the previous example to produce the source of the example UNIT.

Select the E key from the COMMAND mode to enter the editor. In response to the file prompt, type PROC (the name of the INCLUDE file created in the previous example). The contents of the file PROC.TEXT are read into the text buffer and appear on the screen. Modify the text in the following way:

```
(*$S+*)
UNIT MATHUNIT;

INTERFACE

FUNCTION FACTORIAL ( N : INTEGER ) : INTEGER;

IMPLEMENTATION

FUNCTION FACTORIAL;

BEGIN
   IF N = 0
    THEN
       FACTORIAL : = 1
    ELSE
       FACTORIAL := N * FACTORIAL ( N – 1)
END;

BEGIN
END.
```

Next, press the Q key to select the QUIT command. Now press the W key to select the WRITE option. Type in the file name MATHUNIT, and press RETURN. This writes the source of the UNIT out to the text file, MATHUNIT.TEXT. Press the E key to return to the COMMAND mode.

Now that we have created a UNIT, let's look at its structure.

The Structure of a UNIT   UNITS have four parts: the UNIT heading, the INTERFACE, the IMPLEMENTATION and the INITIALIZATION. Let's examine each part.

UNIT Heading   The UNIT heading consists of the reserved word UNIT, the UNIT name and a semicolon. The UNIT heading is the first section of a UNIT. It tells the compiler what to name the UNIT. In some systems, a SWAP directive must appear before the UNIT heading. A SWAP directive, discussed in Part Three of this chapter, is included in this example.

```
(*$S + *)
UNIT MATHUNIT;

INTERFACE

FUNCTION FACTORIAL ( N : INTEGER ) : INTEGER;

IMPLEMENTATION

FUNCTION FACTORIAL;

BEGIN
   IF N = 0
     THEN
        FACTORIAL := 1
     ELSE
        FACTORIAL := N * FACTORIAL ( N - 1 )
END;

BEGIN
END.
```

INTERFACE The INTERFACE part of a UNIT contains the procedures, functions and declarations that can be used by a main program. The INTERFACE begins with the reserved word INTERFACE, followed by a section of declarations. In this section, you declare all the UNIT's constants, types, variables, procedures, and functions which will be used by the main program. The procedure and function declarations consist of only the procedure or function headings. You specify the bodies and local declarations of the procedures or functions in the IMPLEMENTATION section. In this example, the only object visible to the main program is the function FACTORIAL. (*Note:* If there had been more than one procedure or function in this example, we would have listed each heading, separated by semicolons.)

```
(*$S+*)
UNIT MATHUNIT;


INTERFACE


FUNCTION FACTORIAL ( N : INTEGER ) : INTEGER;


IMPLEMENTATION


FUNCTION FACTORIAL;


BEGIN
   IF N = 0
     THEN
        FACTORIAL := 1
     ELSE
        FACTORIAL := N * FACTORIAL ( N - 1 )
END;


BEGIN
END.
```

IMPLEMENTATION The IMPLEMENTATION part of a UNIT contains the definitions of the procedures and functions declared in the INTERFACE, as well as any procedures, functions or declarations used only within the UNIT. The IMPLEMENTATION section begins with the reserved word IMPLEMENTATION, followed by any local procedures, functions or declarations, and the bodies of the procedures and functions declared in the INTERFACE. In this example, there are no local procedures, functions or declarations; the IMPLEMENTATION contains only the body of the function FACTORIAL declared in the INTERFACE.

```
(*$S+*)
UNIT MATHUNIT;

INTERFACE

FUNCTION FACTORIAL ( N : INTEGER ) : INTEGER;

IMPLEMENTATION

FUNCTION FACTORIAL;

BEGIN
  IF N = 0
    THEN
      FACTORIAL := 1
    ELSE
      FACTORIAL := N * FACTORIAL ( N - 1 )
END;

BEGIN
END.
```

INITIALIZATION The last part of a UNIT, the INITIALIZATION section, contains a block of Pascal statements within a BEGIN-END pair. These statements are executed at the start of the main program in order to provide any initialization that the UNIT may require. In this example, there is no initialization required, so we have left blank the section between the last BEGIN and END. (*Note:* Version IV.0 of UCSD Pascal allows a termination section, as well as an initialization section. Consult your user's manual for the details on your system.)

```
(*$S+*)
UNIT MATHUNIT;


INTERFACE


FUNCTION FACTORIAL ( N : INTEGER ) : INTEGER;


IMPLEMENTATION


FUNCTION FACTORIAL;


BEGIN
  IF N = 0
    THEN
       FACTORIAL := 1
    ELSE
       FACTORIAL := N * FACTORIAL ( N - 1 )
END;

BEGIN
END.
```

Now that we have examined the four parts of a UNIT, let's learn how to use it.

Compiling A UNIT   Before we can use the MATHUNIT with a program, we must first compile it.

Press the C key, while in the COMMAND mode, to invoke the compiler. Now, in response to both prompts, type MATHUNIT and press RETURN:

Compile what text ? **MATHUNIT**⌐

To what codefile ? **MATHUNIT**⌐

Compilation of the MATHUNIT begins. When the compilation is finished, MATHUNIT is ready to be used with a program. Let's now modify the file MAIN.TEXT in the previous example, so that it uses MATHUNIT.

Press the E key to select the EDIT command. Answer the file prompt by typing MAIN. The contents of the file MAIN.TEXT are read into the text buffer, and they appear on the screen. Now, modify the text as shown here:

```
(*$L LISTING.TEXT*)

PROGRAM PRINTFACTORIAL ( INPUT, OUTPUT );

(*$U MATHUNIT.CODE*)

USES
   MATHUNIT;

VAR
   NUMBER : INTEGER;

BEGIN
   REPEAT
      WRITE ( 'INPUT A NUMBER: ' );
      READLN ( NUMBER );
      WRITELN ( NUMBER, ' FACTORIAL IS ', FACTORIAL ( NUMBER ) );
      UNTIL NUMBER = 0
END.
```

Now, press the Q key to select the QUIT command. Press the W key to select the WRITE option. Type in the file name MAIN, and press RETURN. This writes the main program out to the text file, MAIN.TEXT. Press the E key to return to the COMMAND mode.

The Use Library Directive

With this last modification, we have deleted the INCLUDE directive, and added a new directive: (*$U MATHUNIT*). This directive tells the compiler where to find the libraries that contain the UNITs that we use in this program. If the compiler is not told which library to use, then it uses the default library, SYSTEM.LIBRARY on the root volume. (*Note* that the .CODE version of the UNIT (the object code) is used as the library, not the .TEXT version (the source code).)

The USES Declaration

The USES declaration tells the compiler which UNITs in the library the program will use. The USES declaration appears between the program heading and any other declarations in the main program. Note that our program example uses only one UNIT. If we had listed multiple UNITs in our USES declaration, we would have separated them with semicolons.

Let's now compile the main program.

Press the C key, while in the COMMAND mode, to invoke the compiler. Type in MAIN and press RETURN in response to both prompts:

Compile what text ? **MAIN**⌐
To what codefile ? **MAIN**⌐

Note that since the file MATHUNIT.CODE on the prefix volume was the library that contained the UNIT, MATHUNIT, and since the compiler must read the INTERFACE part of the UNIT to compile the main program, then the MATHUNIT.CODE file *must* be on the prefix volume while the main program is being compiled.

Linking

You can link programs in two ways: automatically, by using the RUN command, and manually, by using the LINK command. If you use the RUN command to *automatically* LINK and RUN a program, then all the UNITs to be linked with the program must be in the system library file, SYSTEM.LIBRARY, on the root volume. (*Note:* you can insert UNITs into the system library and other libraries by using the p-System LIBRARIAN utility, LIBRARY.CODE (see Appendix E).)

Let's now link MAIN and MATHUNIT to form a complete, executable program. Since we have not inserted MATHUNIT in the system library, we cannot use the RUN command—we must use the LINK command to link the two files.

Select the LINK command by pressing the L key while in the COMMAND mode. The LINKER responds with the following prompt:

Host file ? ☐

The LINKER is asking for the name of the file that contains the main program to which the other files will be linked. Type MAIN in response to the prompt, and press RETURN.

The LINKER now opens the MAIN.CODE file, verifies that it is a code file requiring linking, and displays a message that the file is ready for linking. The linker then prompts for the names of the files to be linked with the MAIN.CODE:

```
Host file ? MAIN⟩
Opening MAIN.CODE
Library file ? ☐
```

Respond to the prompt by typing the name of one of the files that you want to link with the main program. In this example, you have *only* one library file: MATHUNIT. Therefore, type MATHUNIT, and press RETURN. The LINKER opens the specified file, verifies that it is a library file, and displays a message that the file is ready for linking:

```
Host file ? MAIN
Opening MAIN.CODE
Library file ? MATHUNIT⟩
Opening MATHUNIT.CODE
Library file ? ☐
```

The LINKER will continue to ask for more library files, until you press RETURN without specifying a library file. Press RETURN to tell the LINKER that there are no more library files. The LINKER then prompts for the map file:

```
Host file ? MAIN
Opening MAIN.CODE
Library file ? MATHUNIT
Opening MATHUNIT.CODE
Library file ?⟩
Map file ? ☐
```

The *map file* receives information from the LINKER about the sizes and locations of the sections of the program being linked. If you want to generate a map file, type in a file name and press RETURN. If you do not, simply press RETURN. For this example, we do not want to generate a map file.

Press RETURN. The LINKER reads in the main program and the sections to be linked. As it reads in each section, it displays the name of each UNIT linked. After it reads in all the sections, the LINKER prompts for the name of the output file:

```
Host file ? MAIN
Opening MAIN.CODE
Library file ? MATHUNIT
Opening MATHUNIT.CODE
Library file ?
Map file ?
Reading PRINTFAC
Reading MATHUNIT
Output file ? ▢
```

You may either respond with the name of the output file that will hold the linked version of the program, or press RETURN without specifying a file name. (*Note:* if you give the output file the same name as the host file, the unlinked version of the program will be destroyed and replaced with the linked version.)

For this example, press RETURN without specifying a file name. This tells the LINKER to use the work file, SYSTEM.WRK.CODE, as the output file.

The linking takes place. As the LINKER links each section, it displays the name and segment number of the UNIT or main program being linked:

```
Host file ? MAIN
Opening MAIN.CODE
Library file ? MATHUNIT
Opening MATHUNIT.CODE
Library file ?
Map file ?
Reading PRINTFAC
Reading MATHUNIT
Output file ?
Linking PRINTFAC # 7
Linking MATHUNIT # 1
```

When the linking is complete, the linked version of the program is in the work file, and the system returns to the COMMAND mode.

Let's now execute the MAIN program. Press the R key, while in the COMMAND mode, to invoke the RUN command. (*Note:* If we had specified any output file other than the work file, we would have used the EXECUTE command in the COMMAND mode (rather than the RUN command) to execute the program.)

SOURCE MANAGEMENT SUMMARY

We have now learned how to use the INCLUDE directive and UNITs to combine several small files into one large program. These useful techniques, however, will not solve all the problems we will encounter when creating large programs. In Part Two we will discuss other approaches to the problems often encountered when creating, compiling, and running large programs.

PART TWO: COMPILING LARGE SOURCE PROGRAMS

A chief problem when compiling large programs is the lack of memory space available for holding the UCSD Pascal compiler and the symbol table. (The *symbol table* is a section of main memory used by the UCSD Pascal compiler to store the symbols used in programs.) If, during compilation, the memory space is exhausted, the compiler will halt and indicate a *stack overflow error*. It is then up to you to take the appropriate actions to get the program to compile. You may be able to compile it, without modification, by using the swapping options, which provide additional space in main memory for the symbol table. However, if this does not work, you may also need to restructure the program, so that it requires less symbol table space. We will discuss both options in this section. Let's first examine swapping.

Swapping

Swapping (or overlaying) allows a large program, such as a compiler, to run in a small amount of main memory. This technique involves sharing a section of main memory between two or more parts of a program, called *overlays*. Each overlay must be read into main memory before the code in that overlay can be executed. This is known as *swapping in the overlay*. Overlays that are not being executed do not need to reside in main memory. Overlays not currently in main memory are called *swapped out*.

The UCSD Pascal compiler can operate in a mode in which part of the compiler is overlayed. This opens up more main memory space for use by the symbol table; however, it also causes the compiler to run more slowly, since parts of the compiler must be swapped in from disk during the compilation. Let's now examine this process in greater detail.

Overlays In The Compiler

There are two large sections of code in the UCSD Pascal compiler. One section processes declarations; the other processes executable statements. When the compiler is executing in the normal (non-swapping) mode, both sections of the compiler are loaded into main memory (see Figure 6.2). Note that even though the compiler is only executing one part of the code at any one time, all of the code is in main memory.

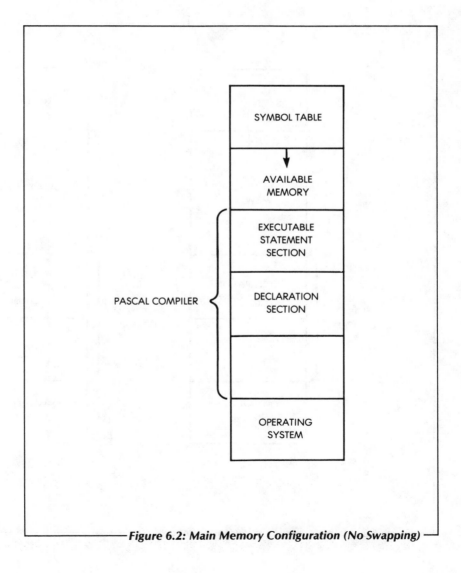

Figure 6.2: Main Memory Configuration (No Swapping)

When the compiler is executing in the swapping mode, *only one* of the two large sections of the compiler is in main memory at any one time. When the compiler encounters a section of declarations, the appropriate part of the compiler is swapped into main memory from the disk and executed (see Figure 6.3). When the compiler finishes compiling a section of declarations and begins to compile a section of executable statements, the other part of the compiler is swapped into the same section of main

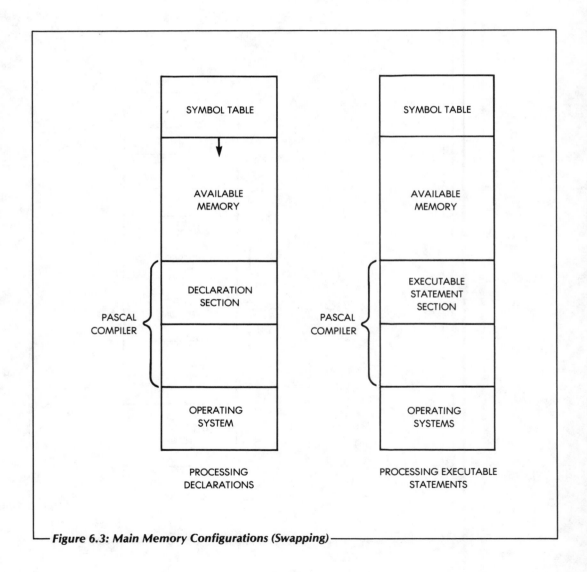

Figure 6.3: Main Memory Configurations (Swapping)

memory and executed. Thus, one section of main memory is continually swapping back and forth between the two sections of the compiler. Since the two large sections of the compiler are sharing one section of main memory, a large section of main memory is now free for use by the symbol table.

It takes time to swap the sections of the compiler from disk each time the compiler switches parts. Therefore, using the swapping mode slows compilation.

The Swapping Options

We will now examine the three swapping options available on various versions of the p-System. We will start with the SWAP directive, because it is available on every version of the system.

The SWAP Directive

The SWAP directive occurs at the beginning of a source program and instructs the compiler to use the swapping mode. This option slows compilation, but frees more main memory space for use in the symbol table. Here are two examples of SWAP directives.

(*$S + *)

and

{$S +}

The SWAP directive must appear at the beginning of a source program, before any Pascal code.

Some versions of the p-System support additional levels of swapping. If you use the SWAP directive and still do not have enough memory for the symbol table, check your system's documentation to see if your version supports other swapping options.

Extended SWAP Directive

Some systems have an extended SWAP directive of the form:

(*$S + + *)

or

{$S + +}

This directive activates even further swapping in the compiler, and, consequently, slows compilation even more.

The SWAP Command

Some versions of the p-System also have a SWAP command in the COMMAND mode. This command causes part of the operating system (rather than the compiler) to be swapped in and out of main memory. If your system supports it, you can toggle this command on and off by typing the letter S while in the COMMAND mode. You can use the SWAP command in conjunction with the regular or extended SWAP directives to obtain the largest possible free memory for the symbol table.

How Much Space Does Swapping Save The amount of main memory available for use by the symbol table on your system depends on the version of the p-System that you are using and the amount of main memory in your system. If you are using Version II.1, the swapping options will provide the following:

- The *SWAP directive* can provide about 5000 words of additional space for the symbol table.

- The *extended SWAP directive* can provide about 6500 words of additional space for the symbol table.

- The *SWAPPING command* can provide about 1000 words of additional space for the symbol table.

- The *SWAPPING command* and the *SWAP directive* together can provide about 6000 words of additional space for the symbol table.

- The *SWAPPING command* and the *extended SWAP directive* together can provide about 7500 words of additional space for the symbol table.

Remember that not all of these options are available on all versions of the p-System.

If you have tried all the swapping options available on your system and your program still requires more symbol table space, then you must reduce the number of symbols stored in the symbol table. To do this, it is necessary to understand how the compiler manipulates the symbol table, and to know the properties of the Pascal language that affect the symbol table.

Symbol Table Management

The symbols stored in the symbol table are called *identifiers*. Identifiers are used in a program to name constants, types, variables, procedures, functions, parameters, and the main program. All identifiers are stored in the symbol table. Whenever an identifier appears in a statement, the compiler looks up the identifier in the symbol table to determine what it represents. When compiling a statement, it is, therefore, necessary for the symbol table to hold all the identifiers that might legally appear in that statement.

To better understand when and how the identifiers are put into and taken out of the symbol table, we need to understand some concepts of identifier usage in the Pascal language. In particular, we need to learn about *blocks* and *scope*.

Blocks

A *block* is a section of code. In Pascal there are three types of blocks: procedures, functions, and programs. A block may contain other blocks. However, a block may not overlap the edges of other blocks. *Block structured* means composed of non-overlapping blocks.

Scope

Scope is a property of identifiers. The scope of an identifier is the section of the program that the identifier can be used in. If an identifier can be used in a particular statement, the identifier is said to be visible from that statement. Outside of the scope of an identifier, where the identifier is not visible, the identifier is undefined. Using an identifier outside of its scope results in an undefined identifier error message from the compiler. In Pascal, the scope of an identifier is the block where the identifier is declared and any blocks nested within that block. An example will help to clarify these concepts.

Example of Blocks and Scopes of Identifiers　In the following nonsense program, we have outlined the blocks. Let's examine each block.

```
PROGRAM SCOPES ( INPUT, OUTPUT );

    VAR
       W : INTEGER;

              PROCEDURE A;

                  VAR
                     X : INTEGER;

                         PROCEDURE B;

                             VAR
                                Y : INTEGER;

                             BEGIN
                                Y := X;
                                X := W;
                                W := Y
                             END;                    BLOCK B    BLOCK A

                  BEGIN
                     X := W + 1;
                     B;
                     W := W + X
                  END;

              PROCEDURE C;

                  VAR
                     Z : INTEGER;

                  BEGIN
                     Z := W DIV 2;
                     W := SQR ( Z * W )           BLOCK C
                  END;

    BEGIN (* SCOPES *)
       W := 5;
       A;
       C;
       WRITELN ( W )
    END.
```

BLOCK SCOPES

In this program, the scopes of the identifiers include the blocks shown in the following table:

Identifier	Blocks in the Scope
A	SCOPES, A, B, C
B	A, B
C	SCOPES, C
W	SCOPES, A, B, C
X	A, B
Y	B
Z	C

As you can see from this table, the scope of an identifier is the smallest block that contains the identifier and any smaller blocks contained within that block.

Note that the name of a procedure or function is defined in the block that surrounds the procedure or function. Thus, the scope of a procedure or function is the block outside of the definition, not just the procedure or function block itself. The scope of any variable declared in a block consists of the block itself and any blocks contained within that block.

Symbol Table Management Revisited

From the previous section, we can conclude that *an identifier must remain in the symbol table in which it was declared, while the block that it was declared in, and any blocks nested within that block, are being compiled.* The compiler implements this rule in the following way:

- Symbols become visible at the beginning of the blocks. The compiler puts the visible symbols into the symbol table at this time.

- The symbols remain in the symbol table and are visible throughout compilation of the block and any nested blocks.

- Symbols cease to be visible at the end of their defining block and are removed by the compiler at that time.

The key feature of this technique is that symbol table space is freed at the end of each block.

Now that we know how identifiers are managed in the symbol table, let's learn how we can reduce the symbol table requirements of a program.

Reducing Symbol Table Size

To reduce the size of the symbol table, you must reduce the number of identifiers visible at any point in the program. (*Note:* the total number of identifiers in the program does not need to be reduced, only the number *visible at any point* in the program.) To reduce the number of visible symbols, you must structure the program so that most of the identifiers are declared in different, non-nested blocks. The compiler can then reuse the symbol table space that holds the identifiers in each block.

The easiest way to implement this technique is to restrict the scope of the variables to the procedures that use them. You can do this by declaring the variables local to (contained within) the procedures that use them. *Note that you should declare variables global only when necessary, as global variables take up symbol table space that can never be reclaimed.*

There are several benefits to restricting the scope of the variables:

- Symbol table space can be reclaimed more easily.

- Memory can be used more efficiently at run-time (see the section on run-time memory management in this chapter).

- Variables are protected from accidentally being changed by a section of the program that does not need to use them, thus making a program easier to debug, since this type of error is prevented.

The most important step in reducing the symbol table requirements of a program is to structure the program carefully. There are other ways to save memory in the symbol table, including shortening the parameter lists associated with procedures and functions, using named types, and using local procedures and functions.

Parameter Lists

Parameters are used to pass information into procedures and functions. Parameter lists associated with the procedures and functions are stored in the symbol table with the procedure or function identifier. Long parameter lists use alot of symbol table space. Therefore, it may be possible to save symbol table space by making the parameter lists as short as possible.

There are only two ways to pass information to a procedure or function: by using parameters and by using global variables. It is generally undesirable to use global variables (as previously explained), unless, for example, a value is passed to several procedures and must be declared as a parameter in each procedure. Since this process requires a large amount of symbol table space, it makes more sense to declare the value in only one place (as a global variable) and, thus, save symbol table space.

Un-named Types

Each time we declare a variable of an un-named type, the description of the type is entered into the symbol table. However, when we declare a variable of a named type, only a reference to the type identifier is entered into the symbol table. A type description takes up more symbol table space than a reference to a type identifier. Thus, named types require less symbol table space than un-named types.

Let's look at two examples of types descriptions. In this example,

```
VAR
    X : ARRAY [1..10] OF INTEGER;
    Y : ARRAY [1..10] OF INTEGER;
    Z : ARRAY [1..10] OF INTEGER;
```

the type description ARRAY [1..10] OF INTEGER is entered into the symbol table three times.

However, in this example,

```
TYPE
    A = ARRAY [1..10] OF INTEGER;

VAR
    X : A;
    Y : A;
    Z : A;
```

the type description is stored only once in the symbol table, with the name "A." This arrangement uses less symbol table space. In addition, we can easily declare additional variables of this type. Also, since the type is declared in only one place, it is much easier to modify the program.

Local Procedures And Functions

Procedure and function declarations take up space in the symbol table in the same manner as variables and other identifiers. Although we usually declare most procedures and functions to be global in scope, we can declare them local to other procedures and functions if they are used only within them. Remember that if we declare the procedures and functions local, the compiler can remove them from the symbol table when they are no longer useful.

COMPILING SUMMARY

We have learned several techniques for compiling large programs, including increasing the size of the space available to the symbol table and reducing the symbol table requirements of a program. Our next step is to learn how to make a large program run in a limited amount of memory.

PART THREE: RUNNING LARGE PROGRAMS

In this section, we will examine the ways a program uses main memory, and we will learn how to fit a program efficiently into main memory at run-time.

How Main Memory Is Used

Programs have two main parts: code and data. The data are the variables used by the code. The codes are the instructions to be executed. Both data and code use main memory at run-time. Let's first look at the data part of the program.

Data

The data used by a program are kept in variables. There are three types of variables in UCSD Pascal: global, local and heap.

Global Variables   Recall that you declare global variables in the main body of a program. Global variables are accessible throughout the execution of a program and, therefore, continously use main memory space. Since the memory space they use cannot be reused, it is best to keep the use of global variables to a minimum.

Some variables *must* be global. For example, all variables used in the body of the main program must be global. Also, variables that must retain their values between the calls to the procedures that use them, cannot be local to those procedures (although, it may be possible to make them local to a surrounding procedure or function), and, therefore, it may be necessary to make them global (if there is no convenient procedure or function that encloses all usages of the variable).

Local Variables   You declare local variables in the body of a procedure or function. These variables are accessible only when the procedure or function is executing. When the procedure or function finishes executing, the main memory space used to hold the local variables can be reused. Local variables are the ideal way to allocate memory automatically when it is needed. A program that makes extensive use of the procedures, each with a few local variables, uses less main memory space than a program that uses many global variables, even though they may both use the same number of variables.

Heap Variables   You can use variables of type POINTER to refer to heap variables. Programs explicitly allocate and de-allocate the space for their heap variables using the UCSD Pascal procedures: NEW, DISPOSE, and RELEASE. You can use heap variables to create dynamic data structures, such as linked lists and trees. You normally use heap variables only when the other types of variables are insufficient. Heap variables give you the greatest freedom for controlling exactly when main memory is allocated and de-allocated.

Data Memory Allocation

Memory allocation is the process of assigning main memory locations to the variables. All variables must be assigned locations before you can use them. Before we learn how memory is allocated in the p-System, let's examine stacks, since the p-System uses a stack to allocate most of the main memory.

Stacks   A stack is a data structure that grows and shrinks at one end. Items may be placed (allocated) on the top of the stack and removed (de-allocated) from the top of the stack. A stack is frequently called a push-down stack, because its operation is similar to the operation of the spring loaded plate dispensers often found in a cafeteria. (With this device, you can take the top plate off a stack of plates and the next plate will pop up ready to be dispensed. If you put a plate on top of the stack of plates, the weight of the plates will push the spring down, so that the top plate is level with the dispensing surface.) Thanks to this analogy, the operations of adding and removing items on a stack have been called *pushing* and *popping* the stack.

To allocate sections of main memory on a stack, the sections of memory must meet two requirements:

1. any section of memory to be de-allocated must be on the top of the stack, and

2. once allocated, a section of memory may not change in size.

The global and local variables of a Pascal program meet these requirements; therefore, they may be stored on a stack.

The Run-Time Stack   In the p-System, the global and local variables are allocated on a stack, called the *run-time* stack. The run-time stack is usually referred to as simply the STACK.

At the beginning of program execution, the system allocates the space to hold the global variables at the bottom of the STACK. This space remains allocated throughout the execution of the program. When a procedure is called, the system allocates the space to hold the local variables of the procedure on the top of the stack, above the global variables.

When the procedure is finished executing and the program returns to the caller, the system de-allocates, from the top of the STACK, the space used to hold the local variables for the procedure. Since there is no longer any use for the procedure's local variables, it is reasonable to de-allocate the space they occupy.

If several procedures call each other, then each time a procedure is called, the system allocates a new set of local variables on top of the STACK. Each time one of the procedures finishes executing and returns, the space used to hold its local variables is reclaimed from the top of the STACK. Let's look at an example.

Example of the Run-Time Stack   The program below contains procedures with local variables:

```
PROGRAM EXAMPLE ( INPUT, OUTPUT );

PROCEDURE ZZZ;
VAR
   ALPHA : INTEGER;
BEGIN
END;

PROCEDURE YYY;
VAR
   BETA : REAL;
BEGIN
END;

PROCEDURE XXX;
VAR
   GAMMA : BOOLEAN;
BEGIN
   YYY;
   ZZZ;
END;

BEGIN
   XXX
END.
```

We will now step through the execution of this program and observe how the STACK grows and shrinks with each procedure.

The p-System maintains the *stack pointer* variable to control the allocation of the memory on the stack. The stack pointer points to the top of the STACK. Space is allocated above the stack pointer, and the stack pointer is moved to point to the memory location at the top of the newly allocated space. Space is de-allocated by moving the stack pointer down. Then, the next allocation will reuse the de-allocated space. At the start of the program, the stack is empty. First, space is allocated for the global variables. Then the stack pointer is moved up to point to the top of the global variables. This is illustrated below:

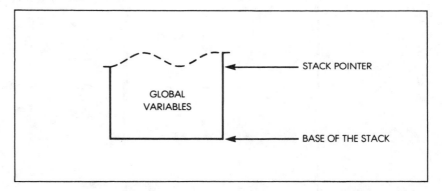

As the program executes, the first statement is a procedure call to procedure XXX. Procedure XXX has local variables. Space for these local variables is allocated on the STACK, above the global variables, and the stack pointer is moved to point to the top. The STACK now looks like this:

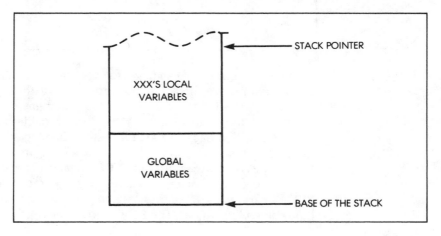

Then execution of procedure XXX begins. The first statement in procedure XXX is a procedure call to procedure YYY. Procedure YYY also contains local variables. So the system allocates space for the local variables of procedure YYY on the STACK above the local variables for procedure XXX and moves the stack pointer to the top of the stack. The STACK now looks like this:

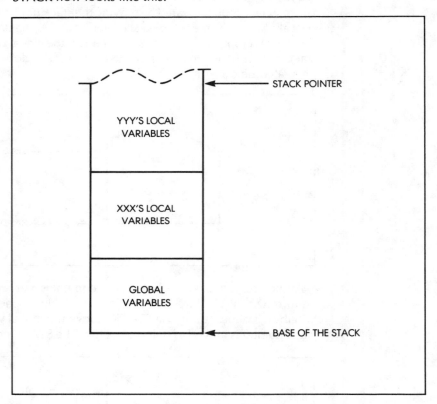

Then procedure YYY can begin to execute. When all the statements in the body of YYY have executed, control returns to the statement following the call of YYY—in this case, to the second statement in procedure XXX. There is no longer any use for YYY's local variables. Therefore, before control is passed back to XXX, the system de-allocates the space on the STACK that held YYY's local variables by moving the stack pointer down to point just below the bottom of YYY's local variables. Moving the stack pointer does not change the values of the memory locations that held YYY's local variables. But these memory locations may now be reused to hold some other values. The STACK now looks like this:

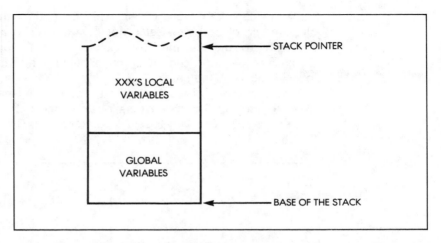

Execution continues in procedure XXX. The next statement in procedure XXX is a call to procedure ZZZ. Procedure ZZZ also contains local variables which must be allocated on the STACK. The system allocates space for the local variables for procedure ZZZ in the same memory locations that were used for the local variables of procedure YYY. The STACK now looks like this:

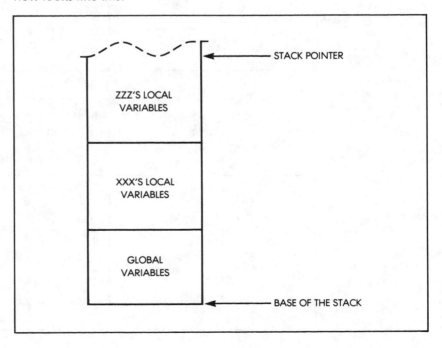

If procedure YYY were called again later, then the system would allocate space for a new set of local variables. Local variables don't necessarily use the same memory locations each time a procedure is called. Because of this, a procedure cannot expect to find the old values of its local variables on the next call.

The statements of procedure ZZZ are executed and then control returns to procedure XXX. The system de-allocates space for the local variables of procedure ZZZ by moving the stack pointer down. The STACK now looks like this:

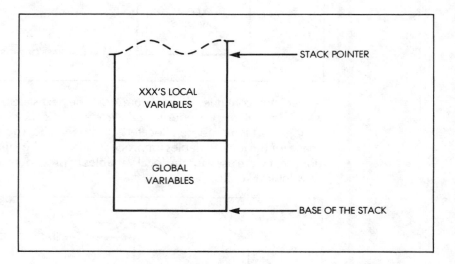

We now find that we are at the end of procedure XXX. Control returns to the main program. The system moves the stack pointer down to the "top" of the global variables, effectively de-allocating the memory space that had been reserved for XXX's local variables. The STACK now looks like this:

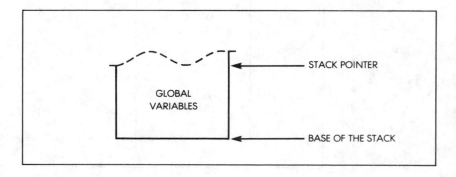

Back in the main program, the next statement is a procedure call to procedure ZZZ. Before the procedure can begin executing, the space must be allocated for the local variables. The local variables are allocated on the top of the STACK, and the stack pointer is moved up, as usual. The STACK now looks like this:

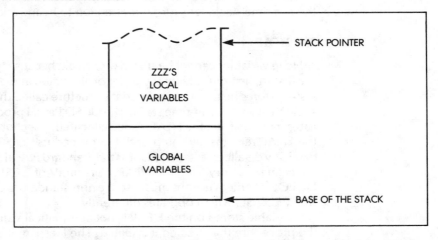

Note that the local variables of procedure ZZZ are now in a different location on the STACK than they were the last time ZZZ was called. In fact, they are now stored in the same locations that the local variables from procedure XXX were stored. This does not cause a problem since XXX no longer needs the variables. Procedure ZZZ knows where to find its local variables, because when they are allocated, they will always be on the top of the STACK.

Procedure ZZZ now executes using its local variables in their current positions on the STACK. When it has finished executing, ZZZ de-allocates those variables from the STACK and returns to the main program. The STACK is then in the configuration shown below:

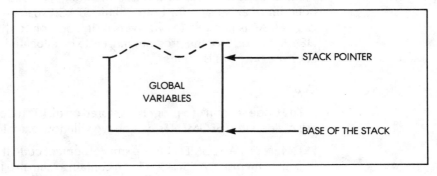

Since the procedure call of XXX was the only statement in the main program, the program is now finished. Before control returns to the operating system, the system de-allocates the global variables, thus leaving an empty STACK.

Now that we have seen how local and global variables are allocated on the run-time stack, let's turn our attention to heap variables.

The HEAP

Heap variables cannot be stored on a stack, because they do not follow the first-in, first-out rule for the order of allocation and de-allocation. The system stores heap variables in a data structure called the HEAP, which is separate from the run-time stack. The UCSD Pascal procedure NEW allocates memory from the HEAP. Once allocated, a section of memory from the HEAP remains allocated until the procedures DISPOSE or RELEASE explicitly de-allocate it. (DISPOSE is the Standard Pascal procedure for de-allocating memory from the HEAP. Version IV of UCSD Pascal includes DISPOSE. Earlier versions must use the non-standard UCSD Pascal extension RELEASE, which operates differently.)

A variable stored on the HEAP is not automatically de-allocated when the procedure that created it is exited. The lifespan of a heap variable is under the control of the program. This is both useful and dangerous. For example, if you forget to de-allocate the heap variables after you are done with them, and continue to allocate more, you will quickly exhaust the memory space.

Now let's see where the STACK and HEAP are allocated in main memory.

Main Memory Allocation

The STACK and the HEAP start at opposite ends of the free space in main memory, as shown in Figure 6.4. Both the STACK and the HEAP can dynamically expand and contract during program execution. By placing them at opposite ends of the free memory, you allow for the greatest freedom of expansion for both. If little STACK space is required, then a large HEAP is possible (or vice versa). In addition to the STACK and the HEAP, the code for the program must also be allocated in main memory. Let's see how this is done.

Code

The Code section of a program is stored on disk in a Code file. Code files are divided into SEGMENTs, which we will now examine.

SEGMENTs   A SEGMENT is the smallest unit of code that can be loaded into main memory. A SEGMENT can contain a main program, a SEGMENT

PROCEDURE, a SEGMENT FUNCTION or a UNIT. SEGMENTs are swapped in and out of main memory as needed. We have already discussed two of the four types of SEGMENTs: main programs and UNITs. We will now look at SEGMENT PROCEDUREs and SEGMENT FUNCTIONs.

SEGMENT PROCEDUREs and SEGMENT FUNCTIONs allow a program to specify how it is divided into SEGMENTs. SEGMENT PROCEDUREs and SEGMENT FUNCTIONs are UCSD Pascal extensions to Standard Pascal. These extensions let you place a procedure or function in a separate SEG-MENT. Ordinary procedures and functions are included in the main program SEGMENT. Because SEGMENT PROCEDURES are in their own SEGMENTs, independent of the main program SEGMENT, the system can load them into memory independently from the main program. Only those SEGMENTs needed at a particular moment have to be in memory; unused SEGMENTs can remain on disk. This economizes on the use of main memory space.

When a program begins to execute, its SEGMENT PROCEDUREs are not in main memory. When a SEGMENT PROCEDURE is called, the system loads into main memory from disk the SEGMENT that contains the SEGMENT PROCEDURE, and the SEGMENT PROCEDURE begins to execute. When the SEGMENT PROCEDURE has finished executing, the system can then ''remove'' the SEGMENT from main memory by using the space it occupies.

(*Note:* the main program SEGMENT and the SEGMENTs holding UNITs are generally loaded into main memory at the start of the program. These

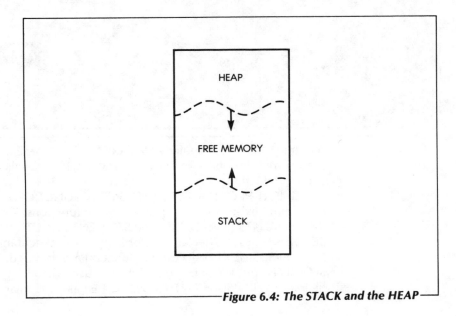

Figure 6.4: The STACK and the HEAP

SEGMENTs usually remain in main memory while the program executes. Normally, only the SEGMENTs that hold SEGMENT PROCEDUREs and SEGMENT FUNCTIONs are swapped. Check your system's documentation for details on your version of the p-System.)

Now let's specify SEGMENT PROCEDUREs and SEGMENT FUNCTIONs in a program.

Example of SEGMENT PROCEDUREs SEGMENT PROCEDUREs and SEGMENT FUNCTIONs are written exactly like regular procedures and functions, except that the reserved word, SEGMENT, precedes the word FUNCTION or PROCEDURE. Here is an example of a SEGMENT PROCEDURE:

```
SEGMENT PROCEDURE READARRAY ( VAR DATA : DATARRAY; NAME : FILENAME );

VAR
    X, Y : INTEGER;
    DATAFILE : TEXT;

BEGIN
    RESET ( DATAFILE, NAME );
    FOR X := 1 TO XSIZE
        DO
            FOR Y := 1 TO YSIZE
                DO
                    READLN ( DATAFILE, DATA [X, Y] );
    CLOSE ( DATAFILE )
END;
```

Assuming that the identifiers DATARRAY, FILENAME, XSIZE and YSIZE are all properly defined in the main program, this is a valid SEGMENT procedure definition.

SEGMENT PROCEDURES and SEGMENT FUNCTIONS have restrictions that do not exist with other procedures or functions. For example, all of the SEGMENT PROCEDURES and SEGMENT FUNCTIONS in a particular SEGMENT must be declared *before* any of the executable statements of any non-SEGMENT procedure or function are declared. This means that SEGMENT PROCEDURE definitions must precede other procedure definitions. If a SEGMENT PROCEDURE calls a regular procedure, the regular procedure must have appeared in a FOREWARD declaration, prior to the SEGMENT PROCEDURE definition. The actual body of the regular procedure must appear after all the SEGMENT PROCEDURES.

Now that we have seen how the SEGMENTs are swapped in and out of main memory, let's examine how the memory for the SEGMENTs is allocated.

Code Pool   The CODE POOL is the section of main memory that contains the currently loaded SEGMENTs. A SEGMENT cannot be executed unless it is loaded into the CODE POOL.

The CODE POOL is managed in two different ways depending on the version of UCSD used. Version IV.0 uses a different technique than the previous versions.

Versions of the System   In Version IV of UCSD, the system keeps the CODE POOL separate from the STACK and HEAP. The CODE POOL is located between the STACK and the HEAP (see Figure 6.5). When the system loads a new SEGMENT into the CODE POOL, it puts it at either end of the CODE POOL.

If either the STACK or the HEAP tries to expand into the area of memory used by the CODE POOL, the system can move the CODE POOL to the

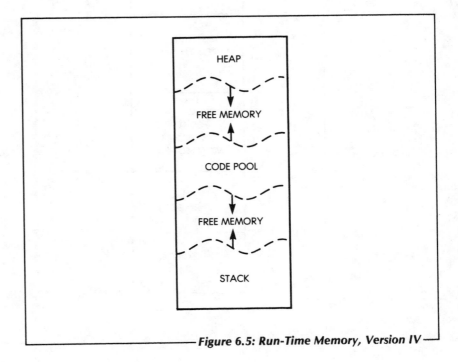

HEAP

FREE MEMORY

CODE POOL

FREE MEMORY

STACK

Figure 6.5: Run-Time Memory, Version IV

side, thus, allowing more space. If there is not enough room available to move the CODE POOL and leave a large enough free space, then the part of the CODE POOL not being used can be discarded. In fact, if space is in short supply, only the SEGMENT that is currently executing needs to be in the CODE POOL.

In versions of the p-System prior to Version IV, the CODE SEGMENTs are *not* stored in a CODE POOL between the STACK and the HEAP. They are stored on the STACK.

When a procedure is called that is in a different SEGMENT than the caller's SEGMENT, the system reads in the new SEGMENT from disk and loads it onto the STACK. It then allocates the local variables for the SEGMENT procedure. At that point, the STACK looks like this:

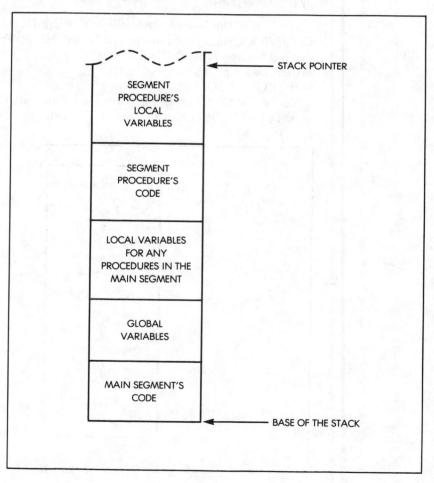

When control returns from the procedure in the "different" SEGMENT, the system de-allocates the space on the STACK that holds the code for the SEGMENT. This provides for a first-in, first-out allocation of SEGMENTs, similar to the first-in, first-out allocation of local variables.

The Version IV method generates more free space, since it is not necessary to keep any SEGMENTs, except the one currently executing, in memory. In the earlier versions, the main SEGMENT must *always* be in memory, and any nested SEGMENTs must remain in memory while the innermost SEGMENT executes. The more segments kept in memory, the less SEGMENT swapping from disk, while the program is running. The program runs faster, but there is less memory space available for the STACK and the HEAP. If more space is needed for the STACK and HEAP, then the program must sacrifice speed for space and keep fewer SEGMENTs in memory.

We have now seen how memory is managed at run-time by the p-System. Let's use this information to make large programs run in a small amount of space.

Reducing Data Memory Size

UCSD provides two methods for reducing the data memory requirements of a program: local variables and packed data structures.

Local Variables   You can reduce the data memory requirements of a program by making extensive use of local variables. If you use local variables, all the data does not need to be in main memory at the same time. As we have seen, this technique also reduces the symbol table requirements during compilation. This is the most important technique for reducing main memory requirements.

PACKED Data   In addition to being able to control when the data is in main memory, you can also control the size of the data for some types of data. UCSD Pascal provides a mechanism for reducing the size of certain types of data. This method is called PACKING. UCSD Pascal allows the reserved word PACKED to appear in a type specification for a FILE, ARRAY or RECORD. If you specify that the data is PACKED, the compiler will use the minimum amount of main memory to hold each of the components of the FILE, ARRAY or RECORD. If your program uses large data structures, packing may save a significant amount of main memory space.

Now that we know two ways to reduce the memory requirements of the data section of a program, let's examine some techniques for reducing the memory requirements of the code section of a program.

Reducing Code Memory Size

You can run a large amount of code in a small space by dividing it into small pieces with the SEGMENT feature. However, this step should be your last attempt at squeezing a large program into a small machine, because it greatly affects the performance of the program. The more you divide your program, the slower it runs.

The key to the successful division of a program is independence between the sections of the program. If the sections are independent, then they can be divided into SEGMENTs, and only a few segments need to be in main memory at any time. This saves much memory space. However, if the sections of the program are all dependent on each other, then you can save only a little memory space, since several SEGMENTs must be in main memory at a time.

The structure of your program is critical to the SEGMENTing process. If it uses five or six big procedures, each containing forty or fifty little procedures, then the task is simple. The big procedures become SEGMENT PROCEDUREs that contain forty or fifty little procedures. As long as the code in one SEGMENT does not call the code in other SEGMENTs, you can significantly reduce memory usage.

If, on the other hand, your program has two or three hundred little procedures that call each other in an unstructured manner, your task is more difficult. Probably the best thing to do is to start over and rewrite the program from the beginning with SEGMENTS in mind.

A significant fact about the run-time memory usage in all versions of the p-System is that *all* the memory is shared; it is traded between the STACK, the HEAP and the CODE POOL, as necessary. As a consequence, you can often solve a problem in memory allocation in one area by reducing the memory requirements in another.

SUMMARY

In this chapter, we have examined several features of the p-System and the UCSD Pascal compiler. We have seen how the compiler processes INCLUDE FILES and UNITs; how it manages the symbol table; and how programs manage main memory at run-time. We have also learned how to structure programs so that they make efficient use of symbol table space at compile-time and main memory space at run-time.

Armed with the techniques learned in this chapter, you should now be able to run many large Pascal programs on your computer system using the p-System. Good luck in your programming ventures!

APPENDIX **A**

DISK VOLUME SIZES

Disk Type	Number of Blocks	System
Single density soft-sectored 8″ floppy	494 blocks	CP/M DEC Terak
Double density soft-sectored 8″ floppy	1102 blocks 988 blocks	NorthWest Micro DEC
Single density hard-sectored 8″ floppy	608 blocks	Zilog
Single density soft-sectored 5¼″ floppy	280 blocks	Apple
Single density hard-sectored 5¼″ floppy	168 blocks	NorthStar
RK05 Disk pack	4872 blocks	DEC

APPENDIX **B**

SYSTEM CONFIGURATION

System configuration is the process of tailoring the p-System software to work with the hardware on a specific computer system. Information about this process is stored in a data file, called SYSTEM.MISCINFO. When the p-System is booted-up, the operating system reads this file and stores the values of the system parameters in main memory. Changing the values in this file changes the configuration of the system. System parameters included in this file describe: the character codes to invoke the CRT functions, the keys to invoke the p-System functions, and some parameters of the CPU.

There are three steps to configuring a system. The first is to boot the system. If your system does not boot initially, you may have to write a bootstrap loader and/or an I/O package to get it to boot. This procedure is beyond the scope of this book and should be attempted by only the very experienced user. Most systems will not require this task.

The second step in the configuration process is to run a program called SETUP. SETUP is a p-System utility that creates a file, called NEW.MISCINFO. This file is a new version of the file SYSTEM.MISCINFO. You then rename the NEW.MISCINFO file SYSTEM.MISCINFO, to complete this stage of the configuraton.

The third step is to write a GOTOXY routine and bind it to the system. A GOTOXY routine is a Pascal procedure that moves the terminal's cursor to a specified location on the screen. Most terminals have a special character code that will do this. Others do not; but you can simulate this effect with other cursor control functions. You must create, compile and bind your GOTOXY routine before you can use the screen oriented editor. (*Note:* the system comes with a GOTOXY routine already bound in place. If this is the proper routine for your terminal, then you can skip this step.)

We will begin by assuming that you have your system booted up and are ready to start with step two: running SETUP.

SETUP

SETUP is a program stored in the file SETUP.CODE. You execute SETUP by using the EXECUTE command. Type X to invoke the EXECUTE command. Then type SETUP, and press RETURN:

Exécute what file? **SETUP**⟩

After initialization, SETUP displays the following prompt:

SETUP: C(HANGE) T(EACH) H(ELP) Q(UIT) ☐

There are four commands available in SETUP. CHANGE allows you to change the values of the various system parameters. TEACH offers a short explanation of how to perform the SETUP process. HELP displays a description of each command. QUIT terminates the SETUP program.

We want to change the values associated with the system. Type C to select the CHANGE command. The following prompt appears:

CHANGE: S(INGLE) P(ROMPTED) R(ADIX) H(ELP) Q(UIT) ☐

The SINGLE command allows you to change the value of a single parameter. PROMPTED prompts you for all the values and allows you to change or leave each one. RADIX allows you to change the default radix that you use to enter values; you can set the default radix to octal, hexadecimal or decimal. The HELP command, again, displays a description of the various commands available here.

We want to use the PROMPTED command to reconfigure the system. Press P to select the PROMPTED command. SETUP displays the prompt for the first value:

FIELD NAME = BACKSPACE

OCTAL	DECIMAL	HEXADECIMAL	ASCII	CONTROL
10	8	8	BS	^H

WANT TO CHANGE THIS VALUE? (Y,N,!) ☐

This display shows the current setting of the character code that is sent to the terminal to cause the cursor to move one space to the left. The value is displayed in five different formats. You are now given the option of changing this value. There are three possible responses to this prompt. Typing Y causes the system to prompt for a new value for this parameter. Typing N causes the value to remain unchanged. Typing ! (exclamation point) causes the value to remain unchanged and the system to return to the CHANGE prompt.

If your terminal uses a different character code for this function, type Y to change the value. SETUP will prompt with the following message:

NEW VALUE: ☐

In response to this prompt, you can type in a value in one of three formats:

- a number, in either octal, decimal or hexadecimal, that represents the ASCII character code for the value

- the ASCII abbreviation for the character

- the character itself.

SETUP will then display the new value in all five formats and prompt you for any change you may want to make.

Once you have entered the desired value, answer the prompt by typing N. The display for the next value will appear. Repeat this process for each parameter that SETUP prompts you for. Here is a list of these parameters, including a description of each parameter. (*Note:* different versions of the p-System have slightly different parameter lists. The parameter list for your system may differ slightly from the one listed here.)

BACKSPACE
> the code that is sent to the terminal to move the cursor one space to the left.

EDITOR ACCEPT KEY
> the key that you type to accept modifications in the editor (called ETX in this book).

EDITOR ESCAPE KEY
> the key that you type to abort modifications in the editor (called ESCAPE in this book).

ERASE LINE
> the code sent to the terminal to erase a line.

ERASE SCREEN
the code sent to the terminal to erase the screen.

ERASE TO END OF LINE
the code sent to the terminal to erase from the current cursor position to the end of the line.

ERASE TO END OF SCREEN
the code sent to the terminal to erase from the current cursor position to the end of the screen.

HAS 8510A
TRUE, if your computer is a Terak 8510a.

HAS BYTE FLIPPED MACHINE
TRUE, if the byte address of the low order half of a word is different from the word address; FALSE, for machines with PDP-11, LSI-11, 8080, Z80, 8086, 8088, and 6502 processors; TRUE, for machines with 6800, 9900 and GA440 processors.

HAS CLOCK
TRUE, if there is a clock in the system from which the p-System can read the time of day. If this is set TRUE and there is no clock in the system, the compiler will have a run-time error as it attempts to calculate the number of lines compiled per minute.

HAS LOWER CASE
TRUE, if the terminal can display lower case characters.

HAS RANDOM CURSOR ADDRESSING
TRUE, if the terminal supports mechanism for rapidly moving the cursor to any specified location on the screen (GOTOXY).

HAS SLOW TERMINAL
TRUE, if you do not want alot of output sent to the terminal, normally FALSE.

HAS WORD ORIENTED MACHINE
TRUE, if successive addresses refer to different words; FALSE, if they refer to different bytes in a word.

KEY FOR BREAK
>   the key that you type to stop a program that is running.

KEY FOR FLUSH
>   the key that you type to cause all the output to the console to be discarded, rather than displayed.

KEY FOR STOP
>   the key that you type to suspend and restart the output to the console.

KEY TO ALPHA LOCK
>   the key that you type to enable or disable the input of lower case characters from the console.

KEY TO DELETE CHARACTER
>   the key that you type to backspace over a character that is in error.

KEY TO DELETE LINE
>   the key that you type to backspace over an entire line that is in error.

KEY TO END FILE
>   the key that you type to signal that the console is in an end of file state.

KEY TO MOVE CURSOR DOWN
>   the key that you type to move the cursor down a line in the editor.

KEY TO MOVE CURSOR LEFT
>   the key that you type to move the cursor left a space in the editor.

KEY TO MOVE CURSOR RIGHT
>   the key that you type to move the cursor right a space in the editor.

KEY TO MOVE CURSOR UP
>   the key that you type to move the cursor up a line in the editor.

LEAD IN FROM KEYBOARD
> the code that the terminal sends as a prefix to any special function keys.

LEAD IN TO SCREEN
> the code that precedes special function codes sent to the terminal.

MOVE CURSOR HOME
> the code that causes the terminal to move the cursor to the upper left corner of the screen.

MOVE CURSOR RIGHT
> the code that causes the terminal to move the cursor one space to the right.

MOVE CURSOR UP
> the code that causes the terminal to move the cursor one line up.

NON PRINTING CHARACTER
> the character displayed to show that there is a non-printable character in a file.

PREFIX [EDITOR ACCEPT KEY]
> TRUE, if there is a lead-in character generated by the terminal when you push the editor accept key.

PREFIX [EDITOR ESCAPE KEY]
> TRUE, if there is a lead-in character generated by the terminal when you push the editor escape key.

PREFIX [ERASE LINE]
> TRUE, if there is a lead-in character needed on the code that is sent to the terminal, that erases a line.

PREFIX [ERASE SCREEN]
> TRUE, if there is a lead-in character needed on the code that is sent to the terminal, that erases the screen.

PREFIX [ERASE TO END OF LINE]
> TRUE, if there is a lead-in character needed on the code that is sent to the terminal, that erases to the end of a line.

PREFIX [ERASE TO END OF SCREEN]
> TRUE, if there is a lead-in character needed on the code that is sent to the terminal, that erases to the end of the screen.

PREFIX [KEY TO DELETE CHARACTER]
> TRUE, if there is a lead-in character generated by the terminal when you push the delete character key.

PREFIX [KEY TO DELETE LINE]
> TRUE, if there is a lead-in character generated by the terminal when you push the delete line key.

PREFIX [KEY TO MOVE CURSOR DOWN]
> TRUE, if there is a lead-in character generated by the terminal when you push the key to move the cursor down.

PREFIX [KEY TO MOVE CURSOR LEFT]
> TRUE, if there is a lead-in character generated by the terminal when you push the key to move the cursor left.

PREFIX [KEY TO MOVE CURSOR RIGHT]
> TRUE, if there is a lead-in character generated by the terminal when you push the key to move the cursor right.

PREFIX [KEY TO MOVE CURSOR UP]
> TRUE, if there is a lead-in character generated by the terminal when you push the key to move the cursor up.

PREFIX [MOVE CURSOR HOME]
> TRUE, if there is a lead-in character needed on the code that is sent to the terminal, that moves the cursor to the upper left corner.

PREFIX [MOVE CURSOR RIGHT]
> TRUE, if there is a lead-in character needed on the code that is sent to the terminal, that moves the cursor one space to the right.

PREFIX [MOVE CURSOR UP]
> TRUE, if there is a lead-in character needed on the code that is sent to the terminal, that moves the cursor one line up.

PREFIX [NON PRINTING CHARACTER]
TRUE, if there is a lead-in character needed on the code that is sent to the terminal, which displays the symbol indicating a non-printable character.

SCREEN HEIGHT
the number of lines on the screen.

SCREEN WIDTH
the number of characters on a line of the screen.

STUDENT
TRUE if you are using a restricted mode of the operating system (usually FALSE).

VERTICAL MOVE DELAY
the length of time that the system must wait after moving the cursor, before sending the next command (the number of null characters to send after a cursor move).

The p-System allows single character or two character sequences for most of the terminal functions. If you use a two character sequence, the first character is called the lead-in character. The lead-in character signals that the next character is a special function. If your terminal uses a lead-in character in the code for one or more of the functions listed previously, then you must enter the value of the lead-in character in the LEAD-IN FROM KEYBOARD or LEAD-IN TO SCREEN parameter. Then, all the parameters that use a lead-in character should be set to the value of the second character in the sequence, and the PREFIX [ ] parameter that corresponds to the parameter should be set to TRUE. The PREFIX [ ] parameters are set to FALSE if the corresponding parameter is a single character code.

After SETUP has prompted you for all of these parameters, and you have changed them to correspond to your hardware configuration, it is time to SAVE the configuration and exit SETUP.

Type Q to quit the CHANGE command. The SETUP prompt appears again:

SETUP: C(HANGE) T(EACH) H(ELP) Q(UIT) ☐

Now type Q again to select the QUIT command of SETUP. The QUIT prompt appears:

QUIT: D(ISK) OR M(EMORY) UPDATE, R(ETURN) H(ELP) E(XIT) ☐

There are five options on this prompt. DISK UPDATE writes the new values out to the file NEW.MISCINFO. MEMORY UPDATE changes the currently active system parameters to the new parameters that you have just created (until the next boot, when the values in SYSTEM.MISCINFO will be read in again). RETURN aborts the quit command and returns you to the SETUP prompt. HELP displays a description of the commands now available. EXIT terminates the SETUP program and returns the system to the COMMAND mode.

Now that you have created your new parameters, type M for a memory update, so that the new values will be used in the system. Type D to write the values out to a file, so that you can use them the next time you boot the system. Then type E to exit the program and return to the COMMAND mode.

You now have a file called NEW.MISCINFO. This file contains the values of the system parameters that are configured to your system. To actually install this file you must use the FILER to change its name to SYSTEM.MISCINFO.

The GOTOXY Procedure

The last step in configuring a system is to create and install the GOTOXY procedure. This procedure provides for the placement of the cursor at any location on the screen. This feature varies widely between terminals; therefore, the p-System implements it as a procedure.

Your terminal's documentation offers precise instructions on which characters must be sent to the terminal, in order to move the cursor to any location. You must write a Pascal procedure that outputs the characters, given X and Y coordinates of the location as parameters.

The exact format of the procedure varies with the type of terminal you are using. The sequence of steps necessary for binding this procedure to the system varies with the different versions of the p-System. The newer versions of the p-System use the librarian to insert a UNIT containing the GOTOXY procedure into the system library. Earlier versions use a special utility called a binder, that links the procedure with the operating system's code. Consult your documentation to learn how to bind the GOTOXY routine for your system.

APPENDIX **C**
PASCAL COMPILER ERROR MESSAGES

1: Error in simple type
2: Identifier expected
3: Unimplemented error
4: ')' expected
5: ': ' expected
6: Illegal symbol (terminator expected)
7: Error in parameter list
8: 'OF' expected
9: '(' expected
10: Error in type
11: '' expected
13: 'END' expected
14: ';' expected
15: Integer expected
16: '=' expected
17: 'BEGIN' expected
18: Error in declaration part
19: Error in <field-list>
20: '.' expected
21: '*' expected
22: 'INTERFACE' expected
23: 'IMPLEMENTATION' expected
24: 'UNIT' expected

50: Error in constant
51: ': =' expected
52: 'THEN' expected
53: 'UNTIL' expected
54: 'DO' expected

55: 'TO' or 'DOWNTO' expected in for statement
56: 'IF' expected
57: 'FILE' expected
58: Error in <factor> (bad expression)
59: Error in variable

60: Must be of type 'SEMAPHORE'
61: Must be of type 'PROCESSID'
62: Process not allowed at this nesting level
63: Only main task may start processes

101: Identifier declared twice
102: Low bound exceeds high bound
103: Identifier is not of the appropriate class
104: Undeclared identifier
105: Sign not allowed
106: Number expected
107: Incompatible subrange types
108: File not allowed here
109: Type must not be real
110: <tagfield> type must be scalar or subrange
111: Incompatible with <tagfield> part
112: Index type must not be real
113: Index type must be a scalar or a subrange
114: Base type must not be real
115: Base type must be a scalar or a subrange
116: Error in type of standard procedure parameter
117: Unsatisfied forward reference
118: Forward reference type identifier in variable declaration
119: Re-specified params not OK for a forward declared procedure
120: Function result type must be scalar, subrange or pointer
121: File value parameter not allowed
122: A forward declared function's result type can't be re-specified
123: Missing result type in function declaration
124: F-format for reals only
125: Error in type of standard procedure parameter
126: Number of parameters does not agree with declaration
127: Illegal parameter substitution
128: Result type does not agree with declaration
129: Type conflict of operands

130:    Expression is not of set type
131:    Tests on equality allowed only
132:    Strict inclusion not allowed
133:    File comparison not allowed
134:    Illegal type of operand(s)
135:    Type of operand must be Boolean
136:    Set element type must be scalar or subrange
137:    Set element types must be compatible
138:    Type of variable is not array
139:    Index type is not compatible with the declaration
140:    Type of variable is not record
141:    Type of variable must be file or pointer
142:    Illegal parameter solution
143:    Illegal type of loop control variable
144:    Illegal type of expression
145:    Type conflict
146:    Assignment of files not allowed
147:    Label type incompatible with selecting expression
148:    Subrange bounds must be scalar
149:    Index type must be integer

150:    Assignment to standard function is not allowed
151:    Assignment to formal function is not allowed
152:    No such field in this record
153:    Type error in read
154:    Actual parameter must be a variable
155:    Control variable cannot be formal or non-local
156:    Multidefined case label
157:    Too many cases in case statement
158:    No such variant in this record
159:    Real or string tagfields not allowed
160:    Previous declaration was not forward
161:    Again forward declared
162:    Parameter size must be constant
163:    Missing variant in declaration
164:    Substitution of standard proc/func not allowed
165:    Multidefined label
166:    Multideclared label
167:    Undeclared label
168:    Undefined label
169:    Error in base set
170:    Value parameter expected

171: Standard file was re-declared
172: Undeclared external file
173: FORTRAN procedure or function expected
174: Pascal function or procedure expected
175: Semaphore value parameter not allowed

182: Nested UNITs not allowed
183: External declaration not allowed at this nesting level
184: External declaration not allowed in INTERFACE section
185: Segment declaration not allowed in INTERFACE section
186: Labels not allowed in INTERFACE section
187: Attempt to open library unsuccessful
188: UNIT not declared in previous uses declaration
189: 'USES' not allowed at this nesting level
190: UNIT not in library
191: Forward declaration was not segment
192: Foward declaration was segment
193: Not enough room for this operation
194: Flag must be declared at top of program
195: Unit not importable

201: Error in real number—digit expected
202: String constant must not exceed source line
203: Integer constant exceeds range
204: 8 or 9 in octal number
250: Too many scopes of nested identifiers
251: Too many nested procedures or functions
252: Too many forward references of procedure entries
253: Procedure too long
254: Too many long constants in this procedure
256: Too many external references
257: Too many externals
258: Too many local files
259: Expression too complicated

300: Division by zero
301: No case provided for this value
302: Index expression out of bounds
303: Value to be assigned is out of bounds
304: Element expression out of range
398: Implementation restriction
399: Implementation restriction

400:    Illegal character in text
401:    Unexpected end of input
402:    Error in writing code file, not enough room
403:    Error in reading include file
404:    Error in writing list file, not enough room
405:    'PROGRAM' or 'UNIT' expected
406:    Include file not legal
407:    Include file nesting limit exceeded
408:    INTERFACE section not contained in one file
409:    Unit name reserved for system
410:    Disk error

500:    Assembler error

APPENDIX **D**

RUN-TIME ERROR MESSAGES

0   System error   ... FATAL
1   Invalid index, value out of range
2   No segment, bad code file
3   Procedure not present at exit time
4   Stack overflow
5   Integer overflow
6   Divide by zero
7   Invalid memory reference <bus timed out>
8   User break
9   System I/O error   ... FATAL
10 User I/O error
11 Unimplemented instruction
12 Floating point math error
13 String too long
14 Halt, Breakpoint
15 Bad Block

All runtime errors cause the System to I(nitialize itself; FATAL errors cause the System to re-bootstrap. Some FATAL errors leave the System in an irreparable state, in which case the user must re-bootstrap by hand.

APPENDIX **E**

THE LIBRARIAN

This appendix shows you how to use the p-System librarian utility. The *librarian* is a program that combines compiled SEGMENTs from various code files into a library file, which can then be linked with your compiled main programs. You can use the librarian to construct libraries of SEGMENTs that you can use with different application programs. If you add SEGMENTs to the system library, then you can automatically compile, link, and run programs that use these SEGMENTs, by using the RUN command.

In this appendix, we will create a new library that consists of an existing system library, plus an additional SEGMENT. We can use this same procedure to create an entirely new library.

Note that the displays that appear on your screen may differ from those shown here, depending on the versions of the p-System, the librarian, and the system library you are using. But, in any case, all the displays should be very similar, and you should be able to follow along easily.

Using the Librarian

The librarian is stored in the file LIBRARY.CODE. There is no *single letter* command that will invoke the librarian—you must use the EXECUTE command.

Type X to invoke the EXECUTE command. Then type the librarian's file name, without the suffix LIBRARY, and press RETURN:

Execute what file? **LIBRARY**

(*Note:* If this file is not on the prefix volume, you must precede it with a volume specification.)

The librarian program begins to execute. The screen displays:

```
Pascal System Librarian [II.0]




Output code file --> ☐
```

The librarian is asking for the name of the library file that it will create. To add a SEGMENT to the system library, you would type in SYSTEM.LIBRARY in response to the prompt. To create a new library, you would type in the name of the new library, in response to the prompt. In this example, we will add a SEGMENT to the system library.

Type in SYSTEM.LIBRARY, and press RETURN. The screen displays:

```
Pascal System Librarian [II.0]



Link Code File --> ☐



Output code file --> SYSTEM.LIBRARY
Code file length -- 1
```

The librarian opens the new file and displays its current length. It then asks for the name of the file that contains the SEGMENTs you want it to read into the library file. Note that whenever you add a SEGMENT to an existing library, the first file to be read in is the old version of the library:

Type in SYSTEM.LIBRARY, and press RETURN. The screen responds by displaying a map showing the contents of the file SYSTEM.LIBRARY:

```
Segment # to link and <space>, N(ew file, Q(uit, A(bort

□


Link Code File --> SYSTEM.LIBRARY
  0--              0    4--SCONTROL 2202    8--         0   12--       0
  1--PASCALIO   1824    5--            0     9--         0   13--       0
  2--DECOPS     2092    6--            0    10--         0   14--       0
  3--EDITORUN     16    7--            0    11--         0   15--       0


Output code file --> SYSTEM.LIBRARY
Code file length -- 1
```

This map gives alot of information about the library. Note that there are a maximum of 16 SEGMENTs in the library, numbered from 0 to 15 (in this version of the p-System) and that this SYSTEM.LIBRARY file uses four of them. SEGMENT 0 is always reserved for the SEGMENT that contains the main program. In this library, there is no main program, so this SEGMENT is empty. The SEGMENTs 1 through 4 contain the SEGMENTs that comprise this library—the name and length of each SEGMENT is shown.

Adding a SEGMENT

To add a SEGMENT to the library, we must first put all the old SEGMENTs into the new library. Some versions of the p-System have a command in the librarian that will transfer all the SEGMENTs from the link file to the output file. The version shown here, however, does not have this convenient feature, so we must transfer the SEGMENTs one by one.

To transfer a SEGMENT to the output file, type the number of the SEGMENT in the link file. For this example, type 1 for the SEGMENT called PASCALIO. The number appears near the top of the screen:

Segment # to link and <space>, N(ew file, Q(uit, A(bort

1☐

Link Code file --> SYSTEM. LIBRARY

0--	0	4--SCONTROL	2202	8--	0	12--	0
1--PASCALIO	1824	5--		9--	0	13--	0
2--DECOPS	2092	6--		10--	0	14--	0
3--EDITORUN	16	7--		11--	0	15--	0

Output code file --> SYSTEM.LIBRARY
Code file length -- 1

After typing the number of the SEGMENT in the link file, press the space bar. The librarian then asks for the number of the SEGMENT in the output file into which it should place this SEGMENT:

Segment # to link and <space>, N(ew file, Q(uit, A(bort

Seg to link into? ☐

Link Code File --> SYSTEM.LIBRARY

0--	0	4--SCONTROL	2202	8--	0	12--	0
1--PASCALIO	1824	5--		9--	0	13--	0
2--DECOPS	2092	6--		10--	0	14--	0
3--EDITORUN	16	7--		11--	0	15--	0

Output code file --> SYSTEM.LIBRARY
Code file length -- 1

Type in the SEGMENT number that the SEGMENT will have in the output file. In this example, we will give each SEGMENT the same SEGMENT number in the new file, that it had in the old file.

Type 1 and then press the space bar. The librarian then copies the SEGMENT to the output file and displays the map of the output file:

Segment # to link and <space>, N(ew file, Q(uit, A(bort

Seg to link into? **1**

Link Code File --> SYSTEM.LIBRARY

0	0	4--SCONTROL	2202	8--	0	12--	0
1--PASCALIO	1824	5--	0	9--	0	13--	0
2--DECOPS	2092	6--	0	10--	0	14--	0
3--EDITORUN	16	7--	0	11--	0	15--	0

Output code file --> SYSTEM.LIBRARY
Code file length -- 8

0	0	4--	0	8--	0	12--	0
1--PASCALIO	1824	5--	0	9--	0	13--	0
2--	0	6--	0	10--	0	14--	0
3--	0	7--	0	11--	0	15--	0

The output file now contains one SEGMENT. The file is 15 blocks long. The librarian is ready to transfer the next SEGMENT. Repeat this procedure to copy the three remaining SEGMENTs to the output file. When you have copied all four SEGMENTs, the screen displays the following:

Segment # to link and <space>, N(ew file, Q(uit, A(bort

☐

Link Code File --> SYSTEM.LIBRARY

0--	0	4--SCONTROL	2202	8--	0	12--	0
1--PASCALIO	1824	5--	0	9--	0	13--	0
2--DECOPS	2092	6--	0	10--	0	14--	0
3--EDITORUN	16	7--	0	11--	0	15--	0

Output code file --> SYSTEM.LIBRARY
Code file length -- 28

0--	0	4--SCONTROL	2202	8--	0	12--	0
1--PASCALIO	1824	5--	0	9--	0	13--	0
2--DECOPS	2092	6--	0	10--	0	14--	0
3--EDITORUN	16	7--	0	11--	0	15--	0

The output file is now a copy of the link file. Let's add a SEGMENT from a different file to our new output file. We must first establish a new link file.

Press N to invoke the NEW FILE command. The system prompts for the name of the new link file:

```
Segment # to link and <space>, N(ew file, Q(uit, A(bort


N


Link Code File --> ☐
  0--              0   4--SCONTROL   2202    8--          0   12--        0
  1--PASCALIO   1824   5--                0   9--          0   13--        0
  2--DECOPS     2092   6--                0  10--          0   14--        0
  3--EDITORUN     16   7--                0  11--          0   15--        0


Output code file --> SYSTEM.LIBRARY
Code file length -- 28
  0--              0   4--SCONTROL   2202    8--          0   12--        0
  1--PASCALIO   1824   5--                0   9--          0   13--        0
  2--DECOPS     2092   6--                0  10--          0   14--        0
  3--EDITORUN     16   7--                0  11--          0   15--        0
```

Type in the name of the file from which you wish to copy the SEGMENTs. In this example, we will copy the MATHUNIT SEGMENT from the file MATHUNIT.CODE.

Type the name MATHUNIT.CODE, and press RETURN. The following display appears:

Segment # to link and <space>, N(ew file, Q(uit, A(bort

☐

Link Code File --> **MATHUNIT.CODE**

0--	0	4--	0	8--	0	12--	0
1--	0	5--	0	9--	0	13--	0
2--	0	6--	0	10--MATHUNIT	38	14--	0
3--	0	7--	0	11--	0	15--	0

Output code file --> SYSTEM.LIBRARY
Code file length -- 28

0--	0	4--SCONTROL	2202	8--	0	12--	0
1--PASCALIO	1824	5--	0	9--	0	13--	0
2--DECOPS	2092	6--	0	10--	0	14--	0
3--EDITORUN	16	7--	0	11--	0	15--	0

We are now ready to add the new SEGMENT to the system library. Type the number 10, which is the number of the new SEGMENT, and press the space bar. The system prompts for the number of the SEGMENT in the output file to which it will copy:

Segment # to link and <space>, N(ew file, Q(uit, A(bort

Seg to link into? ☐

Link Code File --> MATHUNIT.CODE

0--	0	4--	0	8--	0	12--	0
1--	0	5--	0	9--	0	13--	0
2--	0	6--	0	10--MATHUNIT	38	14--	0
3--	0	7--	0	11--	0	15--	0

Output code file --> SYSTEM.LIBRARY
Code file length -- 28

0--	0	4--SCONTROL	2202	8--	0	12--	0
1--PASCALIO	1824	5--	0	9--	0	13--	0
2--DECOPS	2092	6--	0	10--	0	14--	0
3--EDITORUN	16	7--	0	11--	0	15--	0

For this example, we will put the new SEGMENT in slot 5—the lowest free SEGMENT slot available. Type the number, 5, and press the space bar. The librarian then adds the new SEGMENT to the system library:

```
Segment # to link and <space>, N(ew file, Q(uit, A(bort

Seg to link into? 5

Link Code file --> MATHUNIT.CODE
    0--            0   4--           0   8--            0   12--       0
    1--            0   5--           0   9--            0   13--       0
    2--            0   6--           0   10--MATHUNIT  38   14--       0
    3--            0   7--           0   11--           0   15--       0

Output code file --> SYSTEM.LIBRARY
Code file length -- 31
    0--            0   4--SCONTROL 2202   8--           0   12--       0
    1--PASCALIO 1824   5--MATHUNIT   38   9--           0   13--       0
    2--DECOPS   2092   6--           0   10--           0   14--       0
    3--EDITORUN   16   7--           0   11--           0   15--       0
```

Our new library, containing the previous SEGMENTs, plus one new SEGMENT, is complete. We will now finalize this new file and exit the librarian.

Type Q to invoke the QUIT command of the librarian. The librarian displays:

Segment # to link and <space>, N(ew file, Q(uit, A(bort

Q

Link Code file --> MATHUNIT.CODE

0--	0	4--	0	8--	0	12--	0
1--	0	5--	0	9--	0	13--	0
2--	0	6--	0	10--MATHUNIT	38	14--	0
3--	0	7--	0	11--	0	15--	0

Output code file --> SYSTEM.LIBRARY
Code file length -- 31

0--	0	4--SCONTROL	2202	8--	0	12--	0
1--PASCALIO	1824	5--MATHUNIT	38	9--	0	13--	0
2--DECOPS	2092	6--	0	10--	0	14--	0
3--EDITORUN	16	7--	0	11--	0	15--	0

Notice? ☐

This rather cryptic prompt is asking you to enter any copyright notice that you want want to include in the library. Each code file in the p-System contains a section that is reserved for a copyright notice. You can enter a copyright notice by typing the notice, followed by RETURN. If you do not want to enter a copyright notice, simply press RETURN. The librarian then closes the output file, and the system returns to the COMMAND mode:

```
Command: E(dit, R(un, F(ile, C(omp, L(ink, X(ecute, A(ssem, D(ebug, ? [II.0] □

Q


Link Code File --> MATHUNIT.CODE
    0--            0   4--              0   8--              0   12--          0
    1--            0   5--              0   9--              0   13--          0
    2--            0   6--              0   10--MATHUNIT    38   14--          0
    3--            0   7--              0   11--             0   15--          0
Output code file --> SYSTEM.LIBRARY
Code file length -- 31
    0--            0   4--SCONTROL   2202   8--              0   12--          0
    1--PASCALIO 1824   5--MATHUNIT     38   9--              0   13--          0
    2--DECOPS   2092   6--              0   10--             0   14--          0
    3--EDITORUN   16   7--              0   11--             0   15--          0

Notice? (c) 1982 by John Q. Public
```

Your new library file is now safely stored on disk. In some systems, you must re-boot the system after changing the system library file. If this is the case for the version of the p-System that you are using, then re-boot the system, and it will use your new library.

INDEX

ADJUST command, 25,
    141–143, 177
Apple Pascal, 13
Arrow keys, 115
Arrowheads, 203
ASSEMBLE command, 18
Assembler, 5, 7
Assembling, 7
Assembly language, 7
Asterisk, 13, 15, 30, 43–44
Auto-indent feature, 27, 130,
    156, 159–160, 182
Auxiliary prompt, 9
Backspace, 23, 26, 28, 33, 177,
    179
BACKSPACE key, 127, 129,
    131, 133, 186, 189
Backup, 77, 99
Bad block, 82, 86, 104
BAD BLOCKS command, 40,
    80–81, 86
BASIC, 7, 8, 18
Basic concepts, 1
BEGINNING, 123, 190
Bit, 2
Block, 44, 243, 245
Block structure, 243
Block structured volume, 13
Boot, 22
Booting, 13, 22
Bootstrap loading, 13
BUFFER, 138
Byte, 2
BYTES, 158, 183
Cathode Ray Tube (CRT), 4
Central Processing Unit (CPU), 2

CHANGE command, 13, 15,
    40, 60–61, 87
Code, 248, 256
Code file, 12, 14, 256
Code pool, 259
Colon, 13, 43–44
Comma, 179
COMMAND mode, 8, 10, 22,
    225, 229
COMMENT, 220
COMPILE command, 18, 31,
    34, 201–204, 209
Compile-time error, 215
Compiler, 5, 7, 202
Compiler directive, 211, 220
Compiling, 7
Components, 1
Console, 4
Copy, 70, 99
Copy buffer, 135, 138
COPY command, 25, 138–141,
    171, 175, 178
CP/M, 43
CPU, 2, 7
CRT, 4
CRT screen, 4, 9, 22, 109
Cursor, 9, 114, 118
Cursor keys, 179–180
Data, 248
    textual, 4
Data file, 12, 14
DATE command, 22, 84, 88,
    158, 183
Default file, 18
DEL, 127, 189
Delete, 97

DELETE command, 25
DELETE mode, 134–135, 181
Delimiter, 148
Device, 12
Direction marker, 24–25, 119, 179
Directory, 6, 15, 105
Disk drive, 4, 12
Disk volume, 13
DISPOSE, 256
Dollar sign, 71, 203
Down arrow, 118, 142, 177, 179
Duplicate directory, 69
EDIT command, 9, 18, 24, 112
EDIT mode, 9, 24, 112
    prompt, 25, 113
EDITOR, 5, 6, 109
    commands, 25, 111, 144
End, 123, 190
ENVIRONMENT, 155–156, 158, 162, 182, 197
    prompt, 166, 163
Equal sign, 15–16, 103
EQUALS command, 126, 185
Error message, 44, 53, 57
ESC, 32, 127, 131, 135, 138, 149, 152, 186, 189–190
Escape command, 9–10
ETX, 28, 34, 127, 131, 135, 142, 177, 184, 186, 189
EXAMINE command, 40, 82–83, 104
EXCHANGE mode, 131–132, 186
EXECUTE command, 201, 210
EXIT option, 24, 29, 146, 194
EXTENDED DIRECTORY
    command, 15, 29–30, 35–36, 40, 44–45, 66, 89, 92
Extended SWAP directive, 241
File, 6, 11
File name, 6, 13, 15, 59–60, 87
File specification, 13–14
File system, 5–6, 11–13
FILER, 39
FILER command, 10, 22, 39–41
FILER mode, 10, 14, 23, 29–30
FILLING, 156, 159
FIND command, 147, 149–150, 187

FLIP, 220
Floppy disk, 3
Floppy disk drive, 4
Fortran, 7, 8, 18
FROM FILE, 138
Functions, 247
GET command, 40, 48, 50, 90
Global variable, 248
GOTO, 220
GOTOXY procedure, 275
Greater-than symbol, 179
HALT command, 10, 201
HEAP, 256–257
Heap variable, 249
High-level language, 7
Identifier, 243, 245
IMPLEMENTATION, 231
INCLUDE, 220, 225
INCLUDE directive, 224, 226
INCLUDE file, 223–224, 226–228
INITIALIZATION, 232
INITIALIZE command, 201
INSERT command, 33
INSERT mode, 25, 126–127, 189
INTERFACE, 231–232
Interpretation, 7
Interpreter, 7
IOCHECK, 220
JUMP command, 122, 171, 174, 190
Keyboard, 4
Kilo, 2
KRUNCH command, 40, 78–80, 91
L2, 110
Left arrow, 115, 141, 177, 179
LEFT MARGIN, 156
Less-than symbol, 179
LIBRARIAN, 235, 285
Library, 5, 6, 234
LINK command, 18
Linker, 6, 235
Linking, 6, 228, 235–236
LIST directive, 212, 214, 216
LIST DIRECTORY command, 15, 40, 47, 89, 92
LITERAL, 148, 187
Loader, 5–6
Local variable, 248, 255, 261

Low-level language, 7
Machine language, 2, 7, 12, 18
Main memory, 2, 224,
    239–240, 248–249, 256
MAKE command, 40, 62–63, 93
MARGIN command, 170, 191
MARKER, 158, 171–175, 183,
    190, 192, 197
Marker overflow, 172
Menu, 8
Minus sign, 179
Mode selection commands, 10
Mode tree, 11
Modes, 8
Natural language, 155
Nesting, 227
NEW command, 24, 37, 40, 52,
    94, 256
NO LOAD, 220
Non-resident library, 6
Numerical argument, 119, 147,
    180
Operating modes, 8
Operating system, 5
Overflow, 130
Overlays, 238
P-code, 18
P-machine, 18
PAGE command, 124, 193, 220
PARA MARGIN, 157, 164, 183
Paragraph, 165–166, 170, 191
Parameter, 246
Pascal, 7–8, 18
Period, 179
Plus sign, 179
Pointers, 32, 251
PREFIX command, 14, 40,
    42–43, 95
Prefix
  name, 95
  volume, 14–15, 42, 95
Print, 73, 99
Printer, 4, 46
Procedure, 247
Program, 2
PROGRAM mode, 158
Program translation, 7
Prompt, 8
  auxiliary, 9
Question mark command, 9,
    15–16, 103

QUIET, 211, 220
QUIT command, 10, 24,
    28–29, 40, 96, 145, 194
RAM, 3
Random Access Memory
    (RAM), 3
RANGE CHECK, 220
RELEASE, 256
REMOVE command, 15, 40,
    56–59, 97
Rename, 87
REPLACE command, 147, 151,
    153, 195
RESIDENT, 220
Resident library, 6
RETURN, 26, 121, 146, 179,
    194
  option, 29
  symbol, 26
Right arrow, 117, 141, 177, 179
RIGHT MARGIN, 157
Root volume, 13, 42
RUN command, 18, 35, 201,
    208–209
Run-time error, 35, 215,
    217–218
Run-time stack, 249–250
SAVE command, 35, 40, 53, 55,
    98
Scope, 243–244, 246
Screen oriented editor, 4, 6, 21,
    109
Scrolling, 124, 126
Secondary memory, 3
SEGMENT, 223, 256, 287
SEGMENT FUNCTION, 257
SEGMENT PROCEDURE, 257
Separate compilation, 228
SET command, 155, 197
Sharp sign, 13, 42
Shell, 5–6, 8
SofTech Microsystems, 8
Spacebar, 120, 179, 184
Stack, 249, 252–253, 257
Stack overflow error, 238
Stack pointer, 251
Substitute string, 148, 158
SUBSTITUTES, 158
Suffix, 14
SWAP, 220
SWAP command, 201, 242

SWAP directive, 230, 241–242
Swapping, 223, 238, 240–241
Symbol table, 238, 243,
    245–247
Syntax error, 21, 31, 33, 206
System configuration, 22, 267
SYSTEM.WRK.CODE, 31,
    35–36, 48, 202, 208–209
SYSTEM.WRK.TEXT, 24, 29,
    31–32, 34, 36, 48, 112, 145,
    206
TAB, 122, 179
Target string, 148
TARGETS, 158
Text file, 12, 14
TEXT mode, 158–159, 161, 166
TOKEN, 148, 187
TRANSFER command, 15, 40,
    62, 69–70, 76, 99
Tree structure, 10
UCSD Pascal compiler, 18, 31,
    219, 238
UCSD Pascal programming
    language, 8, 18, 236
UNIT, 223, 228–229, 231, 233
UNIT heading, 230
Unit number, 12
Up arrow, 117, 142, 177, 179
UPDATE option, 29, 145, 194
Use Library directive, 234
USER, 220
USER RESTART, 201
USES, 220, 235

VERIFY command, 176, 198
Version number, 9
Volume, 12, 56
Volume name, 12, 60, 69, 87,
    101
Volume specification, 13
VOLUMES command, 10, 40,
    42, 101
WHAT command, 40, 51, 102
Wild card, 15, 17, 58, 61, 72,
    103
Window, 124, 126
Word, 2
Work file, 16, 18, 47, 90, 94, 98,
    102, 112, 202
WRITE option, 29, 146–147,
    194
YALOE, 109
ZAP command, 176, 199
ZERO command, 62, 68–69,
    105

* 13, 15, 30, 43–44
$ 71, 203
↓ 118, 142, 177, 179
= 15–16, 103
← 115, 141, 177, 179
− 179
+ 179
? 9, 15–16, 103
→ 117, 141, 177, 179
13, 42
↑ 117, 142, 177, 179

The SYBEX Library

BASIC PROGRAMS FOR SCIENTISTS AND ENGINEERS
by **Alan R. Miller**   340 pp., 120 illustr., Ref. B240
This second book in the "Programs for Scientists and Engineers" series provides a library of problem solving programs while developing proficiency in BASIC.

INSIDE BASIC GAMES
by **Richard Mateosian**   350 pp., 240 Illustr., Ref. B245
Teaches interactive BASIC programming through games. Games are written in Microsoft BASIC and can run on the TRS-80, APPLE II and PET/CBM.

FIFTY BASIC EXERCISES
by **J.P. Lamoitier**   240 pp., 195 Illustr., Ref. B250
Teaches BASIC by actual practice using graduated exercises drawn from everyday applications. All programs written in Microsoft BASIC.

EXECUTIVE PLANNING WITH BASIC
by **X.T. Bui**   192 pp., 19 illustr., Ref. B380
An important collection of business management decision models in BASIC, including Inventory Management (EOQ), Critical Path Analysis and PERT, Financial Ratio Analysis, Portfolio Management, and much more.

BASIC FOR BUSINESS
by **Douglas Hergert**   250 pp., 15 illustr., Ref. B390
A logically organized, no-nonsense introduction to BASIC programming for business applications. Includes many fully explained accounting programs, and shows you how to write them.

BASIC EXERCISES FOR THE APPLE
by **J.P. Lamoitier**   230 pp., 80 illustr., Ref. B500
For all Apple users, this learn-by-doing book is written in APPLESOFT II BASIC. Exercises have been chosen for their educational value and application to math, physics, games, business, accounting, and statistics.

YOUR FIRST COMPUTER
by **Rodnay Zaks**   260 pp., 150 Illustr., Ref. C200A
The most popular introduction to small computers and their peripherals: what they do and how to buy one.

DON'T (or How to Care for Your Computer)
by **Rodnay Zaks**   220 pp., 100 Illustr., Ref. C400
The correct way to handle and care for all elements of a computer system including what to do when something doesn't work.

INTRODUCTION TO WORD PROCESSING
by **Hal Glatzer**   200 pp., 70 illustr., Ref. W101
Explains in plain language what a word processor can do, how it improves productivity, how to use a word processor and how to buy one wisely.

INTRODUCTION TO WORDSTAR
by Arthur Naiman   200 pp., 30 illustr., Ref. W105
Makes it easy to learn how to use WordStar, a powerful word processing program for personal computers.

FROM CHIPS TO SYSTEMS: AN INTRODUCTION TO MICROPROCESSORS
by Rodnay Zaks   560 pp., 255 illustr., Ref. C201A
A simple and comprehensive introduction to microprocessors from both a hardware and software standpoint: what they are, how they operate, how to assemble them into a complete system.

MICROPROCESSOR INTERFACING TECHNIQUES
by Rodnay Zaks and Austin Lesea   460 pp., 400 Illustr., Ref. C207
Complete hardware and software interconnect techniques including D to A conversion, peripherals, standard buses and troubleshooting.

PROGRAMMING THE 6502
by Rodnay Zaks   390 pp., 160 Illustr., Ref. C202
Assembly language programming for the 6502, from basic concepts to advanced data structures.

6502 APPLICATIONS BOOK
by Rodnay Zaks   280 pp., 205 Illustr., Ref. D302
Real life application techniques: the input/output book for the 6502.

ADVANCED 6502 PROGRAMMING
by Rodnay Zaks   300 pp., 140 Illustr., Ref. G402
Third in the 6502 series. Teaches more advanced programming techniques, using games as a framework for learning.

PROGRAMMING THE Z80
by Rodnay Zaks   620 pp., 200 Illustr., Ref. C280
A complete course in programming the Z80 microprocessor and a thorough introduction to assembly language.

PROGRAMMING THE Z8000
by Richard Mateosian   300 pp., 125 Illustr., Ref. C281
How to program the Z8000 16-bit microprocessor. Includes a description of the architecture and function of the Z8000 and its family of support chips.

THE CP/M HANDBOOK (with MP/M)
by Rodnay Zaks   330 pp., 100 Illustr., Ref. C300
An indispensable reference and guide to CP/M—the most widely used operating system for small computers.

INTRODUCTION TO PASCAL (Including UCSD PASCAL)
by Rodnay Zaks   420 pp., 130 Illustr., Ref. P310
A step-by-step introduction for anyone wanting to learn the Pascal language. Describes UCSD and Standard Pascals. No technical background is assumed.

THE PASCAL HANDBOOK
by Jacques Tiberghien   490 pp., 350 Illustr., Ref. P320
A dictionary of the Pascal language, defining every reserved word, operator, procedure and function found in all major versions of Pascal.

PASCAL PROGRAMS FOR SCIENTISTS AND ENGINEERS
by Alan Miller   400 pp., 80 Illustr., Ref. P340
A comprehensive collection of frequently used algorithms for scientific and technical applications, programmed in Pascal. Includes such programs as curve-fitting, integrals and statistical techniques.

APPLE PASCAL GAMES
by Douglas Hergert and Joseph T. Kalash   380 pp., 40 illustr., Ref. P360
A collection of the most popular computer games in Pascal challenging the reader not only to play but to investigate how games are implemented on the computer.

INTRODUCTION TO THE UCSD p-SYSTEM
by Charles W. Grant and Jon Butah   320 pp., 110 illustr., Ref. P370
A simple, clear introduction to the UCSD Pascal Operating System for beginners through experienced programmers.

INTERNATIONAL MICROCOMPUTER DICTIONARY
140 pp., Ref. X2
All the definitions and acronyms of microcomputer jargon defined in a handy pocket-size edition. Includes translations of the most popular terms into ten languages.

MICROPROGRAMMED APL IMPLEMENTATION
by Rodnay Zaks   350 pp., Ref. Z10
An expert-level text presenting the complete conceptual analysis and design of an APL interpreter, and actual listings of the microcode.

SELF STUDY COURSES

Recorded live at seminars given by recognized professionals in the microprocessor field.

INTRODUCTORY SHORT COURSES:
Each includes two cassettes plus special coordinated workbook (2½ hours).

S10—INTRODUCTION TO PERSONAL AND BUSINESS COMPUTING
A comprehensive introduction to small computer systems for those planning to use or buy one, including peripherals and pitfalls.

S1—INTRODUCTION TO MICROPROCESSORS
How microprocessors work, including basic concepts, applications, advantages and disadvantages.

S2—PROGRAMMING MICROPROCESSORS
The companion to S1. How to program any standard microprocessor, and how it operates internally. Requires a basic understanding of microprocessors.

S3—DESIGNING A MICROPROCESSOR SYSTEM
Learn how to interconnect a complete system, wire by wire. Techniques discussed are applicable to all standard microprocessors.

INTRODUCTORY COMPREHENSIVE COURSES:
Each includes a 300-500 page seminar book and seven or eight C90 cassettes.

SB3—MICROPROCESSORS
This seminar teaches all aspects of microprocessors: from the operation of an MPU to the complete interconnect of a system. The basic hardware course (12 hours).

SB2—MICROPROCESSOR PROGRAMMING
The basic software course: step by step through all the important aspects of microcomputer programming (10 hours).

ADVANCED COURSES:
Each includes a 300-500 page workbook and three or four C90 cassettes.

SB3—SEVERE ENVIRONMENT/MILITARY MICROPROCESSOR SYSTEMS
Complete discussion of constraints, techniques and systems for severe environmental applications, including Hughes, Raytheon, Actron and other militarized systems (6 hours).

SB5—BIT-SLICE
Learn how to build a complete system with bit slices. Also examines innovative applications of bit slice techniques (6 hours).

SB6—INDUSTRIAL MICROPROCESSOR SYSTEMS
Seminar examines actual industrial hardware and software techniques, components, programs and cost (4½ hours).

SB7—MICROPROCESSOR INTERFACING
Explains how to assemble, interface and interconnect a system (6 hours).

SOFTWARE

BAS 65™ CROSS-ASSEMBLER IN BASIC
8" diskette, Ref. BAS 65
A complete assembler for the 6502, written in standard Microsoft BASIC under CP/M®.

8080 SIMULATORS
Turns any 6502 into an 8080. Two versions are available for APPLE II.
APPLE II cassette, Ref. S6580-APL(T)
APPLE II diskette, Ref. S6580-APL(D)

FOR A COMPLETE CATALOG
OF OUR PUBLICATIONS

U.S.A.
2344 Sixth Street
Berkeley,
California 94710
Tel: (415) 848-8233
Telex: 336311

SYBEX-EUROPE
4 Place Félix-Eboué
75583 Paris Cedex 12
France
Tel: 1/347-30-20
Telex: 211801

SYBEX-VERLAG
Heyestr. 22
4000 Düsseldorf 12
West Germany
Tel: (0211) 287066
Telex: 08 588 163